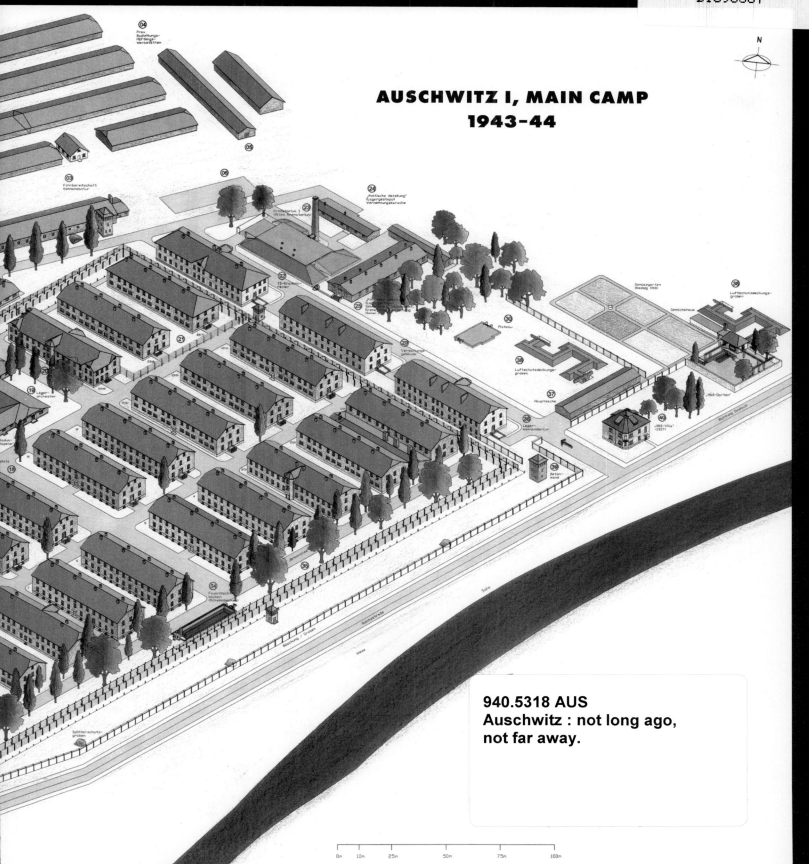

AUSCHWITZ I, MAIN CAMP
1943-44

N

0m   10m   25m   50m   75m   100m

Auschwitz

Not long ago. Not far away.

EDITED BY ROBERT JAN VAN PELT,
WITH LUIS FERREIRO
AND MIRIAM GREENBAUM

Abbeville Press Publishers
New York London

Auschwitz

Not long ago. Not far away.

Contents

AUSCHWITZ
Not long ago. Not far away.

THE ENCOUNTER

BEFORE AUSCHWITZ

AUSCHWITZ

AFTER AUSCHWITZ

Auschwitz: Not long ago. Not far away. at the Museum of Jewish Heritage—A Living Memorial to the Holocaust in New York is made possible with lead support from Bruce C. Ratner, the George and Adele Klein Foundation, Ingeborg and Ira Leon Rennert, and Larry and Klara Silverstein and family. The exhibition is presented in part with support by the David Berg Foundation, Patti Kenner, the Oster Family Foundation, and the Bernard and Anne Spitzer Charitable Trust. The New York premiere is made possible in part by Simon and Stefany Bergson, with additional support from the Knapp Family Foundation.

ENDPAPERS:
These axonometric views of the Auschwitz main camp (front endpapers) and the Auschwitz-Birkenau camp (back endpapers) as they appeared in 1943–44 were made by Peter Siebers, Cologne, on the basis of a new survey of the remains of the Auschwitz camps made by Siebers with the sponsorship of Beate and Serge Klarsfeld, Paris.

Long Shadows: New York Remembers

BRUCE C. RATNER AND MICHAEL S. GLICKMAN
CHAIRMAN, BOARD OF TRUSTEES, AND PRESIDENT AND CEO, MUSEUM OF
JEWISH HERITAGE—A LIVING MEMORIAL TO THE HOLOCAUST, NEW YORK

The crematoria—their brick chimneys spewing smoke. Ash, remains. Train tracks unfolding, scarring the landscape. Steel. *Arbeit macht frei*: work sets you free. Striped uniforms, decimated bodies. Bodies, hanged. The living, standing in rows for hours; counting, counting, re-counting. Thin soup, thickest hunger, hunger with new dimensions. Barbed wire, narrow bunks, rotting planks. Toil. Persistent illness and showers and—choking. We still see the people—choking.

When we envision the Holocaust, Auschwitz rises in our minds. Its long shadows rise.

At Auschwitz, one million Jewish people were murdered. Crammed railcars rumbled the arrival of Jewish people from nearly every country in Europe that was occupied by or allied with Germany. Survivors' stories ask us to witness these losses. Deniers and minimizers of the Holocaust, too, focus on Auschwitz—attempting to edit, rewrite, or stamp out one of the most searing monuments of Holocaust history.

The horrors of Auschwitz have guaranteed it a place in the imaginations of people around the world. But what does it mean that images of Auschwitz reign in Holocaust histories, cultural products, and online forums? What unique responsibilities do Holocaust museums and education centers carry when we teach others about Auschwitz? What can we do to ensure that, precisely because of its infamy, its history becomes more widely known and is presented with accuracy and respect for victims and survivors?

To continue to answer these challenges and responsibilities, the Museum of Jewish Heritage—A Living Memorial to the Holocaust presents the groundbreaking exhibition *Auschwitz. Not long ago. Not far away*. The exhibition opens in New York on May 8,

The Museum of Jewish Heritage—A Living Memorial to the Holocaust, New York, 2017

2019, marking the anniversary of VE Day, or Victory in Europe Day, 1945, when the Allies celebrated Nazi Germany's surrender of its armed forces and the end of the European phase of World War II. During the run of the exhibition, the museum will present related public, educational, and scholarly programming so that people from New York and around the world can responsibly explore the history of Auschwitz.

It feels significant that the Auschwitz exhibition—the most comprehensive Holocaust exhibition ever presented in this country—will open in a museum that completes the cultural and educational landscape it shares with the Statue of Liberty and Ellis Island. Across the water, Lady Liberty lifts her lamp and Ellis Island marks the gateway through which millions flowed into this country seeking refuge. The exhibition will be featured across the three floors of the museum's core building, whose six-sided shape and six-tiered roof are reminders of the six million Jews who perished in the Holocaust. They are also reminiscent of the six-pointed Star of David, symbolizing the museum's dedication to representing Jewish life and culture as it has endured and evolved.

Twenty years ago, the Museum of Jewish Heritage—A Living Memorial to the Holocaust was dedicated by survivors. Since then we have welcomed more than two million visitors. We have emerged as the third-largest Holocaust museum in the world, and the primary resource in the northeastern United States for teaching and learning about the Holocaust. In presenting the *Auschwitz* exhibition in New York, we advance our mission as a place of memory and a place of learning. At the museum, we remember the history of the Holocaust as a history of individuals, and this in itself is an act of resistance.

We All Need Peace. Memory, Meanwhile, Breeds Unrest.

DR. PIOTR M. A. CYWIŃSKI

DIRECTOR, AUSCHWITZ-BIRKENAU STATE MUSEUM

The road to Auschwitz led through frustration, populism, stigmatization of the Jews as scapegoats, dehumanization of fellow human beings, and passivity to institutionalized hatred.

Today, anxiety should be aroused by the fact that the postwar road out of Auschwitz may paradoxically have come full circle. An Auschwitz may occur again, since none of the initial stages of the road that led to Auschwitz have disappeared once and for all. The escalation of populism, xenophobia, antisemitism, and other racist ideologies is discernible in many parts of our world.

Perhaps this unrest is a signpost, urging us to find paths to lasting peace. Today, anyone seeking peace cannot escape the feeling of unrest. Because we know too much.

Today, unawareness is no longer an excuse or justification. We have access to voluminous information and to many tools that influence public discourse.

And yet, our human passivity has not undergone

Railway tracks in Auschwitz-Birkenau, 2017

a profound transformation. Our family, tribal, and national egotisms are still perceived as patriotic virtues. Pride continually prevents us from seeing equality in humans. Maturity is a state that we are still nowhere near.

Memory is, therefore, the fundamental key to responsibility. Memory thus compels us to look into the future.

The world, meanwhile, is changing at a growing pace. For many years, analysts have been unable to keep up with civilization's changing pace. Moreover, it has been difficult for the entire educational system to keep pace with these changes. We therefore need bright lighthouses, indisputable boundary conditions, stable and uncontested points of reference. Hence, of all the events of the recent past, Auschwitz increasingly appeals to us. We cannot cope without this memory.

Auschwitz and the Shoah are not just another single, dramatic event in the linear history of humanity. When we look at everything that happened before, and how much has happened in opposition to this unique experience, it is difficult not to understand that it is a critical point in the history of Europe and perhaps the world.

It was after this war and none other that the legal definitions of *genocide* and *crimes against humanity* were established. It was then that human rights were universally understood as a natural entitlement of all. It is within this perspective that the building of intra-European relations, based on values of community and interdependence, was set in motion. At the same time, a vision of a new civil society was born, one not based on paramilitary models from earlier centuries. This period also gave birth to the large-scale search for ecumenical paths. Auschwitz, as a critical point, has a chance to become a point of no return. However, we can avoid returning to this point only by heeding the lessons of memory. Perhaps we will return after all.

Therefore, through this exhibition, this encounter with the darkest period in the history of Europe, by listening to the words of witnesses, by making contact with such meaningful and authentic objects, by engaging in this time of self-reflection, you are invited to walk on this road full of unrest—desired unrest.

The Heart of the Matter

LUIS FERREIRO

DIRECTOR, MUSEALIA

In April 2009, I received as a birthday gift the book *Man's Search for Meaning*, by Viktor E. Frankl. A few months earlier, my brother Jesús had died suddenly, at the age of twenty-six, and I did not feel I had the strength to begin reading it.

Some months later, one summer night, I held the fairly slim paperback book in my hands. I stared at it for a few minutes, not knowing what to do. After a while, I opened it to read the first few pages. They recounted the story of Viktor, a young Austrian Jew with a promising career in psychiatry, wandering aimlessly around the streets of Vienna, now threatened by the imminent arrival of Nazism. He had to choose between emigrating hurriedly to the United States with his wife or staying in Vienna to be with his parents, despite the very considerable risk this could entail for all their lives. He stood at a personal crossroads, suffering the profound and sincere pain caused by his situation. I was captivated by the story and went on to finish the book.

The way in which Viktor describes his own experiences in various Nazi concentration camps sowed the seed that gave rise to the idea of creating a traveling exhibition about the history of Auschwitz and its impact. The idea became a necessity, borne out of discovering something that I felt had to be shared with as many people as possible and expressed in the only way I could: in an exhibition. I had grown up working in Musealia, my family's company, which conceives, develops, and manages traveling

Auschwitz-Birkenau, 2014. In the foreground is the Pond of Ashes. The ruins of Crematorium 4 are visible to the right. In the background is the Zentralsauna (Central Sauna), the camp's main delousing and disinfection installation.

exhibitions. The longest-running one, reflecting the maritime environment in which I had grown up, concerns the fate of the RMS *Titanic* and its crew and passengers. Our company was not simply a way to make a living. More important, it was a vehicle to tell stories that affected us profoundly.

With the constant and decisive support of José Antonio Múgica and María Teresa Aguirre, the producers at Musealia, I embarked on a long journey that led, in December 2017, to an inaugural exhibition in Madrid and, in May 2019, to the exhibition's opening in New York. A small team of experts, assembled by Professor Robert Jan van Pelt, provided guidance in what was, initially, a strange and difficult terrain.

We approached the Auschwitz-Birkenau State Museum and requested its participation. The talks ended in a much broader agreement than initially planned, transforming the exhibition into an unprecedented coproduction involving the museum's historians, curators, and educators.

Auschwitz: Not long ago. Not far away. features more than six hundred original objects, many of them on display for the first time. Although most of them are drawn from the collections of the Auschwitz-Birkenau State Museum, there are also items on loan from more than twenty museums, institutions, and private collections from around the world. Each object helps us to understand the complex and dramatic history of Auschwitz.

The exhibition's second stop, the Museum of Jewish Heritage—A Living Memorial to the Holocaust, in New York, is the first venue in North America to host the exhibition. This is a reflection not only of a very special partnership but also a remarkable commitment by our host: *Auschwitz* will occupy the space normally reserved for the museum's permanent collection. In addition, the Museum of Jewish Heritage has made significant objects available for display.

Each of the objects in the exhibition has its own voice, its own historical echo. Each is a fragment of history that has been preserved from the past to provide a firsthand account of the terrible events it witnessed. This voice establishes a unique and personal conversation with every visitor.

The exhibition will travel to other cities around the world over the coming years. This will allow us to tell the story to millions of people, offering them an introspective journey through the nature of humanity itself, experienced through the twofold history of the camp: Auschwitz as a physical space and Auschwitz as a symbol and metaphor of unfettered human barbarity.

The attempt to annihilate each and every one of the Jewish men, women, and children in Europe occurred not long ago and not far from any of us, wherever we may dwell. It happened in a modern and educated society. Moreover, it happened with the participation and collaboration of many different sectors of society, including political, legal, bureaucratic, academic, scientific, and cultural elites.

Aleksandr Solzhenitsyn wrote, in this regard: "If only there were evil people somewhere insidiously committing evil deeds, and it were necessary only to separate them from the rest of us and destroy them. But the line dividing good and evil cuts through the heart of every human being. And who is willing to destroy a piece of his own heart?"[1]

History is often a mute cry rising from the very depths of the earth. In the case of Auschwitz, that voiceless cry warns us where a future built on hatred, intolerance, antisemitism,* and racism leads—of just how far that dark half of the human heart can take us.

* In spelling the word for contemporary hatred of Jews as *antisemitism*, not as *anti-Semitism*, our text follows the recommendation of the International Holocaust Remembrance Alliance, issued in its "Memo on Spelling of Antisemitism" (2015): "The unhyphenated spelling is favored by many scholars and institutions in order to dispel the idea that there is an entity 'Semitism' which 'anti-Semitism' opposes. Antisemitism should be read as a unified term so that the meaning of the generic term for modern Jew-hatred is clear."

Auschwitz Stories and the Story of Auschwitz

DR. ROBERT JAN VAN PELT
CHIEF CURATOR

May 19, 1944. A film camera recorded the face of Settela Steinbach, a nine-year-old Roma girl framed by the door of the freight wagon that was to take her and another 451 Jewish and Roma deportees from Westerbork, a Dutch transit camp, to Auschwitz. Twenty minuscule frames are all that remain of her.

The same transport that carried Settela also included the forty-nine-year-old painter, composer, and writer Robert "Bob" Hanf. Born in a fully assimilated Jewish family in Amsterdam, Bob had studied architecture but preferred a life devoted to the arts. In 1942 artist Johan Sybolt "Joop" Sjollema asked

Bob to sit for a portrait. The picture had been completed but for the hands when Bob received a notice of his "labor deployment" in the east. Bob went into hiding. For twenty months he lived three hundred yards from the secret annex where Anne Frank and her family were residing invisibly to the world. On April 23, 1944, Amsterdam police arrested Bob. On May 19 he was loaded on a transport to Auschwitz, with Settela, 206 other Jews, and 244 other Roma. Of the deportees on this transport, 103 were murdered on arrival. The rest, including Bob and likely Settela, who, as a Roma girl, was not yet subject to selection

Settela Steinbach, a nine-year-old Roma girl, staring out of a railway wagon destined for Auschwitz, just before the door closes, 1944. NIOD Instituut voor Oorlogs-, Holocaust- en Genocidestudies, Amsterdam.

for the gas chambers, were admitted to the camp. It is most likely that Settela's turn came on August 2, when the SS liquidated the so-called Zigeunerlager (Gypsy Camp). Bob was murdered in September.

Bob was my mother's uncle. Thirty years ago I went to Oświęcim, Poland, the site of the Auschwitz-Birkenau camp, in search of an understanding of Bob's end, which was so much tied up with my beginning, as I carry his name. I also wanted to see the place that did not swallow my mother, who, at age twelve in May 1944, would not have survived the selection. I became one of the many millions who, since 1947, have visited the original camp site, its buildings, ruins, and exhibitions, as preserved and presented by the Auschwitz-Birkenau State

Museum. As it has been for many, the visit proved to be a life-changing experience for me: it changed the trajectory of my career as a historian.

Unlike the Auschwitz-Birkenau State Museum, a traveling exhibition such as *Auschwitz: Not long ago. Not far away.*—first suggested to me by Musealia's director, Luis Ferreiro, in December 2013—cannot offer the authenticity of place. Yet the very fact that we began with a blank slate, rather than the given inheritance of the original site and its parts, allowed us to focus first and foremost on storytelling and then to assemble a unique treasury of images and artifacts from both public and private collections worldwide with an eye to their narrative potential.

All through the exhibition there are stories— stories about individuals and families, about communities and organizations, about ideologies that teach people to hate and responses that reveal compassion and love. There are stories of victims, perpetrators, and bystanders, stories with heroes and villains— stories that merge into an epic story of a continent marked by war and genocide.

These stories are triggered by images: the minuscule record of the likeness of Settela; a series of photographs of road signs snapped quickly during a trip from the Dutch-German border to Berlin; mug shots of frightened, confused, or undaunted inmates taken in a concentration camp photography studio; an album with dozens of neatly labeled photos recording the arrival of a transport train in the Auschwitz-Birkenau camp and the selection of the deportees; and furtive, badly framed shots taken from the inside of a gas chamber at the risk of the cameraperson's life.

And there are the stories that come with or can be teased from artifacts. The collection of bottles that once held the many liquors produced by the Haberfeld company in Oświęcim tells a story about the continuity of Jewish life in a Polish town that came to symbolize, under a German name, the destruction of European Jewry. An Iron Cross tells the story of a German Jewish war hero murdered in Auschwitz. A

Johan Sybolt "Joop" Sjollema (1900–1990), Portrait of Bob Hanf, 1942. *Oil on canvas. Joods Historisch Museum, Amsterdam.*

German-made Model 2 freight wagon, 1940. Exhibition installation, Centro de Exposiciones Arte Canal, Madrid, 2017.

doctor's coat tells of the betrayal of the Hippocratic oath, when physicians became murderers, tasked to heal the so-called body of the German nation. A camp administrator's desk tells of the bureaucratic routine of organizing the carefully planned murder of "undesirables." A Model 2 freight wagon of the Deutsche Reichsbahn (German National Railway) tells how easy it is to use something that was originally constructed to support human life, by transporting foodstuffs, goods, and livestock, into an instrument of destruction used to transport people deemed superfluous to ghettos, camps, and killing centers. Postcards thrown from deportation trains tell us about the things people write to one another when they face permanent separation. A used tin that contained cyanide pellets and a tall, steel wire-mesh-covered column tell a story about the inventiveness of mass murderers; a blanket that a deaf-mute prisoner grabbed from a bunk in an Auschwitz barrack tells a story of solidarity during a death march; and a housecoat made

after liberation from a bale of SS-uniform cloth by an Auschwitz survivor tells a story of new beginnings. The more than 400 images and 650 artifacts tell many different stories, and they all converge in a single epic story, which is the story of Auschwitz—a story that this exhibition will tell in places all over the world in the next seven years.

In our selection of images and artifacts, and in the sequence and rhythm of themes and topics that shape the narrative line of our exhibition, we aim to tell the history of a town that had three names: Oświęcim (Polish), Oshpitzin (Yiddish), and Auschwitz (German)—names that testify to the efforts three different peoples made to live together. This idea of common ground did not fit the Nazi worldview. Too many people easily assume that places are destined to become one thing or another, forgetting that destinies do not arise from the land but are made by human beings. "Where Auschwitz stands today, three years ago there were villages and farms," Polish prisoner Tadeusz Borowski wrote while imprisoned in Auschwitz. "There were rich meadows, shaded country lanes, apple orchards. There were people, no better nor worse than any other people. And then we arrived. We drove the people out, demolished their houses, levelled the earth, kneaded it into mud. We built barracks, fences, crematoria. We brought scurvy, phlegmon and lice."[1]

With the same purpose we dwell, perhaps to a greater extent than most visitors expect, on other important developments and events that happened before the creation of the Auschwitz camp but which are essential to the understanding of its history: the story of Christian-Jewish relations, the sad parable of the Weimar Republic, the spectacle of Hitler's Third Reich, and the tragedy of German-occupied Poland.

We present the drama of the Auschwitz camp, designed as an instrument of terror and torture to pacify the Polish population; tell the tale of the German invasion of the Soviet Union and the systematic massacre of Jews in conquered Soviet territories; and try to encompass through words, images, and artifacts the apocalypse of the Nazis' "Final Solution to the Jewish Question," which sought to eradicate both Jews and the memory of Jews from Europe, resulting in what is known in English as the Holocaust (from the Greek noun *Holokaustos*, which means "burnt offering"), in Hebrew as *Shoah* ("annihilation"), and in Yiddish as *Khurbn* ("destruction"). We discuss the fate of the Roma, who suffered a genocide that they remember as the *Porajmos* ("great devouring"), and touch on the tragedy of Poles enslaved and killed by the Germans in the *Zagłada* ("destruction"). All these stories help us understand how and why deportation trains left stations all over Europe with the destination Auschwitz.

In May 2019 the exhibition *Auschwitz: Not long ago. Not far away.* opens at the Museum of Jewish Heritage—A Living Memorial to the Holocaust, in New York. At the southern tip of Manhattan, the museum sits close to the place where, in 1654, the first Jews landed in North America—and the Dutch

authorities decided to admit them. These Jews were the descendants of Jewish converts to Christianity who had been expelled from the Iberian Peninsula a century before because of their ancestry. Despite these Spaniards' adherence to Christianity, their very existence violated the Spanish policy that only those who could prove *limpieza de sangre* (cleanliness of blood), which meant a long Christian lineage, could participate in society. Nieuw Amsterdam offered them a new beginning. One of the descendants of that first group, Emma Lazarus, was to articulate the significance of New York as a place of new beginnings 229 years later, in words that are inscribed at the base of the Statue of Liberty.

"Keep, ancient lands, your storied pomp!" cries she
With silent lips. "Give me your tired, your poor,
Your huddled masses yearning to breathe free,
The wretched refuse of your teeming shore.
Send these, the homeless, tempest-tossed to me,
I lift my lamp beside the golden door!"

Lazarus did not just write an immortal poem that summarizes the promise of America. In 1883 she formed the Society for the Improvement and Colonization of East European Jews, who were arriving in ever greater numbers as the result of the de facto expulsion from Russia that had begun in 1880. Any visitor who attends our Auschwitz exhibition might, on exiting the Museum of Jewish Heritage, consider whether the admission into the United States, between 1880 and 1914, of two million Jews, of whom one million settled in New York, prevented a genocide of Russian Jews because, confronted with hatred and pogroms, *they had somewhere to go*. In the early 1940s the Jews of Europe had nowhere to go because too many statesmen in the West had decided that the political price that came with a generous immigration policy was too high. The Jews had nowhere to go—until the Germans made them go, in sealed freight wagons, to an unknown destination.

As the exhibition travels from venue to venue, we

adapt the story of Auschwitz to fit the particularity of the locality. In the case of our exhibition at the Museum of Jewish Heritage, we do so by excluding some of the artifacts we showed in Madrid and including artifacts from the MJH collection, and by focusing on those aspects of the story that have an American or New York connection. An exhibition on Auschwitz shown in New York is undoubtedly framed by a shared understanding of this great city as the example of everything the Auschwitz camp was not: a place that celebrates the plenitude and diversity of human life; a place that is at ease with the unavoidable and also creative friction that comes when different personalities, ethnicities, religions, and worldviews encounter one another. Unlike New York, the Auschwitz camp was built on foundations of hate and loathing created by crude generalizations and reductive slogans targeting other nations, ethnic groups, political opponents, social outsiders, and other "deviants." *Dort wo man Bücher verbrennt, verbrennt man auch am Ende Menschen* (Where they burn books, they will also end up burning human beings), wrote the German Jewish author Heinrich Heine in 1823.[2] This statement appears to have forecast what was to happen a century later—and not simply because the Nazis who were to build Auschwitz with its gas-chamber-equipped crematoria celebrated their 1933 ascent to power with public book burnings held all over Germany. Heine's understanding was not prophetic in a literal sense; instead, it was a profound insight into the formation of a genocidal mentality: by forbidding access to books written by Jewish, Communist, intellectual, homosexual, and other "suspect" authors, the Nazis aimed to prevent the formation of any counter-narrative to the propaganda that defined Poles as laggards, Roma as thieves, intellectuals as infertile, male homosexuality as masculine rot, Communists as subhumans, and Jews as vermin. Nazi propagandists like Joseph Goebbels, who organized the book burnings, knew well that in taking away from Nazi-approved "Aryan" Germans the possibility to discover by means of

books the lives and views of people different from themselves, he would cripple Germans' capacity for empathy and compassion, their ability to appreciate different perspectives, and their willingness to postpone judgment. Adolf Eichmann, the man who oversaw the deportation of Settela Steinbach, Bob Hanf, and a few million others, was in that sense a perfect Nazi. Reading decades later the transcripts of Eichmann's interrogation in Israeli captivity and listening to him in the Jerusalem court, philosopher Hannah Arendt concluded that the key flaw in Eichmann's character was "his almost total inability ever to look at anything from the other fellow's point of view." Thinking in clichés, he "was surrounded by the most reliable of all safeguards against the words and the presence of others, and hence against reality as such."[3]

In our exhibition we focus on the concentration camp Auschwitz, which by the end of 1944 included dozens of subcamps but which centered on three compounds close to what was, before 1939, and what is again since 1945, a town known to most as Oświęcim. We do so in recognition of the fact that the name *Auschwitz* has also become in the past fifty years a shorthand for the German concentration camps as such, for the Holocaust of six million Jews, for the Porajmos and the passion of the Polish nation, for the attempted suicide of European civilization between 1933 and 1945, and for the trauma that remains in our time, which is often referred to as the post-Auschwitz era.

Why did Auschwitz become so central to our understanding of the twentieth century? First of all, there is the number of its victims: 1.3 million people were deported to Auschwitz. Of these, more than 1.1 million perished in that camp: 1 million Jews, from Hungary, Poland, France, and a dozen other European countries; seventy-five thousand non-Jewish Poles; twenty-one thousand Roma; fifteen thousand Soviet prisoners of war; and up to fifteen thousand people who fall into other categories. Second, the victims of Auschwitz came from all over Europe, and

Foreground: luggage brought to Auschwitz by deportees; background: photograph of the arrival in Auschwitz, 1944. Exhibition installation, Centro de Exposiciones Arte Canal, Madrid, 2018.

as such the history of the Auschwitz camp testifies to the continent-wide character of the catastrophe that was mid-twentieth-century Europe. Last, Auschwitz was the place where the technological prowess and bureaucratic discipline that has defined the West for the last two centuries went awry. Only in Auschwitz did modern, well-designed, gas-chamber-equipped crematoria become the sites of continuous murder and corpse disposal. These buildings provide the collective memory of the West with powerful symbolic images of destruction: their chimneys, discharging fire and smoke, directly suggest that the genocide of the Jews was, indeed, a Holocaust.

The core of the symbolic significance of Auschwitz must be located in its survivors and its material remnants. Of the 1.1 million Jews who were deported to Auschwitz, some one hundred thousand left the camp for slave labor in other camps. In addition, there were one hundred thousand non-Jewish, mostly Polish prisoners, who were deported from Auschwitz to other camps. Of these two hundred thousand survivors—a group that also includes the seven thousand prisoners of Auschwitz liberated by the Soviet Red Army on January 27, 1945—around half died before the end of the war, but one hundred thousand were still alive in May 1945. Why are the survivors so important to the memory of Auschwitz? There are various good answers to this and related questions. At the most practical level, the fact that so many Auschwitz prisoners survived—compared to prisoners held in other German extermination camps such as Belzec, Sobibor, and Treblinka, or the victims of the massacres in the German-occupied Soviet Union by means of shootings—has provided a plethora of witness testimony. This has anchored the history of Auschwitz in our collective memory. At a more metaphysical level, one might observe that because Auschwitz was at the center of the Nazi effort to erase the presence and memory of Jews from the record of history, the simple fact of the survival of Jews can be seen as a both politically and historically significant negation of Auschwitz. Finally, Auschwitz prisoners' survival is important to the historically vital relationship between survival and storytelling that is at the core of Jewish identity: the Bible is a record of survival, of storytelling, and of survival through storytelling. The story of survival in Auschwitz thus merges into what many have identified as "the greatest story ever told."

Seen from a narrative perspective, Auschwitz offered a coherent universe in both spatial and temporal terms. The deportation, the arrival, and the selection followed a fixed pattern, as did the initiation process, which included undressing, shaving, showering, tattooing, donning striped prison uniforms, the assignment of billets, the revelation of what happened to those who had been sent the "other way" at the selection, the daily roll calls, the struggle to obtain food, the struggle to remain clean, the tricks to survive the regular selection in the barracks. The grotesque but well-ordered life of the Auschwitz prisoner occurred in an apparently physical and social matrix that could easily be described and of which substantial remains still exist. This allowed for the emergence of a narrative tradition with recognizable plots, predictable characters, conventional tropes, recognizable cues

that build suspense, and so on. Because we have heard so many stories about survival in Auschwitz—all in many ways similar, and each in a particular way special—we remember them.

When we consider the Holocaust, the key catastrophe of the twentieth century, the great majority of people understand it as a single moral and historical disaster and not as a series of sometimes closely connected, sometimes roughly overlapping, and sometimes even contradictory developments. Hence we refer to it as "the Holocaust," with a capital *H*. Labeling the very complex set of events that ended in the death of six million Jewish people, the flight of one million, and the destruction of so much Jewish heritage as "the Holocaust" suggests a historical singularity that, in a sense, calls for a singular place of focus at its core. And while our collective memory struggles to keep track of the countless *Einsatzgruppen* massacres or distinguish between the Belzec, Sobibor, and Treblinka death camps, Auschwitz appears in our understanding as unique, and singular—for the reasons mentioned above and also because so much of it remains available for visits, thanks to the outstanding stewardship of the Auschwitz-Birkenau State Museum.

There is more to the history of the twentieth century than Auschwitz. There is more to World War II, more to the German assault on Polish civic society, more to the German persecution of the Roma, and more to the Holocaust than Auschwitz. Yet, as we show in our exhibition, the story of Auschwitz touches the core of each of these different but interconnected histories and does so in an utterly memorable manner—one that we believe is worth your attention. Thus, *Auschwitz: Not long ago. Not far away.* tells the story of a particular camp, but in doing so it also seeks to provide some measure of knowledge about the Holocaust of the Jews, the genocide of the Roma, and the decimation of the Poles. And it also aims to offer an occasion for reflection on the self-destructive forces within the civilization of the West.

The Encounter

A Dot on the Map

Auschwitz: a time not long ago, a place not far away. A time and place when hope turned to fear, and governments and their citizens turned to genocide: Holocaust or Shoah or Khurbn, Porajmos, or Zagłada.

In the first half of the twentieth century, ideas that were key to the formation of a genocidal mentality were conveyed by the use of terms such as *race* and the adjectives *superior* and *inferior* to describe human beings. This ideology, represented in Germany by Nazism and elsewhere in Europe by various fascisms, was used to exclude political opponents, labor unionists, people with disabilities, homosexuals, "asocial elements," Jehovah's Witnesses, and Roma from society. In occupied Poland, the Germans destroyed the institutions of the Polish state and attempted to decapitate civil society through the systematic elimination of the political, social, religious, and intellectual elites. All through German-ruled Europe, Jews were a special target. In what became a policy known as the Final Solution to the Jewish Question, the Germans aimed not only to kill every last Jew but also to remove all evidence of the Jewish people's contribution to human civilization.

Auschwitz became central to this Final Solution. But how did this happen? And what does it mean for us today?

These are big questions. Paraphrasing the late Raul Hilberg, who established the academic field of Holocaust history, we might do well to leave the big questions alone for now, so we'll not come up with small answers, and instead focus on some of the smaller questions that are encompassed within the bigger one. One small question shapes the beginning of an exhibition that claims that Auschwitz is "not far away," both metaphorically and, in view of the universality of international travel, practically: Where is Auschwitz?

The entrance of the exhibition displays three maps: the first shows Europe in 1937; the second, Europe in 1943; the third, Europe in the present day. In 1937 and the present, Oświęcim is a place in Poland; in 1943, Auschwitz is a place in the Greater German Reich. The maps make a simple point: the atrocities that unfolded in Auschwitz between 1940 and 1945 happened in Europe and are a German legacy, not a Polish one.

1270
Oświęcim receives a municipal charter

1933
Nazis come to power in Germany; first concentration camps are established

1940
Auschwitz concentration camp is established

1942
In the Wannsee Conference, German officials determine who is in charge of the Final Solution; Auschwitz becomes a killing center

Treaty of Versailles seals Germany's defeat in World War I
1919

Germany and the Soviet Union invade Poland; World War II begins
1939

Germany invades the Soviet Union; Japan attacks the United States; Germany declares war on the United States
1941

AUSCHWITZ, A TOWN AND CONCENTRATION CAMP COMPLEX IN THE GREATER GERMAN REICH, EARLY 1943

Maps by Anna Biedermann and Victor Figuerola

- Greater German Reich, 1943
- Areas under German occupation, 1943
- Germany's allies (Italy, Slovakia, Hungary, Romania, Bulgaria, and Finland) and the areas under their occupation, 1943

Auschwitz •

1945
On January 27, the Soviet Army liberates Auschwitz; on May 8, Germany surrenders; on August 15, Japan surrenders

1948
The United Nations adopts the Convention on the Prevention and Punishment of the Crime of Genocide

2005
The European Union and the United Nations designate January 27 International Holocaust Remembrance Day

The Auschwitz-Birkenau State Museum is established

1947

Auschwitz becomes a UNESCO World Heritage site

1979

OŚWIĘCIM,
A TOWN IN POLAND, 1937

This map shows the borders of interwar
(1918–1939) Germany and Poland.

OŚWIĘCIM/AUSCHWITZ, A
TOWN AND MEMORIAL SITE
IN POLAND, 1947–PRESENT

This map shows the borders of postwar
(1945–present) Germany and Poland.

Auschwitz marks a place in space, and it also represents a series of events in time. And this leads to a second small question: What is the basic chronology that allows us to grasp the geography and history of Auschwitz? We have identified twelve important years, shown in the time line on pages 22–23.

In our chronology we focus on a few years. In a fine-grained history of the Holocaust in general and Auschwitz in particular, every day, apparently ordinary, proves extraordinary when considered close-up. As a historian, I have marked July 13, 1943, in my calendar of commemoration. That day the Nazi regime beheaded Munich professor Kurt Huber. Invoking Immanuel Kant's categorical imperative, which postulates an absolute morality in defense of each individual and articulates the duty of resistance, even if one stands alone, Huber had helped some of his students organize the White Rose resistance group, which aimed to make Germans aware of the criminality of the genocidal character of the Final Solution.

In Auschwitz, July 13, 1943, was an unusually quiet day: only forty-eight deportees were brought

into the camp, and the gas chambers and the ovens of the crematoria, which had a *daily* incineration capacity of 4,416 corpses, were idle. Yet too many rumors were circulating in German-occupied Europe about the camp. Therefore, on that very July 13, the Auschwitz SS, on orders of the coordinator of the deportations, Adolf Eichmann, instructed thousands of Jewish inmates to send family and friends a postcard with the message that they were doing well. The return address was "Arbeitslager Birkenau, bei Neu Berun" (Labor Camp Birkenau, near Neu Berun). Yet a stamp instructed recipients to send a reply not directly to the return address but to another one, in Berlin.

Thousands of such cards were sent from Arbeitslager Birkenau. They did not have much effect: the majority of the recipients had been deported themselves, and a small minority was in hiding. Those few who were still at home, and who owned a comprehensive atlas of the German Reich published before 1914, might have found a dot on the map of Upper Silesia marked as Neu Berun or Neuberun (a Polish atlas marked the place as Bieruń Nowy). This dot

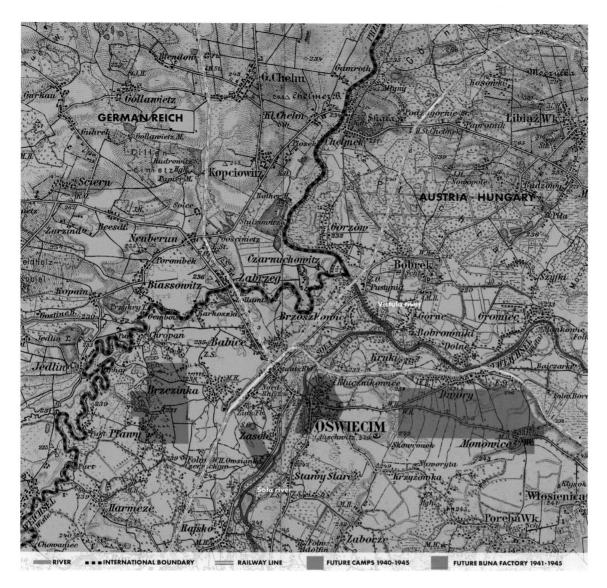

RIVER ▪▪▪ INTERNATIONAL BOUNDARY ▭▭▭ RAILWAY LINE ▮ FUTURE CAMPS 1940-1945 ▮ FUTURE BUNA FACTORY 1941-1945

Map of Oświęcim area, ca. 1900. The international border between the German Reich and the Austro-Hungarian Empire, the main rivers, and the railway lines are enhanced. In addition, the three main compounds of the future Auschwitz-Birkenau concentration camp are indicated, as is the IG Farben Buna (synthetic rubber) plant. Collection of Robert Jan van Pelt, Canada.

Postcard sent by Helene Schwarz with the return address "Arbeitslager Birkenau, bei Neu Berun," 1944. Florence and Laurence Spungen Family Foundation, Santa Barbara, California.

had some importance because, until 1918, the Neu Berun railway station marked the German terminus of the international border crossing, which at its Austro-Hungarian end was marked by the Oświęcim railway station. Not a single atlas, old or contemporary, showed Labor Camp Birkenau.

A Dot on the Map   25

The Wheel Set and the Shoe

In the collective memory of Auschwitz, two artifacts have acquired a dominant place. The first is the train; the second is the shoe. The first room of the exhibition contains a large, iron wheel-and-axle assembly, or wheel set, from a German DRG 50 locomotive used to haul freight trains in the 1940s. And it displays a woman's red dress shoe, found in the warehouses of Auschwitz after the war.

The wheel set raises questions about the role of industrialization in, and the commitment of orga-

Wheel set, 1930–1945. Exhibition installation, Centro de Exposiciones Arte Canal, Madrid, 2017.

nized society as represented by the state, to the five-year catastrophe of Auschwitz. A highly personal artifact, carrying the imprint of the wearer, the shoe seeks to touch the historical imagination by asking about the identity and fate of one deportee—and at the same time of all 1.3 million deportees—brought to Auschwitz to be murdered on arrival or worked to death.

Photograph of wheel sets produced at the Krupp factories, ready for shipment to the Deutsche Reichsbahn (German National Railway), 1920s. Collection of Robert Jan van Pelt, Canada.

Woman's dress shoe, belonging to an unknown deportee to Auschwitz, 1940s. Auschwitz-Birkenau State Museum, Oświęcim, Poland. Exhibition installation, Centro de Exposiciones Arte Canal, Madrid, 2017.

January 27, 1945

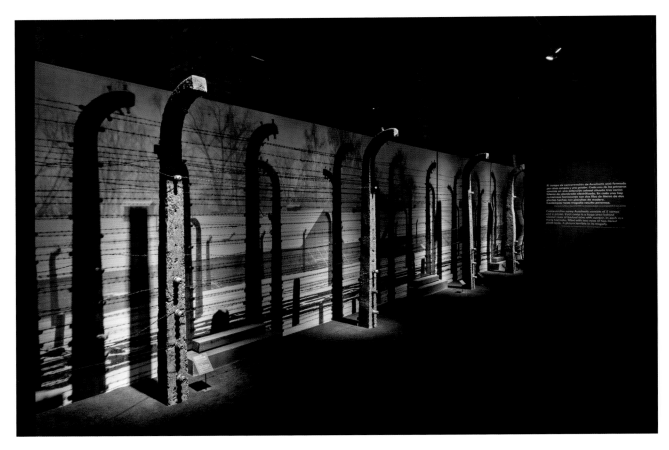

Concrete posts, isolators, and barbed wire that were once part of the fence of the Auschwitz camp, 1940–45. Exhibition installation, Centro de Exposiciones Arte Canal, Madrid, 2017.

When Red Army soldiers arrived at three large barbed-wire enclosures near the town of Auschwitz on January 27, 1945, they discovered seven thousand sick and emaciated men, women, and children, and piles of unburied corpses. Making their way through the camp, the soldiers saw evidence of the lives of another million people who had been brought there from Poland and the rest of Europe: hundreds of thousands of items of clothing, including shoes, and tons of human hair. And they heard what at first seemed unbelievable stories: of daily trains bringing hundreds of thousands of Jews to be murdered in gas chambers; of human ashes used as fertilizer; of

Zinovii Tolkatchev (1903–1977), No Words, *1945. Pencil on paper. Gift of Anel Tolkatcheva and Ilya Tolkatchev, Kiev. Yad Vashem: The World Holocaust Remembrance Center, Jerusalem.*

medical experiments. The Italian prisoner Primo Levi, deported to Auschwitz a year earlier, saw in the faces of these soldiers compassion, confused restraint, and above all shame, "the shame . . . that the just man experiences at another man's crime; the feeling of guilt that such a crime should exist, that it should have been introduced irrevocably into the world of things that exist."[1]

Red Army war artist Zinovii Tolkatchev expressed this sense of shame in a series of drawings he made immediately after his arrival in Auschwitz. Having depleted his own supplies of paper, he drew a sketch of a woman covering her face on letterhead of the Auschwitz commandant's office. Tolkatchev presents us not with an image of hope and joy at the moment of liberation but with a cry of despair: it is unbearable to look at a world in which Auschwitz is possible.

The *New York Times* devoted, on January 28, 1945, on page 3, two sentences to the liberation of Auschwitz: "Fifteen miles southeast of Katowice in industrial Silesia, Marshal [Ivan] Koneff's troops captured Oswiecim, site of the most notorious German death camp in all Europe. An estimated 1,500,000 persons are said to have been murdered in the torture chambers at Oswiecim." Despite the fact that the writer referred to "the most notorious German death camp" and provided a somewhat accurate victim total of one and a half million, this information did not warrant a separate article. For the Allies, closing down the German death camps was not an end in itself but a small part of the war to be won.

The date of the arrival of Marshal Koneff's men at the gates of Auschwitz is remembered worldwide with an awareness that Auschwitz does not simply represent a rupture in our past but also threatens to separate us from our future. "It happened, therefore it can happen again: this is the core of what we have to say," Levi observed, many years after that first encounter with those Red Army soldiers. And, he added, "It can happen, and it can happen everywhere."[2]

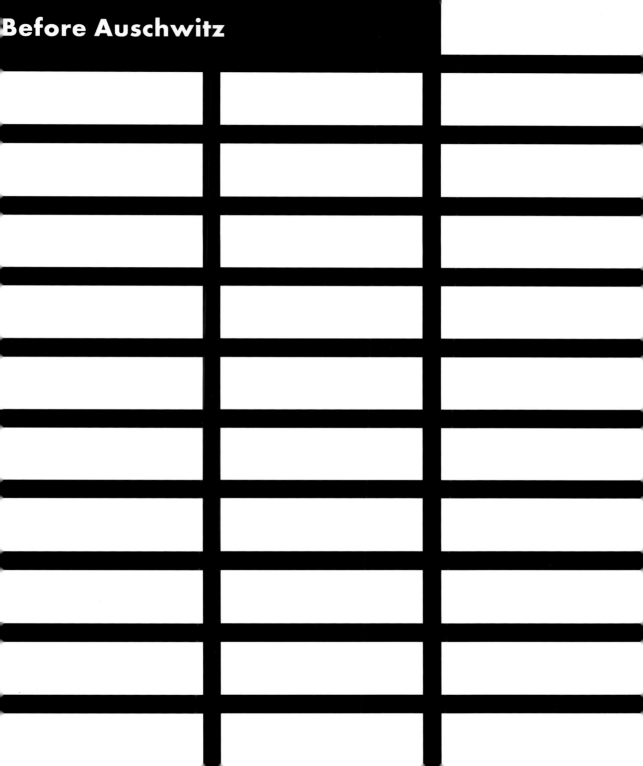

Oświęcim/Oshpitzin/Auschwitz

The name Auschwitz carries a terrible symbolic power: it stands for Holocaust and genocide, for government tyranny, for the condition of bare life, for the collapse of the ideal of progress, and so on. Often these symbolic meanings overshadow our awareness that Auschwitz, the camp and the town from which the camp took its name, was located in a particular place. Knowledge of the history and character of that place helps to anchor our knowledge of Auschwitz in our common world.

Oświęcim dates back to the late eleventh or early twelfth century, when it was a Polish fortified settlement. In the thirteenth century it became a self-governing town that measured within its walls some hundred acres and contained a castle, a parish church, and a large market square. By this time the region immediately to the west of Oświęcim had experienced substantial immigration of German speakers, and Oświęcim became for all practical purposes a border town between German and Polish lands. It was to remain so until the end of World War I. It was the capital of an independent duchy in the fourteenth century that was sandwiched between Hungary in the south, German Silesia in the

Ogólny widok Oświęcimia. — Total-Ansicht von Oświęcim.

View of Oświęcim from the city's castle, ca. 1900. In the right background stands a Roman Catholic church, built on the site of a former Dominican church; in the right foreground is the Haberfeld family's mansion; between these two buildings, on the right, is the Great Synagogue, seen from the side and back; in the background on the left are the houses that line the central market square. Auschwitz Jewish Center, Oświęcim, Poland.

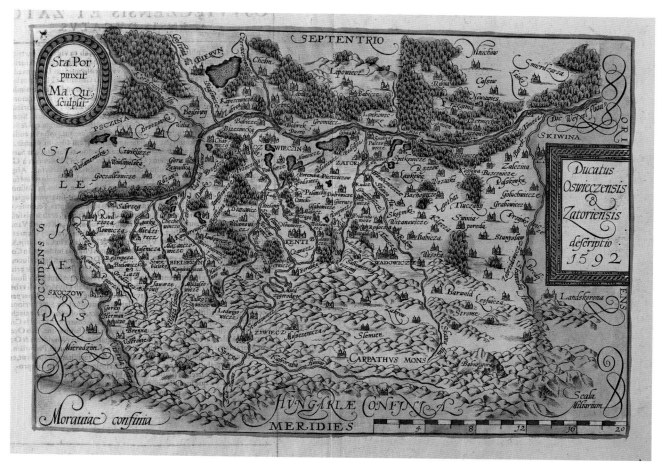

Map of the Polish duchy of Oświęcim and Zator, 1592. This map shows the Carpathian Mountains and the Vistula and Soła Rivers as they come together near Ozwieczin (Oświęcim). The map also shows the many bridges, maintained by and controlled from Oświęcim, that facilitated travel. It also marks the neighboring villages of Bizezimcka (Brzezinka or Birkenau) and Manwicze (Monowice or Monowitz). Collection of Robert Jan van Pelt, Canada.

Photograph of the Oświęcim train station with railway personnel and locomotive, ca. 1900. Collection of Miroslav Ganobis, Poland.

Oświęcim/Oshpitzin/Auschwitz 33

west, and Poland to the north and the east. At this time Dominican friars arrived in the town and built, with the financial help of the duke of Oświęcim, a large church, which was ruined in the seventeenth century and rebuilt 120 years ago. In the fifteenth century the Polish king became duke of Oświęcim, and the duchy became an integral part of the Commonwealth of Poland in the sixteenth. It was never powerful or rich, but many people knew of it because it was located at an important crossroads that connected Vienna to the south, Wrocław (Breslau) to the west, and Kraków to the east.

In 1772 Oświęcim became part of Austria under the House of Habsburg as a result of the First Partition of Poland, and the (German-speaking) Habsburgs assumed the title "duke of Auschwitz." The town Oświęcim itself was of no great significance to the government in Vienna until, in the early 1840s, it began to construct a major railway line to connect the imperial capital Vienna to Lemberg (now Lviv, Ukraine), then capital of the Austrian-ruled part of Poland. The station of Oświęcim marked an important junction, because the Austrian rail lines connected there to the German and Russian railways. As a result, the Oświęcim railway station became, in the 1880s, an important point of connection and transition for emigrants on their way to the ports of Hamburg and Rotterdam; for merchants involved in cross-border trade; and for Polish seasonal laborers seeking jobs in Germany. For the laborers' use, the government constructed in the 1910s a compound of dormitories, located close to the Oświęcim station.

With the end of World War I, in 1918, Oświęcim ceased to be part of the Habsburg empire, becoming part of independent Poland, and was no longer a border town. The dormitories constructed to provide shelter for seasonal laborers awaiting permission to cross the border lost their purpose. They were taken over by the newly established Polish army. In October 1939 the Wehrmacht (Germany's armed forces) took custody of the buildings, transferring them in April 1940 to the SS—the Schutzstaffel (Protection

Squadron), the elite of the Nazi militias, which had been established as Hitler's personal bodyguard and by 1940 had become a key component of the German state's security apparatus.

The concentration camp that became a symbol of the Holocaust was located at the edge of a town that, for centuries, provided testimony of the ability of non-Jews and Jews to live together. Jews first arrived in Oświęcim, which they called Oshpitzin (from the Aramaic word for "guests"), in the sixteenth century. Their community grew rapidly after the construction of the railways, and in 1914 Jews made up half of the town's ten thousand inhabitants. They worshipped in dozens of *shtiebelach* (prayer rooms), which served the ultra-Orthodox Jews, and in the Great Synagogue, located between the Soła River and the market square, which served the rest. The town's Jewish community had a good reputation among

Candlesticks and candelabra excavated by the Polish archaeologist Małgorzata Grupa at the site of the Great Synagogue of Oświęcim, destroyed in 1940 by the Germans, 2004.

Wedding photograph of Alfons Haberfeld and Felicia Spierer, 1936. Rodgers Center for Holocaust Education, Chapman University, Orange, California.

Original liquor bottles produced at the Jakób Haberfeld Steam Vodka and Liquor Factory in Oświęcim, 1804–1939. Collection of Miroslav Ganobis, Poland. Exhibition installation, Centro de Exposiciones Arte Canal, Madrid, 2017.

Jewish peddlers and business travelers who regularly sojourned in Oshpitzin and among the Jewish emigrants who saw the town only once, on their way to the port of Hamburg in search of a better life overseas. The Oshpitzin Jewish community included pious groups that were internal-looking, focusing on the older traditions of Jewish learning, and newer ones of abundant spirituality. Oshpitzin was well known as the westernmost outpost of Hasidism.

Oświęcim also included Jewish families who embraced the modern age. Established in 1804, the Jakób Haberfeld Steam Vodka and Liquor Factory

was by the end of the nineteenth century the largest business in town, producing a wide range of liquors famous throughout the Austro-Hungarian Empire and beyond. By the late 1930s Jakób Haberfeld's grandson Alfons and his wife, Felicia, who were leading citizens in the town, had global ambitions. In July 1939 they traveled to the United States to represent the Haberfeld distillery at the New York World's Fair. Six weeks later Germany occupied Poland. Unable to return home, the Haberfelds became refugees in the United States. They never returned to Oświęcim.

Jews, Judaism, and Anti-Judaism

In September 1935, a twenty-two-year-old Austrian journalist, Hanns Chaim Mayer (later known as Jean Améry), opened a newspaper in his favorite coffeehouse in Vienna to read a report on two laws placing restrictions on German Jews, which had been passed a day earlier during the annual Nazi Party rally in Nuremberg. He immediately realized that it would be only a matter of time before the laws would apply to him also, in Austria. "To be a Jew, that meant for me, from this moment on, to be a dead man on leave, someone to be murdered, who only by chance was not yet where he properly belonged."[3] The youth's intuition was justified: on January 17, 1943, he arrived, with 656 other Jews and 351 Roma, in Auschwitz.

Looking to the future, Mayer saw himself as a "dead man on leave"; for us, looking backward, it is all too easy to foreshadow the Holocaust in the history that preceded it and to consider all prewar European Jews as dead people on leave. Sometimes it is necessary to shake ourselves and to look with fresh eyes at the six million Jewish men, women, and children who perished in the Holocaust (of whom one million died in Auschwitz)—and also to pay some more detailed attention to the prejudice and hatred they encountered.

Originating in the Middle East, Jews are a religious, social, and cultural group that has lived as a minority in various parts of Europe, the Middle East, and northern Africa since the Roman Empire. They trace their ancestry to Abraham and more specifically to Abraham's grandson Jacob, also known as Israel, the name (meaning, "he fought with God") the angel gave to Jacob after a nightlong battle between the two. Thus Jews are sometimes referred to as the Children of Israel. Matrilineal descendants of Jacob/Israel who either adhere to the religious precepts of Judaism or, at least, do not belong to another religion, count as Jews.

Jacob had twelve sons. The great majority of Jews descend from the fourth son, Yehudah (Judah). Hence they are known in Hebrew as *Yehudim* and in English as Jews and their religion as Judaism. Jews believe in one universal God, venerate the five books of Moses, which they know as the Torah ("teaching"), and cherish a series of writings that together form the Tanakh, which roughly corresponds to what Christians call the Old Testament. In addition, from the postbiblical period onward, they accept an oral revelation from God that is contained in the Mishnah (which means, "to study by repetition") and take guidance from a series of commentaries on the Torah and the Mishnah known as the Talmud ("instruction").

At home in the land between the Jordan River and the Mediterranean, Jews scattered two thousand years ago in a wide Diaspora, leading to three major geographic groups, each with its own traditions: the Sephardim (centered on the Mediterranean), Ashkenazim (central and eastern Europe), and Mizrahim (Middle East and northern Africa). These groups, always minorities, centered their lives on an institution that was both a house of worship, a court, a school, and a community center: the synagogue.

Jews have always stood apart from the majority society in which they live. They circumcise boys in memory of the covenant between God and Abraham. They have a special calendar that goes back to the Creation and observe their own holidays, such as the weekly Sabbath on Saturday and the annual observances Rosh Hashanah (New Year), Yom Kippur (Day of Atonement), and Pesach (Passover), which centers on a ritual meal known as the Seder ("order"). The Seder is accompanied by a retelling of the story of the Jewish exodus from Egypt. Special foods, most importantly the unleavened bread known as matzo, are eaten during the meal. In addition, observant Jews follow various dietary restrictions.

Bernard Picart (1673–1733). The Passover Meal of the Portuguese Jews, 1723. Engraving. Collection of Robert Jan van Pelt, Canada.

The world-historical significance of biblical Judaism has been the articulation of monotheism—embodied also in Christianity and Islam. However, the unique character of postbiblical Judaism can be found in a continuous debate and process of decision-making on ethics known as Halakhah (meaning, "the way of walking"). It focuses on issues of behavior, not faith. The relation between Halakhah and the biblical revelation embodied in the Torah has been the object of much reflection. "Man must rely upon himself, and not upon God, to fashion a Halakhic system that is conclusive and categorical from a revelation that was purposefully inconclusive and indeterminate," observed Auschwitz survivor

Rabbi David Weiss Halivni, who has devoted his life to the historical origins of the Talmud, the key source of Halakhah. Dispute leads to debate, and debate to a majority opinion that is the basis of decision. Halivni continued, "Man is thereby empowered and commissioned by God to consummate the process of revelation, to make tangible and exact what has been revealed only in outline."[4]

Christianity evolved from biblical Judaism and, in order to find its own identity, opposed postbiblical or rabbinical Judaism with a hateful ideology that is known as anti-Judaism. From Christianity's early days, Christian theologians proclaimed the Church and the teachings of Jesus of Nazareth to be the

Jews, Judaism, and Anti-Judaism   37

A German imperial proclamation, signed by Holy Roman emperor Ferdinand I in 1551, and record of its being given as a gift to Hermann Göring in 1940. The imperial proclamation orders Jews to wear a circle on their clothing. In 1939 Reinhard Heydrich, architect of the Final Solution, obtained the proclamation for senior Nazi Göring's forty-seventh birthday, on January 12, 1940. In 1938 Heydrich and Göring had initiated the discussion among Nazi leaders about forcing German Jews to wear a distinctive sign. The George and Adele Klein Foundation Collection, Museum of Jewish Heritage—A Living Memorial to the Holocaust, New York.

only fulfillment of biblical Judaism and the only gate to salvation for both Gentiles and Jews. They considered postbiblical Jews to be blind to the truth proclaimed by the Church and placed the burden of Jesus's crucifixion—a Roman form of punishment—firmly on the Jews. These teachings concluded: Jews were to be tolerated only in a state of misery that, incidentally, was to provide proof of God's judgment against the Children of Israel.

Their fallen state was assured by Christian society through the many restrictions Jews faced through the ages and into the early modern era: they were not allowed to own land, and any of the trades or professions that required guild membership were closed to them. This left them with the immoral, in the eyes of the Church, trade of moneylending and marginal

occupations such as rag collecting. Jews were forced to live in crowded ghettos, and like lepers they were made to wear a special sign or hat. From time to time Christians subjected Jews to pogroms, massacres, and expulsions. However, at the price of a complete severance of relations with family and community, individual Jews could escape these restrictions, and worse, through (timely) conversion.

One of many artifacts in this part of the exhibition is a tallit (prayer shawl) owned by Solomon Krieser, a native of Oświęcim. Like every Jewish boy, Solomon received his tallit at his bar mitzvah. Like every Jewish man, he also wore his tallit during the marriage ceremony, and he expected, as is custom among Jews, to be buried wrapped in his tallit. In 1923, Solomon married Perla Katz, who came from the village of Sborov in eastern Poland, and the couple moved from Oświęcim to Antwerp a few years later. In the Belgian city they made a modest living and raised daughters Hilda and Hannah. In 1940, in the wake of the German invasion of Belgium, the Kriesers fled to France. Like many other refugees, they ended up in a French internment camp. Eventually, due to the intervention of a Swiss volunteer working in the camp, the children found refuge in Switzerland. Their parents weren't as fortunate. In the summer of 1942, the French handed Perla and Solomon to the Germans. Solomon was able to send his tallit to his daughters. Then the Germans locked the Kriesers and a thousand others in a deportation train that left for an unknown destination in the east. It proved to be Solomon's place of birth—only now it had a different name.

The Krieser family in Antwerp, 1936. From left to right: Solomon Krieser, Hilda Krieser, Avigdor Aichel, Hannah Krieser (foreground), and Perla Krieser-Katz. Yad Vashem: The World Holocaust Remembrance Center, Jerusalem.

Tallit (prayer shawl) and bag of Oświęcim native Solomon Krieser, ca. 1910. Yad Vashem: The World Holocaust Remembrance Center, Jerusalem.

Jews and Non-Jews in Modern Europe

Cover of the French humor magazine Le Rire *(The Laughter), April 16, 1898. By the late 1890s, anti-semites had begun to peddle the paranoid fantasy that the Jews secretly controlled the world. Charles Léandre (1862–1934) concisely depicts this notion in his portrait of the Jewish banker James Mayer de Rothschild wearing a crown embellished with the golden calf and holding the globe. Musealia, San Sebastián, Spain.*

The French Revolution (1789–99) proclaimed liberty, equality, and fraternity, and initiated in Europe processes of secularization and of political, civic, and economic emancipation that extended citizenship to the Jewish population, first in France and later elsewhere in Europe. An emphasis on the importance of education, an intellectual comfort with fierce and open-ended argument rooted in the study of the Talmud, and an ability to deal with uncertainty had prepared Jews for the challenges of the modern age. Within two generations, they moved from the margins of European society to its center, playing key roles in shaping the modern world in terms of finance, commerce, industry, science, medicine, politics, and the arts. This led to a backlash among the majority society that, increasingly, defined the national identity in terms of a shared ethnic descent. Outsiders because they remembered their origins in the Holy Land, Jews were a convenient Other who were easily blamed for all the problems that came with capitalism, urbanization, industrialization, and cultural modernism.

In the second half of the nineteenth century, ideologues began to mix traditional anti-Judaism with newly articulated racial theories that postulated the existence of different human races unequal in potential and achievement. While Jews may have been held socially and politically suspect before, now, labeled "Semites," they were declared to be racially different and inherently inferior to other Europeans, who could claim "Aryan" stock. This racial difference, so the argument went, could not be overcome through conversion or its secular counterparts such as socioeconomic integration and assimilation. Miscegenation, or race mixing, between the superior "Aryans" and other, lesser races should be prevented at all cost, as it was believed to be a cause of degeneration and a threat to the future of Western civilization.

The result was a hateful "anti-Semitic" (or, better, "antisemitic"; see footnote, page 12) discourse in which Jews were defined as an alien, rootless, and degenerate people whose very presence polluted the health of the European nations. Heinrich von Treitschke, an influential German opinion maker, summarized the German reaction to the arrival of "a host of hustling, pants-peddling" Jews from the "inexhaustible Polish cradle" in what became a favorite slogan of the Nazis: *Die Juden sind unser Unglück* (The Jews are our misfortune).[5]

In addition, antisemites (who did not include other Semites, such as Arabs, in their fantasies) pointed to the internationalist outlook of many Jews as proof that "the Jew" controlled through a global conspiracy the fate of the modern world. Thanks to sensationalist mass media, such ideas penetrated quickly in the collective imagination of the European continent and spelled catastrophe down the road. While anti-Judaism had offered an escape hatch for individual Jews through conversion, antisemitism called for radical measures. In 1885 the German nationalist Paul de Lagarde suggested a comprehensive territorial solution: ship most of Europe's Jews to the African island of Madagascar.

In the nineteenth century Jews—in Europe and

Engraving of immigrants arriving in New York, published in Frank Leslie's Illustrated Newspaper, *July 7, 1887. Library of Congress, Washington, DC.*

Russian-Jewish portable Sabbath candlesticks, 1875. These candlesticks, used for holding the candles lit at the beginning of Sabbath, consist of four pieces: two dishes and two attachable receptacles for the candles. For travel, the two dishes are screwed together, making a sphere. Five years after these candlesticks were made, the great exodus of Russian Jews to the West began. Collection of Miriam Greenbaum, Canada.

the Americas—adopted several strategies for dealing with both the challenges they faced in the modern age and the antisemitism they experienced. Pessimists among them trusted that by means of negotiation, accommodation, and patience they could cope with adversity, while optimists believed that the new liberal and increasingly democratic order would bring an end to antisemitism. Both groups included reform-minded Jews, who sought to modify traditional practices and teachings to accommodate modern life; religiously observant Jews, who sought to preserve tradition under the social and economic conditions of modern society; and ultra-Orthodox Jews, who sought to resist the challenges of modernity and preserve a traditional way of life.

Some Jews opted to improve the lot of their people by seeking more or less radical change in the societies in which they lived. Of note is the Algemeyner Yidisher Arbeter Bund (General Jewish Labor Bund), which called for Jewish autonomy within a socialist state. The bundists were optimists about the future of Jews in Europe. Zionists were pessimists: there was no future for Jews as either individuals or as an official minority in Europe; Jews ought emancipate themselves by moving to the ancient homeland of

41

Photograph from the bar mitzvah of Mario Modiano, Salonika (now Thessaloníki), Greece, 1939. Jewish religious observance in mid-twentieth-century Europe ranged from ultra-Orthodox to secular. In 2005, what Mario Modiano (front row, in glasses and shorts) would remember of his religious coming-of-age ceremony was the difficulty of learning the Hebrew text well enough to recite it in the service in the synagogue—and the bicycle he received as a gift. Centropa, Vienna.

Palestine playing cards, 1920. This card game, produced in Germany, tried to inculcate a love for the Zionist project in children while teaching them the Hebrew language, which was revived as a language for everyday use. Museum of Jewish Heritage—A Living Memorial to the Holocaust, New York.

Poster, Algemeyner Yidisher Arbeter Bund (General Jewish Labor Bund), Kiev, 1918. The text, in Yiddish, reads: "Here, where we live, here is our country! A democratic republic! Full political and national rights for Jews. Ensure that the voice of the Jewish working class is heard at the Constituent Assembly." YIVO Institute for Jewish Research, New York.

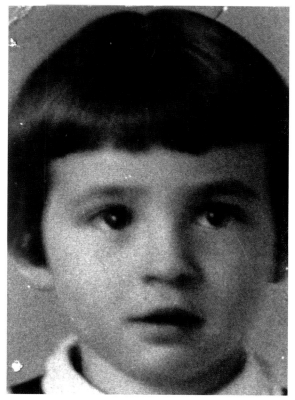

Dress that belonged to Gaby Klipper, late 1930s. In 1939 Jacob Klipper left Vienna for Palestine to prepare a foothold for his family. He expected that his wife, Klara-Kayla Klipper, and his children, Heinz and Gaby, would soon follow. He took with him most of their belongings, including this dress. The outbreak of war made it impossible for Klara and the children to leave Vienna. On September 6, 1943, they were murdered in Auschwitz. Yad Vashem: The World Holocaust Remembrance Center, Jerusalem.

Gaby Klipper, late 1930s. Yad Vashem: The World Holocaust Remembrance Center, Jerusalem.

Palestine, working the land as settlers and farmers. Zionists got wind in their sails when, in 1917, the British government issued a declaration supporting the Zionist aspiration and, five years later, the League of Nations established Mandatory Palestine. Entrusted to Great Britain, the mandate explicitly aimed at the establishment of a Jewish national home. This meant opening Palestine to Jewish immigration. Under the mandate, the British decided every year how many immigrants the economy could absorb, while Zionist officials decided who would be allowed in under the quota.

Most Jews who believed that their future depended on leaving Europe looked not to Palestine but to the New World—especially the United States and above all New York. Beginning in the early 1880s, pogroms and systematic antisemitic policies triggered the movement of two million Russian Jews westward. They filled the steerage sections of steam liners crossing the Atlantic. They arrived penniless

JEWISH POPULATION IN EUROPE BEFORE THE HOLOCAUST

PERCENTAGE OF JEWS AMONG THE TOTAL POPULATION

NORWAY 1,700 (0.02%)

FINLAND 2,000 (0.05%)

SWEDEN 7,050 (0.2%)

ESTONIA 4,500 (0.4%)

DENMARK 7,800 (0.2%)

LATVIA 91,500 (5%)

IRELAND 5,000 (0.2%)

DANZIG 10,000 (2.7%)

LITHUANIA 168,000 (7.3%)

THE NETHERLANDS 112,000 (1.4%)

SOVIET UNION 2,864,250 (1.5%)

UNITED KINGDOM 385,000 (0.8%)

BELGIUM 65,700 (0.8%)

GERMANY 524,000 (0.8%)

POLAND 3,250,000 (10%)

LUXEMBOURG 3,500 (1.2%)

CZECHOSLOVAKIA 354,000 (2.6%)

FRANCE 300,000 (0.9%)

SWITZERLAND 18,000 (0.4%)

AUSTRIA 185,000 (2.8%)

HUNGARY 401,000 (4.9%)

ROMANIA 757,000 (4.2%)

YUGOSLAVIA 70,000 (0.5%)

PORTUGAL 1,000 (0.01%)

ITALY 42,500 (0.1%)

BULGARIA 49,000 (0.75%)

SPAIN 4,000 (0.02%)

ALBANIA 200 (0.02%)

TURKEY 81,460 (0.6%)

GREECE 77,380 (1%)

but were able to make the most of a unique opportunity: in the 1880s off-the-rack clothing became a key consumer good, and having learned to survive at the margins of the premodern economy in the rag trade and the rehabilitation of second-hand clothing, immigrant Jews found it easy to find employment in New York City's booming garment industry.

Finally there were those Jews who assimilated into majority society. In the German city of Osnabrück, the Nussbaum and van Pels families were German patriots, and their nationality took precedence over their *mosaische Glaube* (Mosaic faith), as German Jews who sought assimilation defined it. Felix Nussbaum, who was to become an important painter (pages 75, 83, and 116), did not think much about

his Jewish identity. He was first and foremost an artist. The same applied to Peter van Pels (page 128), who ended up as a refugee in the Netherlands, and to Amsterdam-born Bob Hanf (page 14), who fully identified as a Dutchman, had no interest in what he referred to as his Jewish "background," and focused his considerable talents on making paintings, writing poems, composing music, and being at the center of a large circle of like-minded friends—almost all non-Jewish.

To the Germans, Nussbaum's, van Pels's, and Hanf's disassociation from Judaism did not matter. The only thing that counted was their descent—and it would bring Nussbaum, van Pels, and Hanf to Auschwitz.

World War I

Before 1914, European schoolchildren learned about past wars as both necessary and discrete episodes in the formation of their nations. Only one war stood out for a different reason: the Thirty Years' War (1618–48). While it had an immense political impact in producing, in the Peace of Westphalia (1648), a new concept of state sovereignty, the memory of this political innovation was overshadowed by the death and destruction the war brought to central Europe. It is no accident that perhaps the greatest antiwar play, Bertolt Brecht's *Mother Courage and Her Children*, is set in the Thirty Years' War. Significantly, Brecht wrote it in the fall of 1939, in direct response to the German invasion of Poland. When in 1945 World War II came to an end, both political leaders (Charles de Gaulle and Winston Churchill, for example) and historians (such as Sigmund Neumann) interpreted the two world wars and the interwar period as a second thirty years' war—that is, as a single catastrophe interrupted by an armistice. This vision persists.

"The Second World War, when it came in 1939, was unquestionably the outcome of the First, and in large measure its continuation," observed John Keegan in his classic study *The First World War*. And, in his view, this also applied to the German death camps: "A child's shoe in the Polish dust, a scrap of rusting barbed wire, a residue of pulverised bone near the spot where the gas chambers worked, these are as much relics of the First as of the Second World War."[6]

The social and economic change brought by industrialization had created enormous stress within European society. The democratic aspirations of the many faced the ambitions of social and political elites seeking to defend their positions by enhancing national prestige, by war if necessary. In 1914 the assassination of Archduke Franz Ferdinand, the heir to the throne of the Austro-Hungarian Empire, by a Serb nationalist provided the spark to set the continent ablaze. Vienna declared war on Belgrade; Berlin came to the side of Vienna; Moscow supported

Aerial photo of German gas attack near the Somme, France, 1916. Canadian War Museum, Ottawa.

45

German World War I gas mask, 1917. Musealia, San Sebastián, Spain. Exhibition installation, Centro de Exposiciones Arte Canal, Madrid, 2017.

World War I marked a decisive break with the way a war was fought, when in April 1915 the German army began to use poison gas as a weapon. Until that time, soldiers targeted the bodies of enemy soldiers with swords, lances, bows and arrows, muskets, cannons, bayonets, rifles, and guns; now the target ceased to be the body and became the environment of the enemy. Breathing is the most primary of all human actions. The understanding that we all breathe the same air, friend and foe, has always been the foundation of a shared humanity. In April 1915, thanks to an utterly modern product—bottled chlorine gas, researched and developed in a scientific laboratory and manufactured in a factory—air lost its innocence, and as soldiers of one army breathing through gas masks advanced through a terrain in which soldiers of the opposing army were dying of asphyxiation, the most vital common bond between human beings was both practically and symbolically severed.

But another and perhaps even more important bond dissolved. Until the Enlightenment, Europeans, like many people elsewhere in the world, had lived with a faith in God and in tradition. With secularization and modernization, a new faith had provided a new compass: it assumed in the reality of progress an inexorable convergence between the order of the world and the hopes of human beings. Scientific research combined with industrial prowess would fill in the details. From the circumstances of its beginning to the limitless slaughters that carried no military benefits, World War I had been a senseless war, and it resulted in a widely shared nihilism. When in November 1918 the fighting stopped, Europe counted 17 million dead, 20 million wounded, millions of stateless refugees wanted by none, large stretches of the continent in ruins, endless hatred, and bad faith triumphant. In such conditions the tide of demagoguery could easily sweep up the masses.

The result was that "the war to end war" turned out to be merely the first act of a thirty-year-long tragedy.

Belgrade; Paris and London were bound to aid Moscow and therefore turned on Berlin. Nations that had been peaceful neighbors for a century now engaged in a ruthless and continuous war of attrition, made possible by the very advances in science and technology that had established Europe as the dominant continent.

Within the belligerent countries a rising tide of nationalistic hysteria triggered profound xenophobia, which in turn led to a rapid deterioration of the position of the Jews in central and eastern Europe. The Russian government initiated massive deportations of six hundred thousand Jews from Russian Poland. As they spoke Yiddish, which has close relations to the German language, Jews were considered to be pro-German agents. In Germany antisemites circulated rumors that Jews either shirked military service or were successful in finding comfortable jobs in military offices. A statistical investigation undertaken by the army clearly demonstrated that this accusation was unfounded, but it did not have any effect on public perception.

The Aftermath of the Great War

In 1917 Russia descended into chaos as the result of two revolutions, the first in February and the second in October (both Julian calendar). This allowed Germany to force on Russia a peace that left Germany in control of Poland, much of Ukraine, Belarus, and the Baltic countries. Germans were dreaming of a large empire in the east. However, a series of military defeats initiated the disintegration of the multination Austro-Hungarian Empire. Now Germany stood alone, and when the German army suffered decisive defeats in the west, a mutiny in the German navy and strikes in factories showed that the German nation desired a cessation of hostilities. In November 1918, Kaiser Wilhelm II fled to the Netherlands, and a new German leadership composed of Socialists and Social Democrats accepted the tough terms of the Armistice. German generals refused to concede that their mistakes had caused the defeat and tried to save their reputations by claiming that the striking workers had "stabbed the army in the back."

By 1919 Germany, unofficially known as the Weimar Republic, after the city where the new constitution had been written, had no choice but to accept the Treaty of Versailles, which left it with a huge reparation bill and the loss of its merchant fleet, its colonies, and its border territories. On paper the losses were immense: 20 percent of Germany's territory, 10 percent of its population, one-third of its coal production capacity, and so on. However, in reality, a large part of the land lost was in poor agricultural areas in which farming had been unsustainable, and most of the population lost was the Polish minority, which the German majority had not trusted. Yet German nationalists did not consider this a blessing in disguise: they assiduously nurtured German grievances and in myriad ways demanded that the lands in the east that had become part of the newly established Polish Republic ought to be returned to Germany, if possible through negotiation, if necessary through another war.

Austrian antisemitic postcard, 1919. Antisemites identified Jews as the instigators of the military debacle that brought an end to World War I. The George and Adele Klein Foundation Collection, Museum of Jewish Heritage—A Living Memorial to the Holocaust, New York.

Dokumente einer irrsinnigen Zeit! *(Documents of an insane era), 1923.*
The commemorative sheet contains twenty-eight stamps that show the
cost to mail a postcard between 1920 (ten pennies) and December 1923
(five billion marks). Collection of Robert Jan van Pelt, Canada.

But in the early 1920s Germany had no power: it was a disarmed and bankrupt pariah among the Western nations. Its citizens were left humiliated and uncertain. Added to a sense that Germany had lost its honor was a fear of Communism and the daily experience of a social and economic chaos that culminated in a hyperinflation in which, at its height (lasting from January to November 1923), prices doubled every four days. This inflation bankrupted the middle classes and also provided, in the ridiculous nominal value of the banknotes issued—the highest being the 100 trillion (100,000,000,000,000) mark note, which equaled around forty US dollars when issued—a bitter symbol of Germany's weakness and shame.

Concurrent with the inflation was another humiliation: in 1923 the French occupied the Rhineland province to force the German government to pay its reparations in hard currency. The occupation army included African soldiers from Senegal. Many Germans considered the occupation of white people by black soldiers an utter violation of the laws of European civilization. Yet the reality in the Rhineland cities was more complex, and human. Some German women and Senegalese soldiers fell in love, and around six hundred children were born of these relationships. Before 1914 Germany had maintained colonies in Africa, and a small number of black men from these colonies had settled in Germany. Some had married local women. While these interracial couples had faced discrimination, they were few in number, embedded in German society through ties of family, and hence had been overlooked by the politics of the day. But in 1924, when the first so-called Rhineland Bastards were born (page 55), there were many Germans who desired to exploit the very existence of those children. Writing at that time, the World War I veteran and political agitator Adolf Hitler had no difficulty assigning blame for the miscegenation in the Rhineland: it was all the result of a Jewish conspiracy to destroy the German race.

Hitler was the leader of the Nationalsozialistische Deutsche Arbeiterpartei (National Socialist German Workers' Party), which claimed to offer a social and political vision inspired by life in the trenches. There comrades had shared hardship in a national form of socialism—which in its original form was decisively international in its outlook. The National Socialists, or Nazis, identified with the soldiers of World War I, because they considered life an eternal and merciless war for *Lebensraum* (living space). In a hostile world, the German nation should mobilize itself on a continuous basis. They believed the German nation could survive only if it practiced positive selection, which would ensure the success of the racially superior and would also cull all those who weakened Germany's power to fight.

Exploiting the chaos caused by the hyperinflation, Hitler attempted, on November 9, 1923, a coup against the democratic Weimar Republic. He failed and was imprisoned but served only nine months of a five-year sentence. He used this time to expound his political philosophy in the form of a memoir, entitled *Mein Kampf* (My struggle). In it he articulated, among other things, his belief that the removal of Jews from German society was key to Germany's revival. Hitler also explained his political technique to gain power by legal means and to hold on to it. "The art of all truly great national leaders at all times consists among other things primarily in not dividing the attention of a people, but in concentrating it upon a single foe."[7] Hitler, who appears not to have been an antisemite before he turned to politics, decided to portray "the Jew" as the root of all Germany's problems. "The Jew" was responsible for the stab in the back by striking workers and mutinying sailors (1918), the short-lived and bloodily suppressed Communist revolution in Bavaria (1919), the Rhineland occupation (1923), and the financial collapse (1920–23). And too many people believed this lie.

Yet while the Nazis played on the fears and resentments of the population, others considered the political and social changes brought about by

National Sozialist: Oder umsonst waren die Opfer
*(National Socialist: Or otherwise their sacrifices were
in vain), 1928. This poster called on German citizens
to vote for the Nazi Party because it carried on the
legacy of the soldiers who had sacrificed their lives for
Germany in World War I. Bundesarchiv, Berlin.*

of the modern age. The young painter and graphic
artist Richard Grune, a student of Paul Klee and
Wassily Kandinsky, was energized by the optimism
he saw around him and became a key figure in the
Social Democratic youth movement. Grune helped
create the Kinderrepublik Seekamp (Children's
Republic at Seekamp), a self-governing community
of twenty-three hundred working-class children
who convened in hundreds of tents pitched at the
Seekamp estate in northern Germany near the Baltic
Sea. The Children's Republic expressed confidence
in the potential of every single person and in democratic procedures to deal with friction and conflict.

The Nazis remained a largely marginal group
until 1930, when the Great Depression hit Germany.
At this time, when pessimism reigned, the Nazis
projected a boundless confidence. The bold design
of the swastika, the uniforms and salutes adopted
from Italian fascism, the processions copied from
the military, the mass rallies lifted from the sports
world, and the language and relics of martyrdom all
suggested unity, purpose, and above all victory. (*Sieg*
means "victory" in German—hence the Nazi chant
Sieg Heil!, or "Hail Victory!") In the early twentieth
century the Germanist Guido von List had interpreted the sig rune (ᛋ)—a letter in the early-medieval
Scandinavian rune alphabet—as a symbol of *Sieg*,

the collapse of the old order as an opportunity to be
embraced. The Weimar Republic became a laboratory
of social innovation and artistic discovery. Writers
such as Alfred Döblin and Thomas Mann, poets such
as Walter Mehring and Else Lasker-Schüler, drama-
tists such as Ernst Toller and Bertolt Brecht, com-
posers such as Kurt Weill and Alban Berg, painters
such as Max Beckmann and Elfriede Lohse-Wächtler,
architects such as Walter Gropius and Erich Mendel-
sohn, philosophers such as Martin Heidegger and
Ernst Cassirer, scientists such as Albert Einstein and
Werner Heisenberg—all of them helped to shape the
Weimar years into one of the most exciting periods

*Adolf Hitler, in Munich, surrounded by young comrades,
late 1920s. Collection of Robert Jan van Pelt, Canada.*

Richard Grune (1903–1983), The Children's Republic at Seekamp, *1928. Lithograph. Collection of Robert Jan van Pelt, Canada.*

and the Hitler Youth, which was to shape the German future, thus adopted a single sig rune as its symbol. As unemployment rose to 30 percent of the German workforce, many became convinced that Hitler might be Germany's savior.

In the Weimar Republic, the five-hundred-thousand-strong Jewish community did well, and for the first time in German history Jews enjoyed full access to the highest political offices. They seemed fully acculturated and assimilated into a German society that, at least officially, embraced democracy. Yet, throughout this period, antisemitism remained alive. During the hyperinflation, many referred to money as "Jew confetti." Their argument against their Jewish compatriots was based on the fact that at the time the mark bottomed out, a Jew was minister of finance. They ignored the facts that German Jews suffered equally and that finance minister Rudolf Hilferding laid the foundation for the new currency, the *Rentenmark*, which brought the inflation to an end and introduced five years of economic growth. The false charge that German Jews had shirked service at the front also continued to circulate. Throughout the 1920s Jewish veterans' organizations demanded from German society an acknowledgment of the sacrifice of the Jewish community. The appeal fell on deaf ears. In 1932, when the Nazi Party became the largest party in the Reichstag (legislature), the Reich Federation of Jewish Front Soldiers made a last attempt to remind the nation of the sacrifice made by the German Jewish community during World War I, by publishing the name, address, military unit, rank, and day of death of each German Jew killed in the service of the fatherland.

On January 30, 1933, German president Paul von Hindenburg appointed Adolf Hitler as Reich chancellor. A decade later Salli Joseph, who like Hitler had served at the front, and who like Hitler had earned an Iron Cross for personal courage, was deported with his wife, Martha, to Auschwitz, where both were murdered. Salli's Iron Cross survived the Holocaust; in 1940 he had entrusted it to his daughter, Margot, when she was able to get a passage for Palestine.

Iron Cross, second class, awarded to Salli Joseph for his service in World War I, 1914–18. United States Holocaust Memorial Museum, Washington, DC.

Margot, Salli, and Martha Joseph, March 1940. Less than three years after this photo was taken, Salli and Martha Joseph were murdered at Auschwitz. United States Holocaust Memorial Museum, Washington, DC.

The Third Reich: A Nation of Comrades

When the Nazi Party came to power in 1933, it promised to solve the crisis the nation faced by abandoning austerity policies and reflating the economy. The party's agenda was presented through carefully choreographed mass events—including nocturnal gatherings illuminated by countless torches and framed by pillars of light produced by powerful searchlights—that provided in their Wagnerian splendor an intoxicating sense of communion, adventure, and shared destiny. The seduction achieved by these rallies was an essential part of Nazism.

Nazism was also characterized by the proliferation of organizations, all with their own distinctive uniforms that suggested unity of purpose and, depending on one's rank, status and power. At the same time these organizations promised instant comradeship. "[The Nazis] have made all Germans everywhere into comrades, and accustomed them to this narcotic from their earliest age: in the Hitler youth, the SA, the Reichswehr [army], in thousands of camps and clubs," German lawyer Raimund Pretzel (using the pseudonym Sebastian Haffner) wrote from exile in Britain, five years after his own stint in a Nazi boot camp for junior judges. "They are terribly happy, but terribly demeaned; so self-satisfied, but so boundlessly loathsome; so proud and yet so despicable and inhuman. They think they are scaling high mountains, when in reality they are crawling through a swamp."[8]

Among all Nazi organizations, the paramilitary Schutzstaffel (Protection Squadron), usually abbreviated as SS, stood out as a self-declared elite. It originated within the SA, or Sturmabteilung (Storm Troopers), which before 1933 provided men to beat up opponents and conquer the streets. The SS

Dienſt- und Paradeanzug der Allgem. ⚡⚡
⚡⚡-Oberſcharführer

Traditionsanzug der ⚡⚡
⚡⚡-Unterſcharführer

Tafel 47

SS uniforms depicted in Organisationsbuch der NSDAP (Organization book of the National Socialist German Workers' Party), 1937. Collection of Robert Jan van Pelt, Canada.

SS belt buckle, 1933–45. This buckle, inscribed with the SS motto, was found in Auschwitz after 1945. Auschwitz-Birkenau State Museum, Oświęcim, Poland.

originally served as Hitler's personal bodyguard. The group's motto was *Meine Ehre heisst Treue* (My honor is loyalty). In a state organized on the *Führerprinzip* (leader principle), the SS claimed preeminence because each member had sworn unconditional loyalty and obedience to Hitler. The symbol of the SS was a double sig rune (ᛋᛋ), proclaiming "victory, victory."

Membership in the SS was open to physically fit and generally tall, blond, and blue-eyed German males who could prove they had pure "Aryan" ancestry. Led by Reichsführer-SS Heinrich Himmler, SS men wore deliberately expensive and elegant uniforms designed by artist Karl Diebitsch and graphic designer Walter Heck and tailored by Hugo Boss.

SS men were supposed to look good and to act ruthlessly and without question. In 1934 the SA began to demand the social revolution Hitler had promised in the 1920s. Wishing to maintain his new relationships with Germany's economic and military elites, Hitler decided to eliminate the top leadership of the SA. In the Night of the Long Knives (June 30), Himmler's SS obediently arrested and executed dozens of senior SA men. Having proven his mettle, Himmler was now entrusted with the leadership of the German police, including the Secret State Police (Geheime Staatspolizei, or Gestapo). Members of the SS came to occupy crucial positions in the German state security apparatus. And Himmler was not a bureaucrat but an ideologue. "History dictates that as long as there are people on earth, humans will struggle with subhumans," he declared in 1935. "One can calmly reach the conviction that this struggle for life or death is as much a natural law as the battle of the bacillus that causes the plague against the healthy body."[9] As to the identity of those subhumans, Himmler had no doubt: the Communists and, above all, their master, the Jew.

By 1935 antisemitic propaganda permeated daily life in Germany. It was aimed not only at adults but also at schoolchildren—and none of it elicited a protest from teachers or parents. Published in 1938,

Der Giftpilz (The poisoned mushroom) tells the story of a mother and her young son gathering mushrooms in the forest. Mother's guidance to distinguish edible from poisonous mushrooms quickly leads to a lesson on the Jewish Question. "Jews are Jews, and remain so. For our people they are a poison. . . . Our boys and girls must learn to know the Jew. They must learn that the Jew is the most dangerous poison-mushroom in existence."[10] Even preschoolers were to be exposed to this message of hate. Twenty-one-year-old kindergarten teacher Elvira Bauer produced a picture book in 1936 that took its title from one of Martin Luther's sayings: *Trau keinem Fuchs auf grüner Heid und keinem Jud auf seinem Eid* ("Trust no fox on the green heath! And no Jew on his oath!"). Its first line set the tone: "The Devil is the father of the Jew." It provided a long history of the world, beginning at the Creation, in which the Jew continuously appears as the single source of all corruption. Yet the book ended on a happy note: Germans had finally become aware of the rot, and a solution was at hand, expulsion. Germany was going to be made safe for German

Illustration from Trau keinem Fuchs auf grüner Heid und keinem Jud auf seinem Eid *(Trust no fox on the green heath! And no Jew on his oath!), a picture book by Elvira Bauer, 1936. Museum of Jewish Heritage—A Living Memorial to the Holocaust, New York.*

youth. In the penultimate picture, Bauer showed her children the ideal: a marching formation of Hitler Youth, "husky, tough, and strong," in a Jew-free Germany.[11]

Books like these shaped a new generation of Germans and also could not but shape a new generation of Jews. "Daily, for years on end, we could read and hear that we were lazy, evil, ugly, capable only of misdeed, clever only to the extent that we pulled one over on others," Hanns Mayer (aka Jean Améry) observed after the war. "We were not worthy of love and thus also not of life. Our sole right, our sole duty was to disappear from the face of the earth."[12]

In the pretty picture of the New Germany, not only Jews but also "Aryan" Germans deemed to be less than perfect had no place. In early 1933 the Nazi government had adopted the Law for the Prevention of Offspring with Hereditary Diseases. Ordering the sterilization of the mentally handicapped, schizophrenics, manic-depressives, persons with inherited epilepsy, and the blind, deaf, and alcoholic, this edict was followed by the Law against Dangerous Habitual Criminals, which provided for the castration of serious moral offenders. Initial estimates suggested that some four hundred thousand people would be sterilized or castrated. The Nazi government found use for such laws beyond the originally intended target groups. In 1937 it decided that they could be used to address the problem of the so-called Rhineland Bastards as well as the few other Afro-Germans born at other times and places. Socially shunned, Afro-Germans had already been forced to a life on the margins. In 1935 the Nuremberg Laws, which prohibited marriages and extramarital relations between Germans and those of "alien blood," had been officially interpreted to also include Afro-Germans. Hitler had never wavered in his opinion that the French occupation of Rhineland with black soldiers had been part of a Jewish plot to cause through miscegenation the degeneration of the German people, and in 1937 he ordered the sterilization of all the Rhineland Bastards by widening the application of the Law for the

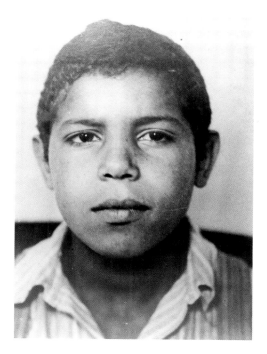

Afro-German boy, 1937. The original caption for this photograph reads: "Hereditary Ill! Bastards along the Rhine. A relic of the Rhineland occupation by colored Frenchmen. Over 600 of these unhappy bastards live in Rhineland. A living symbol of the most tragic betrayal of the white race." Bundesarchiv, Berlin.

Prevention of Offspring with Hereditary Diseases to these children of mixed race. With the help of the Gestapo, which ensured the delivery of the targeted to medical offices and clinics, physicians sterilized more than four hundred Afro-German children.

The fate of these children was kept hidden from the population. Most Germans knew that behind the uplifting image of Germany presented in the rallies, parades, and propaganda there was reality— one that they should not inquire about. And they didn't. Domestic and international successes seemed to confirm the claims of the Nazi propagandists. These included full employment, cheap holidays on newly constructed cruise ships, the introduction of new consumer goods such as affordable radios

Ballot for the 1936 parliamentary election, offering the German people a single-party option, 1936. Wiener Library, London.

(which served to spread Goebbels's propaganda), the promise of an affordable car (the forerunner of the Volkswagen Beetle) that would allow German families to discover the beauty of the German land while driving over the new highways—Adolf Hitler's roads—and the promise of the transformation of the life of workers through the destruction of tenements and the construction of pleasant single-family homes, specially designed for large families. And then there were the successes in the international sphere: the reestablishment of the military draft and the rapid growth of the army (1935); the Summer Olympics in Berlin (1936); and the annexation of Austria (1938), the Sudetenland (1938), and Czech lands (1939).

And it might be argued that the uniformed, comradely world the Nazis sought to create—a world in which people encounter only people like themselves and in which privacy is destroyed—eliminated the very possibility of critical thought itself. At least this is what Hannah Arendt postulated thirty years after her own escape from Germany: in the Third Reich the distinction between fact and fiction, which allows people to judge the reality of experience, and the distinction between true and false, which is a basic standard of thought, collapsed—and this destroyed the German people's capacity for action. According to Arendt, we are able to experience reality when we are in the company of people who are different from us but whom we trust, and who may challenge or confirm our experiences. Yet the Nazis had worked hard to make such people absent. "In this situation, man loses trust in himself as the partner of his thoughts and that elementary confidence in the world which is necessary to make experiences at all."[13] Within the Third Reich, facts did not matter. "The Nazi impress on the German mind consists primarily in a conditioning whereby reality has ceased to be the sum total of hard inescapable facts and has become a conglomeration of ever-changing events and slogans in which a thing can be true today and false tomorrow." The result of this was not indoctrination, "but the incapacity or unwillingness to distinguish altogether between fact and opinion." And this, Arendt postulated, was the core of the Nazi assault on civilization.[14]

Culling the Nation

After his appointment as chancellor of the Reich in January 1933, Hitler used a February arson attack on the Reichstag building, the home of the national parliament, as an excuse to suspend basic civil rights indefinitely. In the weeks that followed, regular police, reinforced with SA and SS Nazi Party militia, rounded up more than ten thousand political opponents from the left and imprisoned them, without any legal recourse, in improvised detention facilities run in a haphazard fashion mostly by the SA and characterized by gratuitous violence. These were the conditions under which a general election was held on March 5 and under which the new Reichstag adopted, on March 23, the Ermächtigungsgesetz (Enabling Act), which gave Hitler the power to enact laws by decree.

The arrests had two purposes: removing those who might oppose the transformation of a democratic, constitutional state into a dictatorship with arbitrary powers; and cowing the majority into silence. "Unnerving was the disappearance of a number of quite harmless people, who had in one way or

Arrest of Communists by the SA, or Sturmabteilung (Storm Troopers), March 6, 1933. Bundesarchiv, Berlin.

another been part of daily life," German lawyer Raimund Pretzel recalled, from exile in Britain in 1939. "The radio announcer whose voice one had heard every day, who had almost become an old acquaintance, had been sent to a concentration camp, and woe betide you if you mentioned his name. . . . Others just vanished. One did not know whether they were dead, incarcerated, or had gone abroad—they were just missing."[15]

The Nazis claimed that the newly established camps served a pedagogic rather than punitive purpose: to apply a shock to the "errant sons" of the German national community: Communists, Social Democrats, pacifists. And, indeed, from time to time the newspapers reported on mass releases of inmates who had been "reeducated."

In March 1933, operating in his new job as acting chief of police in Munich, Reichsführer-SS Heinrich Himmler established an SS-run concentration camp in the nearby town of Dachau. Himmler believed concentration camps should be run uniformly by a professionally trained and managed staff to be recruited from his own SS. A major step in that direction was the appointment of Theodor Eicke as commandant of Dachau in June 1933. A recent inmate of a mental asylum, Eicke established the so-called SS-Totenkopfverbände (SS Death's-Head Units), which, with their rigid discipline backed up by a comprehensive system of punishments, operated the camp independent of the judiciary. Unlike those incarcerated in jails or prisons, the people admitted into the camps had no rights at all. This became very clear when Eicke authorized, without reference to the laws, the killing of those who tried to escape, practically arrogating a key sovereign power to the SS.

In 1934 Himmler became chief of the Gestapo (an acronym for Geheime Staatspolizei, or Secret State Police). The Gestapo was responsible for imprisoning

Card sent from Dachau by inmate Friedrich Hoyer to his wife for her fiftieth birthday, 1934. The card carries an extract from the camp regulations: "Protective custody prisoners may receive each month one package. . . . Visits are not permitted." Florence and Laurence Spungen Family Foundation, Santa Barbara, California.

Eichmann was made responsible for organizing the expulsion of Jews or dispatching them to ghettos, to concentration camps, and, from 1942 onward, to the extermination camps.

By the end of 1933, some thirty thousand had been arrested and detained in the camps. Upon their release, prisoners were instructed not to speak about their experiences in the camps, and the rest of the Germans, if they dared to say anything at all, did so only in whispers. German exiles did try to turn the world's attention to the abuses, and one of the results was the decision by the Norwegian Nobel Committee to award the 1935 Nobel Peace Prize to anti-Nazi journalist Carl von Ossietzky, who had been imprisoned in the Esterwegen concentration camp since early 1933. The SS did not release von Ossietzky to attend the ceremony in Norway, and three years later, at age forty-eight, he died in police custody. Another well-known attempt to shine a light on the camps occurred in 1936, when athletes from all over the world converged in Berlin to participate in the Summer Olympics. German exiles published a map (*Übersichtskarte über die Konzentrationslager, Zuchthäuser und Gefängnisse in Deutschland*) showing the locations of concentration camps and other places of detention throughout Germany and folded it into what appeared to be a regular travel guide to Germany. It was one of over nine hundred camouflaged anti-Nazi writings hidden in booklets with various titles, in packages of tea and shampoo, and in seed packets.

Between 1933 and 1936, prisoners were put to work only inside the camps; in a time of huge unemployment, prisoner labor was not to compete with free labor. By 1936 there was full employment, and now the SS began to consider the economic potential of the camps. Sachsenhausen, established in 1936 near Berlin, was the first major concentration camp to be run like a business. Hitler was committed to numerous infrastructure projects, and Himmler saw an opportunity to use the concentration camp system to generate building materials. Sachsenhausen,

people in concentration camps, and thus Himmler gained control of who was to be incarcerated in the camps. Until 1934, Himmler had overseen a private spy agency within the Nazi Party, the SD (Sicherheitsdienst, or Security Service). Run by Reinhard Heydrich, the SD had become quite an efficient organization, especially as it monitored so-called enemies of the state, such as Freemasons, Jews, emigrants (those who had left Germany in 1933), and others. When Himmler became responsible for the Gestapo, Heydrich merged the SD, a Nazi Party office, into the Gestapo, a government agency, effectively taking control of its intelligence operations. Adolf Eichmann, who was the SD official in charge of collecting information on Jews, now gained official police authority. It took only a few years before

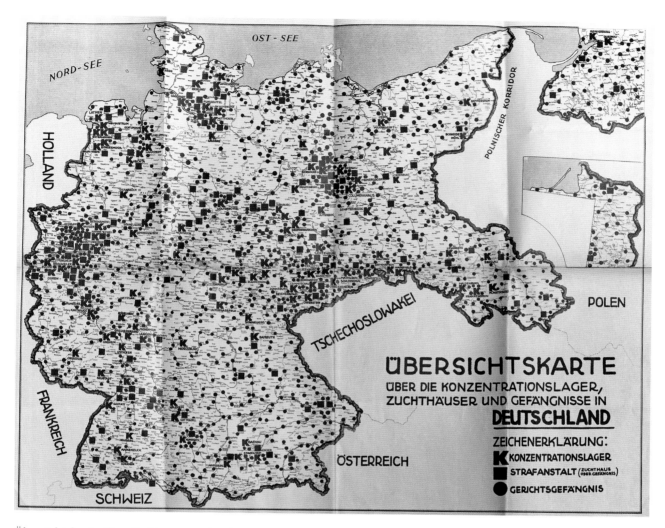

Übersichtskarte über die Konzentrationslager, Zuchthäuser und Gefängnisse in Deutschland *(Map of the concentration camps, prisons, and jails in Germany), 1936. Musealia, San Sebastián, Spain.*

and, in its wake, the new camps of Buchenwald and Neuengamme, were to supply 200 million bricks annually.

By the mid-1930s the regime in the camps, now all run by the SS, was standardized. A punishing daily roll call, lasting many hours and repeated in all the concentration camps, ensured that no prisoners went missing. All prisoners, shaved bald like convicts

(which they were not), were now dressed in standard-issue uniforms made of coarse gray-and-blue-striped material. Each uniform was marked with the prisoner's number and a badge indicating his or her category. The red triangle marked prisoners incarcerated for political offenses, such as membership in the Communist and Social Democratic parties. New categories were soon added. Needing to expand the

Tailors' workshop producing prisoner uniforms in the Sachsenhausen concentration camp, 1941. Gedenkstätte und Museum Sachsenhausen, Oranienburg, Germany.

camp population to increase the prisoner labor force, the Gestapo began to fill the camps with social outsiders, which included anyone not regularly employed or who had caused trouble at work, homeless people, vagabonds, petty criminals, so-called racial defilers, and so on.

In 1933 the population of Germany included some twenty thousand Jehovah's Witnesses. Because their beliefs did not permit them to pledge allegiance to any entity but God, they refused to serve in the army, as the soldier's oath was a personal one to Adolf Hitler. Thus Jehovah's Witnesses became a target of persecution. Some ten thousand were imprisoned, and of these two thousand were sent to concentration camps. While in custody, 1,490 Jehovah's Witnesses died.

Between 1918 and 1933 Berlin had been a center of homosexual culture and, thanks to the pioneering

Photograph of Jehovah's Witness Ernst Schwalm; his wife, Emmy; and their son, Ernst David, 1928. Ernst Schwalm was arrested in late 1937. First imprisoned in Buchenwald, Schwalm ended up in Auschwitz. He was reunited with Emmy in the summer of 1945. Florence and Laurence Spungen Family Foundation, Santa Barbara, California.

Prisoners during a roll call in Dachau concentration camp, 1938. Bundesarchiv, Berlin.

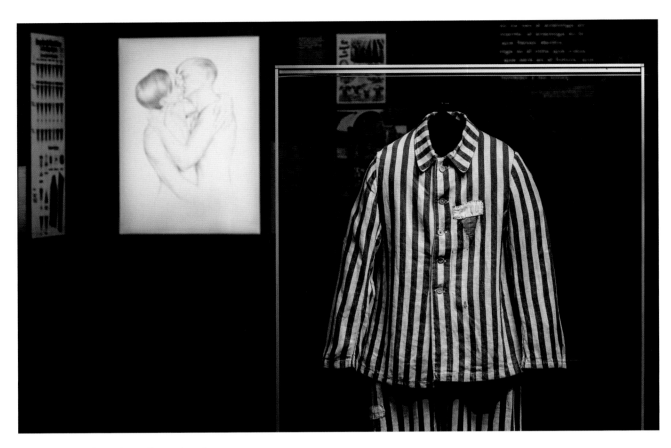

Prisoner's uniform from the Sachsenhausen concentration camp, ca. 1941. In the background, a lightbox showing Christian Schad's drawing Loving Boys, *1928. Uniform: Gedenkstätte und Museum Sachsenhausen, Oranienburg, Germany; drawing: Christian Schad Museum, Aschaffenburg, Germany. Exhibition installation, Centro de Exposiciones Arte Canal, Madrid, 2017.*

work of the physician Magnus Hirschfeld, of a positive gay self-consciousness. In the mid-1930s the Nazis began to target male homosexuals, charging that they undermined the masculine ideal. Some one hundred thousand men were arrested on the basis of Paragraph 175 of the penal code, which criminalized "unnatural fornication." Fifty thousand were convicted, and more than ten thousand ended up in concentration camps. Marked in the camps by a pink triangle, those imprisoned on the basis of Paragraph 175 were the targets of particular abuse. One of the men with the pink triangle was the well-known artist Richard Grune. During the Weimar Republic, Grune had been an organizer of the Children's Republic at Seekamp (page 51). The Social Democratic summer camp had been a good place, a utopia, where children were empowered to take charge of their own lives. Now Grune was committed to a dystopia of total obedience and constant violence. He would spend eight years in the Buchenwald and Flossenbürg concentration camps.

Before the outbreak of World War II (in 1939), concentration camps had had only a marginal role in supporting antisemitic policies, which aimed first at voluntary emigration and later at forced expulsion from Germany. Only 5 percent of the prewar prisoners had been Jews. But when Jews did end up in these camps, they were always exposed to special abuse. Housed in special dormitories, put to work in special labor squads, they were subjected to unique levels of systematic humiliation and sadistic violence that exceeded the treatment meted out to non-Jewish prisoners. In the camps Jews, more than others, faced the likelihood of being murdered.

The special treatment of Jews in the camps provides a missing link between the vicious antisemitic propaganda that permeated German life and the genocidal policy adopted in the early 1940s. In the mid-1930s German Jews, while increasingly excluded from society, still were recognized as a heterogeneous minority that could not simply be understood as "the Jew." But the humiliation and violence Jews experienced in the camps taught the SS to see Jews as a homogeneous entity—"the Jew"—to be excluded from German communal life.[16]

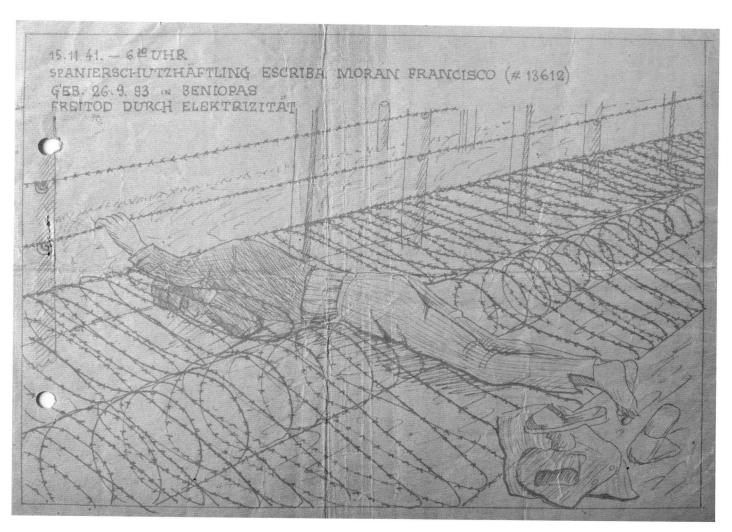

Forensic drawing of the corpse of an inmate of the Mauthausen camp, 1941. Some thirty thousand soldiers and supporters of the Spanish Republic, who had fled to France in 1939, were handed by the Vichy French regime to the Germans, who transported many of them to concentration camps. Mauthausen received more than five thousand, of whom more than forty-two hundred died. This sketch features one of them, Francisco Escribà Morán, who in November 1941 ran into the electrified wire surrounding the Gusen subcamp. Florence and Laurence Spungen Family Foundation, Santa Barbara, California.

Internment Camps for Roma

In 1935 a different kind of camp began to appear in Germany. These camps were not organized and maintained by the SS but by municipalities. Their purpose: to remove Roma people from cities, towns, and villages through internment.

The civil servants and police officials who created these camps called the people to be brought there *Zigeuner* (Gypsies). The people designated by outsiders as Zigeuner, Gypsies, Gitans, or Gitanos refer to themselves, depending on the part of Europe where they live, as Kalo (Spain), Manush (France), Sinti (central Europe), Lalleri (central Europe), and Roma (southern and eastern Europe). They are related but also distinct. Because the Roma group is the largest, the practice has arisen to use its name to designate the totality of Kalo, Manush, Sinti, Lalleri, and Roma.

The Roma originated in India, and groups of them lived in the Byzantine Empire by the end of the first millennium. By the late fourteenth century the Ottomans had taken over most of the Byzantine Empire and began their advance through the Balkans toward the heart of the European continent. The Roma initially followed the Ottoman armies, and then they began to move independently from those armies. A fifteenth-century document records that the Roma, identified as *swartzen getoufte heiden* ("black baptized heathens") had arrived in Bern, Switzerland. The Roma moved frequently, partly out of choice and partly due to the refusal of the majority society to accommodate their presence. Before the modern age, they occupied a small but important economic niche: they were skilled in metalwork, raised and traded horses, tamed and trained bears for public entertainment, and worked as musicians. Few made an effort to understand them and their values. "They have preserved most of the mental characteristics of a nomadic people, including a complete lack of interest in the future and the past," George Orwell observed in 1938. The Roma reminded him of the eighteenth-century ideal of the "noble savage." "And considering their admirable physique, their strict morals—strict according to their own peculiar code, that is—and their love of liberty, one must admit that they have a strain of nobility."[17]

The homogenizing ambition of modern European nation-states created friction with the Roma, because they continued to adhere to their separate language and social structure, which centered on clans. The governments of the German Empire and the Weimar Republic enacted various laws to force the Roma to adopt the way of life of a settled community (which many did) and to impose on them the duties of citizenship, including military service for Roma men. Yet many Roma continued to lead itinerant lives, traveling the countryside in their caravans. Unlike the Jews, the twenty-six thousand Roma living in Weimar Germany were perceived as demographically, politically, socially, and economically irrelevant to the future of the majority society. Hence no *Zigeunerfrage* (Gypsy Question) arose in the nineteenth and early twentieth centuries.

In November 1935 the German government extended the Nuremberg Laws, adopted in September to disenfranchise the Jews, to the Roma. This meant that Roma lost their citizenship and that they were forbidden to marry or have any intimate relations with "Aryan" Germans. Concurrently municipalities began to proceed energetically against the Roma by creating special internment camps at the edges of cities and towns. Cologne set the trend, and Berlin followed suit. In preparation for the 1936 Olympic Games, the police deported the six hundred Roma living in apartments and houses in Berlin to a special internment camp in the suburb of Marzahn. Deportations in the cities of Frankfurt am Main,

Magdeburg, and Düsseldorf followed in succession. In the camps the Roma lived fully segregated from the rest of society: children could not attend school, and Roma men could work only as day laborers. Due to the bad sanitary conditions and lack of medical care, many became ill.

The Rassenhygienische und Kriminalbiologische Forschungsstelle (Research Office on Racial Hygiene and the Biology of Criminality), created by Himmler and led by Dr. Robert Ritter, considered the concentration of so many Roma in Marzahn as an opportunity. Ritter began a pilot project to study the racial

Roma children in the Ravensburg camp, 1937. Bundesarchiv, Berlin. Located near Ravensburg in southern Germany, this internment camp existed from 1937 until 1943, when the remaining thirty-six inmates were sent to Auschwitz. Twenty-nine of them perished there.

Rassenkundliche Bestimmungstafeln für Augen-,
Haar- und Hautfarben *(Racial-determination boards for
eye, hair, and skin colors), 1935. Nazi ethnologists Bruno
Kurt Schultz and Michael Hesch created this tool for
racial fieldwork. Museum of Jewish Heritage—A Living
Memorial to the Holocaust, New York.*

*Eva Justin of the Research Office on Racial
Hygiene and the Biology of Criminality
establishing the eye color of a Roma woman,
ca. 1938. Bundesarchiv, Berlin.*

characteristics of the Roma with the aim to prove that
criminality arose from racial degeneration. Within a
year Ritter had expanded his research to encompass
all Roma in Germany. Ritter's work, and that of his
assistant, Eva Justin, was to be the basis of a program
of persecution that would include, from early 1938
onward, incarceration into regular concentration
camps of "Gypsies and persons travelling in Gypsy
fashion who have shown no desire for regular work
or have violated the law"—a definition that was
interpreted in such a way that it came to be applica-
ble to most Roma adults.[18]

"Perhaps the concentration camps are already
crowded with them," Orwell wrote in December
1938, considering the fate of the Roma in the Third
Reich. He was not sure, as no one appeared interested
in their fate, and therefore no one reported on what
was happening to them. He expressed the hope
that they would survive. "Existing in the teeth of a
civilization which disapproves of them, they are a
heartening reminder of the largeness of the earth and
the power of human obstinacy."[19]

The Expulsion of the Jews

While the persecution of the Roma population began haphazardly, that of the Jews unfolded with speed and purpose. In March 1933, American Jewish organizations called for a boycott of German goods in response to the new German government's antisemitism. Hitler, in retaliation, enacted a one-day boycott against German Jews; they could be held hostage to restrain the behavior of Jews outside Germany— which meant of the world at large. On April 1, 1933, SA men painted Jewish businesses and professional offices all over Germany with yellow stars and the word *Jude* (Jew) and blocked their entryways.

The impact of the boycott was huge. "The unsettling and depressing aspect of [the April boycott] was

Nazi boycott of Jewish businesses, 1933. Deutsches Historisches Museum, Berlin.

that it triggered a flood of arguments and discussions all over Germany, not about anti-Semitism, but about the 'Jewish Question,'" Raimund Pretzel recalled six years later. "Suddenly everyone felt justified . . . to have an opinion about the Jews."[20] But few Germans dared to stand by their Jewish neighbors and friends. "The problem, the personal problem, was not what our enemies did but what our friends did," Hannah Arendt explained to German TV viewers in 1964. "It was if an empty space formed around one."[21]

Within a week after the boycott the government adopted Das Gesetz zur Wiederherstellung des Berufsbeamtentums (the Law for the Restoration of the Professional Civil Service). It allowed for the immediate retirement of all "non-Aryan" civil servants who had entered service before November 9, 1918—the date of the revolution that had toppled the German monarchy. "Non-Aryans" who had entered the civil service after that date were to be summarily dismissed. As to the meaning of the word *Aryan*, it was not that clear. The only thing that *was* clear was that Jews were "non-Aryan." Thousands of Jewish civil servants were fired, but also Jewish teachers, professors, and museum curators—professionals who in Germany enjoyed civil-service status. Even Jewish musicians employed in the many state opera companies found themselves without a job. Shortly thereafter similar laws led to the disbarment of Jewish lawyers, and the government insurance company, which provided the greatest part of physicians' incomes, refused to reimburse invoices issued by Jewish doctors. Universities—all state institutions— began to restrict the number of Jewish students. These laws made history; for the first time since the emancipation of the Jews in Europe, a government had begun to reverse rights gained by legal means. And, beginning in May 1933, works by Jewish authors were burned on pyres all over Germany.

Guidelines for permitted and forbidden marriages under the first
Nuremberg Laws, 1935. Deutsches Historisches Museum, Berlin.

Throughout the country, individuals began to shun their Jewish neighbors; patients ceased to consult Jewish doctors; and libraries, museums, theaters, cinemas, and other places of public entertainment refused admission to Jews. The town limits of many municipalities were marked with a plethora of signs, issued not by some Nazi office in Berlin or Munich but locally designed and produced, a grassroots effort.

THE INHABITANTS OF THIS PLACE DO NOT DESIRE CONTACT WITH JEWS.

JEWS: BEWARE. THE ROAD TO PALESTINE DOES NOT GO THROUGH THIS VILLAGE.

THE JEW IS OUR MISFORTUNE. LET HIM STAY AWAY FROM US.[22]

As German Jews were progressively excluded from civil society, and as they faced harassment, occasional beatings, and vandalization of property, those in smaller communities migrated to large cities, hoping to find safety and opportunity in numbers. There Jewish children could continue to be educated in specially established Jewish schools. Jewish sports clubs located in cities tripled in size, and Jewish adult-education programs became very popular. Intellectual leaders such as Martin Buber and Leo Baeck saw the persecution as an opportunity to deepen Jewish consciousness: if German Jews were persecuted as Jews, they should know themselves as Jews. The often monumental synagogues built during the Jewish emancipation gained a new significance as lifelines to an embattled community. In addition to religious services, they provided space for welfare offices, soup kitchens, emigration counselors, and

Jewish sports-club blouse of Mary Offentier, 1936. In 1938, the parents of ten-year-old Mary sent her and her older sister, Hanna, to the Netherlands. Mary took the Bar Kochba Club sports blouse with her, as it was one of her most beloved possessions. In 1942 Hanna was arrested and sent to Auschwitz, where she was murdered. Mary survived in hiding with her parents. Museum of Jewish Heritage—A Living Memorial to the Holocaust, New York.

a stage for concert and theater performances by Jewish musicians and actors who were forbidden to perform for "Aryan" audiences. Despite all these achievements, most German Jews were increasingly disoriented by the escalating persecution. However, the crisis energized committed Zionists, who had maintained for decades that the only future for Jews was in Palestine. They had a vision and a program.

By the fall of 1933 some fifty thousand Jews had left Germany, most often in a panicked flight to avoid arrest. As political refugees, they were generally welcomed in neighboring countries. Both refugees and hosts assumed that the Nazi regime would not last long and that soon normal conditions would be restored in Germany. By early 1934 it had become clear the Nazis were to stay in power, and the coun-

tries that had taken in refugees began to tighten immigration procedures. At this time, German Jews who saw no future in Germany desired to leave in a well-planned emigration, not in hasty flight. As a result the exodus of Jews from Germany slowed down, to twenty-three thousand in 1934, and twenty-one thousand in 1935. Around a third went to other European countries, a third moved to Palestine, and a third settled overseas. The decision to emigrate always meant leaving most of one's assets behind. Prospective emigrants were forced to sell whatever they had at a great discount; the proceeds were subject to a special tax, and the remaining Reichsmarks were to be deposited into a blocked account, which could be exchanged for foreign currency at between 40 percent (1934) and 20 percent (1936) of the official value.

In the summer of 1935 German officials began to refuse to allow marriages between Jews and non-Jews, and SA men began to harass such couples. Berlin decided it needed to take control of the situation: at a special meeting of the Reichstag during the Nazi Party's annual Nuremberg Rally, held in September, Hitler announced two laws to establish "a tolerable relation" between Germans and Jews. The Gesetz zum Schutze des deutschen Blutes und der deutschen Ehre (Law for the Protection of German Blood and German Honor) and a supplementary decree stipulated that anyone with three or four Jewish grandparents counted as a Jew and could marry only another Jew; anyone with two Jewish grandparents was a "half Jew," and could marry only another "half Jew" (a "half Jew" married to a Jew counted as a full Jew). One Jewish grandparent made a person a "quarter Jew," who could marry only a person without Jewish ancestry. The Reichsbürgergesetz (Reich Citizenship Law) differentiated between Reich subjects and Reich citizens, reserving the second status, which gave political rights, to someone "who is of German or kindred blood and who, through his conduct, shows that he is both desirous and fit to serve faithfully the German people and Reich." A subsequent regulation stated unequivocally: "A Jew cannot be a citizen of the Reich."[23]

In late 1936 the assault began on Jewish entrepreneurs, shopkeepers, and artisans. Government agencies refused to deal with businesses owned by Jews and radically reduced allocations in foreign currency and material. These actions were not always the result of instructions from the top. Throughout Germany, officials had adopted a way of "working toward the Führer," in which they creatively formulated and enacted policies they believed would please Hitler, and which Hitler afterward almost always confirmed. In the case of the Jews, all of these policies had one thing in common: they were ever more radical.[24]

Jews were under increasing pressure to sell whatever was left for bargain-basement prices. The Jewish community now faced a dramatic impoverishment. Many more German Jews were looking for a way out of Germany, preferably as far from Europe as possible. While in 1933 only 8 percent had moved overseas, in 1937 overseas countries absorbed 60 percent of the Jews leaving Germany. When the Nazis came to power, most German Jews had been wary of the United States, which they considered an intensely materialistic country that would not be able to

satisfy their intellectual and cultural aspirations. Yet three years of Nazi rule had made them rethink the American option, and now they lined up at American consulates seeking immigration visas. It was a long shot: the annual US quota of immigrants from Germany was twenty-five thousand. One of those who received a visa was eighteen-year-old Suzanne Bauer from Mannheim. Her father, Ludwig Bauer, had a married sister in New Jersey, and she sponsored Suzanne's immigration through an affidavit. At this time Suzanne's parents, Ludwig and Irma, and her two brothers, Heinz and Werner, decided to remain in Germany. "Our parents (like many others) never believed that conditions could become so disastrous for the Jews and aside from that would have to leave behind all their property," Heinz recalled decades later.[25]

By the beginning of 1938, 140,000 Jews had left Germany, but in March, Germany annexed Austria and thus gained another 180,000 Jews, bringing the total Jewish population to 540,000. The imposition of Nazi rule triggered an eruption of hatred and violence against Austrian Jews, surpassing any such previous display in Germany. In the spring and summer of 1938, some twenty-six thousand Jews left what was now known as Greater Germany—a relatively low number indicating the difficulty of finding refuge abroad. An international conference held in the French resort of Évian-les-Bains was to bring relief to émigrés. But only one country proved willing to allow large-scale immigration of Jews: the Dominican Republic. And it did not have the absorption capacity to do so.

On November 9, 1938, Berlin launched a nationwide, centrally coordinated pogrom, which became known as Kristallnacht (Crystal Night, or Night of Broken Glass). Synagogues were burned all over the Greater German Reich, destroying the only remaining places where Jews had been allowed some measure of communal life. In addition, Nazis looted Jewish-owned businesses and apartments—including the home of the Bauer family. The SA and SS

The philosopher Martin Buber lecturing at an adult-education program in Lehnitz, Germany, 1935.

Torah scroll, 1904. The Bornplatz Synagogue in Hamburg, Germany, dedicated in 1904, was the largest synagogue in northern Europe. On Kristallnacht (November 9–10, 1938), Nazis destroyed its interior, and in 1939 it was demolished. Members of the congregation were able to save some Torah scrolls. When, in March 1940, Dr. Seligmann Bamburger and his family obtained passage to New York, they were able to smuggle one of the Torah scrolls out of Germany. It safely arrived in New York in the spring of 1940. Museum of Jewish Heritage—A Living Memorial to the Holocaust, New York.

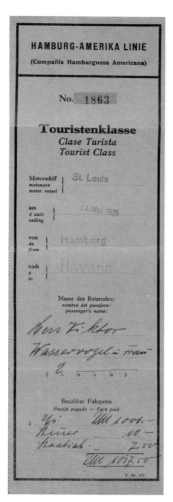

LEFT: Viktor and Irma Wasservogel's ticket for passage on the St. Louis, *1939.* RIGHT: *Viktor and Irma Wasservogel, on the deck of the* St. Louis, *1939. In early 1939 the Wasservogels obtained a visa for Cuba, and in May they joined 935 other, mostly Jewish, passengers on the MS* St. Louis. *However, the government of Cuba did not honor the visas when the ship arrived in Havana, and no safe harbor was offered in the United States. In June the* St. Louis *returned to Europe. Viktor and Irma made a second attempt to reach the Americas nine months later, and this time they were successful. Of the others on the ship, 254 perished—many of them in Auschwitz. Museum of Jewish Heritage—A Living Memorial to the Holocaust, New York.*

rounded up thirty thousand Jewish men and brought them to concentration camps. Ludwig Bauer was one of them. In general, the men's release was made conditional on their families obtaining visas that allowed for immediate departure abroad. Jews were not allowed to collect insurance money. Finally, and cynically, the German government fined the Jewish community with the enormous sum of one billion Reichsmark for the damage caused by Nazis to Jewish property. At the same time the Nazi regime completed the process of disenfranchisement and expropriation: only as forced laborers were Jews allowed to participate in the economy. And all Jewish communal and cultural organizations were shut down.

Emigration turned into flight: some 120,000 Jewish men, women, and children left Germany during the winter of 1938–39. Desperate parents completed questionnaires for the *Kindertransport* (children's transport) to arrange their children's escape out of the Reich. Others stood in lines, hoping to obtain exit visas to Switzerland or England, to find distant relatives in Canada or the United States, or to embrace a whole new and perhaps solitary life in places like Cuba, Uruguay, Paraguay, Brazil, and even Shanghai.

Ludwig Bauer, who had been released from Dachau after a two-week incarceration, had reconsidered his earlier decision to remain in Germany. "We travelled to the nearest US consulate to put our names on the waiting list and were advised that it might take 1 to 2 years before we could get the necessary papers," Heinz recalled.[26] Ludwig and Irma Bauer put in the paperwork for themselves and their young son

五
月
年
三
民
紀
攝
禮
典
業
畢
學
同
期
一
第
練
士
級
校
二
校
醫
部
軍
日
十
五
四
國
念
戲
時
訓
設
高
分
第
學
軍
政

Staff of a hospital in Kunming, China, 1949. Seated in the center are Dr. Hugo Weihs, holding his son, Daniel, on his lap, and his wife, Rozsi Weihs, holding an unidentified girl. Arrested during Kristallnacht in Vienna, Dr. Hugo Weihs was sent to the Buchenwald concentration camp. Rozsi contacted Consul-General Dr. Feng Shan Ho, who issued thousands of visas to Shanghai against the explicit orders of his superiors to desist. His visas not only liberated Dr. Weihs and some three thousand other Viennese Jews but also put Shanghai on the map as a refuge of last resort. The Weihs arrived in China in August 1939, and Hugo found work first in various hospitals. After 1945 the Weihs, like so many Jewish exiles in China, had no option but to remain; return to their native Austria was impossible. The creation in 1948 of the state of Israel and the victory in 1949 of the Chinese Communists over the government army forced a decision, and the Weihs moved to Israel. Collection of Daniel Weihs, Israel.

Werner and then sent Werner to an aunt in Belgium to be out of harm's way until the US visa arrived. Heinz was able to obtain papers for Great Britain and left on April 30, 1939. In November, Heinz received a US visa, sponsored by his American relative, and in February 1940 he arrived with the MS *Veendam* in Hoboken, New Jersey. Within days Heinz, now Henry, had a job in his uncle's butcher shop.

In 1933 Hitler had held German Jews hostage to ensure the good behavior of the United States,

Dr. Feng Shan Ho, Chinese consul-general of Vienna, in 1938. In 2000, Yad Vashem, Israel's Shoah Martyrs' and Heroes' Remembrance Authority, recognized Dr. Ho with the title "Righteous Among the Nations." Feng Shan Ho Family, United States.

Felix Nussbaum (1904–1944), The Refugee, *1939. Oil on canvas. Felix Nussbaum, who had left Germany in 1932 for a scholarship in Italy, and who in 1933 had decided not to return to Germany after Nazis torched his studio in Berlin, visualized the fate of Jewish refugees who know they are welcome nowhere. Museumsquartier Osnabrück, Felix-Nussbaum-Haus, loan from Irmgard and Hubert Schlenke, Ochtrop, Germany.*

a nation that he believed to be controlled by "the Jew." In the fall of 1938, when Hitler prepared for the annexation of the Sudeten area, the Czech border region inhabited largely by ethnic Germans, he feared the possibility of a war with Great Britain and France. Yet the Munich Agreement, in which Great Britain, France, and Italy allowed Germany's annexation of the Sudetenland, averted war. Realizing that

London and Paris had little stomach for an armed conflict, Hitler decided to seek the return of lands Germany had lost in 1918 to Poland. European Jewry was to be held hostage to ensure those countries would not aid Poland. On January 30, 1939, at the occasion of the sixth anniversary of his appointment as Reich chancellor, Hitler told the Reichstag: "I have been a prophet very often in my lifetime. . . . Once again I will be a prophet: should the international Jewry of finance succeed, both within and beyond Europe, in plunging mankind into yet another world war, then the result will not be a Bolshevization of the earth and the victory of Jewry, but the annihilation of the Jewish race in Europe."[27]

The Invasion of Poland and

the Beginning of World War II

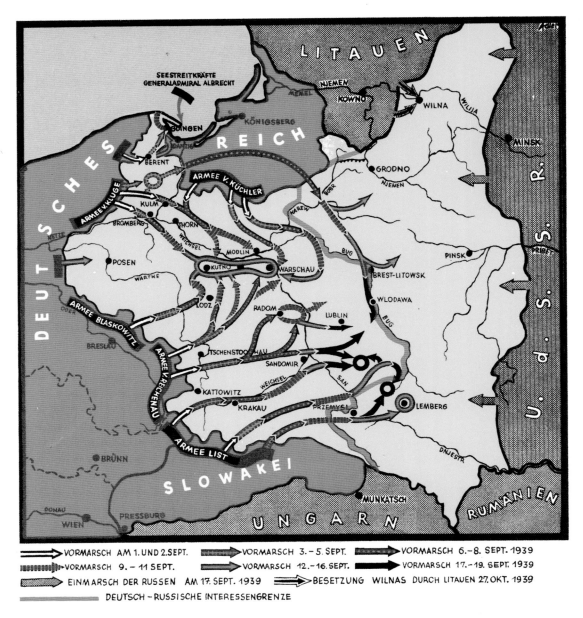

VORMARSCH AM 1. UND 2. SEPT.   VORMARSCH 3.–5. SEPT.   VORMARSCH 6.–8. SEPT. 1939
VORMARSCH 9.–11. SEPT.   VORMARSCH 12.–16. SEPT.   VORMARSCH 17.–19. SEPT. 1939
EINMARSCH DER RUSSEN AM 17. SEPT. 1939   BESETZUNG WILNAS DURCH LITAUEN 27. OKT. 1939
DEUTSCH–RUSSISCHE INTERESSENGRENZE

Map of the German and Soviet invasions of Poland, 1940.
The red line on the right portion of the map, labeled in the key
as Deutsch-Russische Interessengrenze *(German-Russian*
boundary of interests), marks the German-Soviet line of
demarcation. Collection of Robert Jan van Pelt, Canada.

German nationalists had long called for a return of the territories Germany had lost to Poland in 1918–19; more secretly, they hoped for an expansion of *Lebensraum* (living space) in the east beyond the lost territories. In August 1939, Germany concluded a nonaggression pact with the Soviet Union, and on September 1 the German army invaded Poland. Great Britain and France had guaranteed Poland's security and declared war on Germany. But the British and the French did little that was of any practical help to the Poles. The Soviet Union invaded Poland from the east on September 17. Eleven days later Berlin and Moscow ratified a secret agreement to split the country. Invaded from both the west and the east, the Poles had no chance: after five weeks of fighting, which included the heroic resistance of Warsaw, the Polish army capitulated. The Polish government went into exile in London. Moscow annexed all of Poland east of the Curzon Line—the Soviet-Polish border proposed by the Allies after World War I. Berlin annexed the western part of Poland, including Poznań, Łódź, and Oświęcim, and imposed a harsh occupation regime on the remaining lands, which they called Generalgouvernement (General Government). This area included Warsaw, Kraków, and Lublin.

Many Poles, both Jews and non-Jews, escaped from the German-ruled General Government into the territories annexed by the Soviets. Many of these refugees were deported, a year later, to the Gulag camps in the Arctic and Siberia. Lithuania, still independent, also provided a temporary refuge to thousands, including the rabbis and students of a famous Talmudic academy, the Mir Yeshiva. American relief organizations, such as the Va'ad Ha-Hatsala (Rescue Committee), provided support and also sought for ways to help the refugees leave for the United States. In Kovno (Kaunas), then the Lithuanian capital, two diplomats were willing to help. In a coordinated response to the desperation of thousands, the acting Dutch consul, Jan Zwartendijk, and the Japanese consul, Chiune Sugihara, provided visas that allowed more than six thousand people, mostly Jews, safe

Execution of Polish civilians in a forest close to Warsaw, 1939. Institute of National Remembrance, Warsaw.

Students of the famous Talmudic academy Mir Yeshiva learn in the sanctuary of the Beth Aharon Synagogue, in Shanghai, 1943. United States Holocaust Memorial Museum, Washington, DC.

Visa page of the passport of the Goldin family, 1940. Passport of Jakob, Roza, and Isabella Goldin showing a statement by Jan Zwartendijk, acting Dutch consul in Kovno, Lithuania, that no visa is required to enter Dutch colonies in the West Indies (July 30, 1940), and the transit visa subsequently issued by the Japanese consul, Chiune Sugihara (August 5, 1940). Museum of Jewish Heritage—A Living Memorial to the Holocaust, New York.

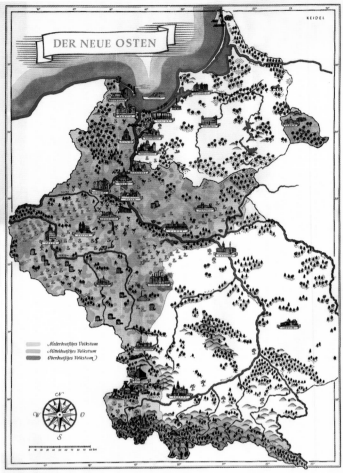

Map of Der neue Osten *(the New East), 1940. This map shows the German-annexed part of Poland (gray) and the German-occupied part of Poland (white). The annexed part, which was often referred to as "the New East," included the now renamed town of Auschwitz and was to be subjected to a radical ethnic cleansing. The occupied part was to serve as a homeland for the Poles. Collection of Robert Jan van Pelt, Canada.*

passage through the Soviet Union to Japan. From there hundreds traveled to the United States before December 1941; the rest ended up in Shanghai. In that city the Mir Yeshiva remained active even under the most difficult conditions.

In the now German-controlled parts of Poland, special units commanded by security chief Reinhard Heydrich arrested, and at times killed, members of the Polish elite. Meanwhile, the Soviets perpetrated a massacre of Polish officers at Katyn and deported over a million Poles to the Gulag and faraway locations in the Soviet Union.

Hitler gave Himmler the authority to Germanize the annexed Polish territories. The first step involved changing the names of towns, villages, squares, and streets. Thus the Polish city of Poznań reverted back to Posen, Katowice to Kattowitz, Oświęcim to Auschwitz, and Łódź became Litzmannstadt. The second was a program of ethnic cleansing that included the deportation of Poles from the annexed territories to the General Government, and the immigration of ethnic Germans from eastern Europe. Himmler also charged land-use planners and architects to design a German makeover of the annexed

territories through reforestation, construction of buildings in a German vernacular, and the demolition of buildings assumed to be too Polish in appearance. Hans Stosberg got the commission to oversee the physical transformation of Polish Oświęcim into German Auschwitz.

With the conquest of Poland, Germany gained control over more than two million Jews. Their continued presence was seen as the greatest obstacle to the Germanization of *Der neue Osten* (the New

East). An SS handbook suggested that German policy toward the Jews might transcend mere expulsion. It warned, "Europe's East is the launching pad and reservoir of Jewry: from there new hordes descend repeatedly on the world." Hence, the reconstruction of this part of Europe involved not only the immigration of Germans and the expulsion of Poles but also *"the solution of the Jewish Problem* as such."[28] In anticipation of this solution "as such," Jews were subjected to systematic humiliation and harassment that included the obligation to wear a distinguishing mark, the forced haircuts of Orthodox men, confiscation, looting and robbery, beatings, and occasional executions.

What was to be the nature of this solution? Initially Hitler insisted that all Jews would be concentrated in a closed "reservation" near the Polish city of Lublin. Infeasible from the start, this project was quickly abandoned, and Nazi officials turned to the possibility of settling all European Jews in Madagascar, in the Indian Ocean. In the summer of 1940 it became clear that the Madagascar option had to be postponed. The Germans began to warehouse Jews

The deportation of Poles from the German-annexed territories to the occupied lands known as the Generalgouvernement (General Government), 1940. Bundesarchiv, Berlin.

Road sign reading AUSCHWITZ KREIS BIELITZ, 1940. It indicates that Auschwitz is part of the Bielitz District of the newly annexed German lands. Collection of Miroslav Ganobis, Poland.

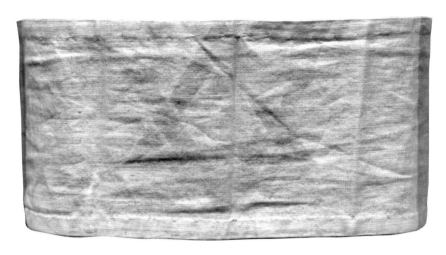

Armband marked with a Jewish star issued to Lazar Chaim Birnbaum in Kraków, 1939–42. Museum of Jewish Heritage—A Living Memorial to the Holocaust, New York.

into ghettos surrounded by walls and barbed-wire fences. Stripped of all their assets, Jews were pushed into these ghettos—the best known are Litzmannstadt in the annexed territories, and Warsaw, Kraków, and Lublin in the General Government. These were terribly overcrowded places: the Warsaw ghetto measured only 1.3 square miles, and initially held four hundred thousand people, who lived nine to a room. Submitting to forced labor, in exchange for food and some worthless ghetto scrip, was the only option for survival. Starvation and a collapse of hygiene due to overcrowding quickly transformed the ghettos into death traps.

From late 1941 onward some Polish ghettos also became dumping grounds for German Jews and Roma people. By that time the mortality in these places was such that some German officials began to consider the possible benefit to the Germans of a wholesale liquidation of both ghettos and their populations.

Jews moving into the Litzmannstadt (Łódź) ghetto, March 1940. Bundesarchiv, Berlin.

"Unworthy of Life"

In the early twentieth century, many Europeans and North Americans believed that human progress depended on eugenics: the concept that only healthy people should reproduce. The Germans made this state policy. A law passed in 1933 gave doctors the power to sterilize patients without their consent. Within six years, more than three hundred thousand people had been forcibly sterilized. At the start of World War II, Hitler decided that society should not care for "useless eaters," as he referred to the disabled, because all resources were needed for the war effort. He signed an authorization that initiated a mass-murder program, Aktion T4, code-named for the address of its headquarters at Tiergarten 4, in Berlin.

Key to the program were carbon monoxide gas chambers, disguised as shower rooms. The brainchild of police captain Christian Wirth, these gas chambers were constructed in existing asylums such as Hartheim Castle, Sonnenstein Castle, and four other "euthanasia" centers. As killings under the T4 program were considered medical treatment, doctors were in charge. One of them was Georg Renno. As a physician in a psychiatric hospital in Leipzig, Renno had become involved with the killing of patients with a lethal overdose of phenobarbital, normally used to treat epilepsy. Subsequently he was transferred to Hartheim Castle, where he prepared his "patients" for the gas chamber. Under the aegis of Aktion T4, Renno also conducted assessments in fifty-plus asylums, nursing homes, and old-age homes, and in the Mauthausen concentration camp, where he identified sick and invalid prisoners who might need a "cure" at Hartheim.

Renno had a special responsibility for the children's ward at Hartheim, which in December 1940 included eleven-year-old Ilse Geuze. A serious illness had left the young Ilse with a learning disability

Hartheim Castle, 1940. The site was a killing center during the Nazi's Aktion T4 "euthanasia" program; the photograph shows the smoke from the small crematorium constructed inside for burning the victims' bodies. United States Holocaust Memorial Museum, Washington, DC.

and continuing health issues. In early 1940 she was taken from her parents and put in a nearby home for children with disabilities. In mid-December her parents received a letter from the director of Hartheim Castle informing them that Ilse had been admitted

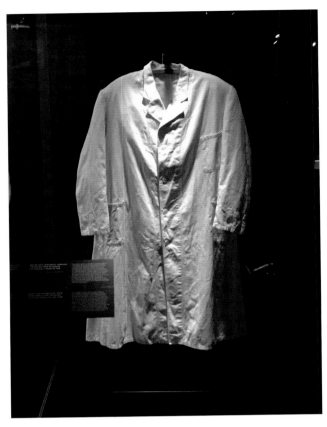

Ilse Geuze, 1930s. At age eleven, after being admitted to Hartheim Castle's children's ward, Ilse died, presumably gassed under the aegis of Aktion T4. Lern- und Gedenkort Schloss Hartheim, Alkoven, Austria.

Georg Renno's doctor's coat, ca. 1940. Dr. Renno was one of the Aktion T4 killers, who collectively put to death tens of thousands of mentally and physically infirm or disabled people—those Hitler deemed "useless eaters." Lern- und Gedenkort Schloss Hartheim, Alkoven, Austria. Exhibition installation, Centro de Exposiciones Arte Canal, Madrid, 2017.

to his institution; it also mentioned that, "under the rules of the Minister of Defense," no visits or phone calls were allowed. A few weeks later Ilse's parents received an urn with her ashes.

By 1941, when news of the killings led to public protest, the initial goal of murdering seventy thousand people had already been exceeded, and Hitler called for an official halt to the program. However, the practice of killing patients continued. In Hartheim another twenty-eight thousand people were killed, mostly Mauthausen prisoners. Other killing centers

added another one hundred thousand victims after the official closing of Aktion T4, bringing the total number of victims to two hundred thousand by the end of the war.

Renno was indicted for war crimes in 1967, but in 1973 a panel of physicians determined that his deteriorating health made him unfit to stand trial, and the court stopped the proceedings against him in 1975. Renno lived another twenty-two years. In the year of his death he told an interviewer that he did not feel guilty, as he had brought his victims relief.

Fear

In 1940, German forces occupied Denmark and Norway in April; captured the Netherlands, Belgium, and Luxembourg in May; and defeated France in June, dividing that country into a zone of German occupation in the north and west, and the unoccupied Free Zone in the south. The French government, committed to a policy of collaboration with the Germans, established itself in the resort of Vichy. Italy, Hungary, Romania, and Bulgaria were now brought into an ever-closer alliance with Germany, and when the Yugoslavs resisted the attempt by Belgrade to ally itself to Berlin, Germany invaded and conquered Yugoslavia—and also Greece. By the beginning of June 1941, all of continental Europe except the remaining neutral countries—Sweden, Switzerland, Spain, and Portugal, and the half-allied Soviet Union—was under direct or indirect German control.

The conquest of western Europe brought another 470,000 Jews under direct or, in the case of the Free Zone in France, indirect German control. This number included one hundred thousand German and Austrian Jews who had found refuge in various European countries between 1933 and 1939. As a result of the war, emigration had ceased to be a viable option: borders were closed, and commercial shipping between the continent and the rest of the world had largely ceased. Assuming that, after Great Britain's expected defeat, the French colony of Madagascar would be ceded to Germany, Reinhard Heydrich aimed to deport all European Jews to that island. Anticipating this solution, the Germans had begun to ghettoize the Polish Jews. In western Europe they decided on a different policy. There the German occupational authorities, with the aid of local civil servants and, where it applied to French territory, the French government in Vichy, issued decree after decree forcing the special registration of Jews, their

Felix Nussbaum (1904–1944), Fear, *1941. Oil on canvas. In exile from Germany, Nussbaum found refuge in Belgium, only to find himself, in 1940, under Nazi rule once again. Living in German-occupied Brussels he painted this self-portrait. In it he is overcome by fear, yet he tries to comfort his niece, Marianne. His fear was prescient: three years later, both were murdered in Auschwitz. Museumsquartier Osnabrück, Felix-Nussbaum-Haus, loan from the Niedersächsische Sparkassenstiftung, Osnabrück, Germany.*

```
            SPECIAL PARCELS FOR INTERNMENT CAMPS
   shipped via parcel post, postage prepaid, arrival guaranteed.
```

For Women	For Men
CERES - $8.50	**MARS - $8.50**
1 Sweater	1 Sweater
1 Sport Shirt (Blouse)	1 Sport Shirt
3 Handkerchiefs	3 Handkerchiefs
2 pairs of Stockings	2 pairs of Socks
2 Bloomers	2 Drawers
Darning Wool and Thread	Darning wool and Thread
DIANA - $10.75	**MERKUR - $10.75**
Contents same as CERES and	Contents same as MARS and
in addition-	in addition-
500 gr. Zwieback	500 gr. Zwieback
500 gr. Soap	500 gr. Soap
500 gr. Cocoa	500 gr. Cocoa
500 gr. Sugar	500 gr. Sugar
JUNO - $10.75	**PLUTO - $10.75**
Contents same as CERES and	Contents same as MARS and
in addition-	in addition-
1 Cotton Blanket,140 x 200 cm.	1 Cotton Blanket,140 x 200 cm.
VENUS - $13.75	**ZEUS - $13.75**
Contents same as CERES and	Contents same as MARS and
in addition-	in addition-
1 heavy Wool Blanket	1 heavy Wool Blanket

```
            When ordering Garments please
                state the size desired
```

List of categories of care packages for inmates in French internment camps made available by the New World Trading Company. Museum of Jewish Heritage—A Living Memorial to the Holocaust, New York.

dismissal from jobs, the expropriation of their businesses and other property, and their removal from civil society. Often a distinction was made between native Jews and those who had arrived as immigrants or refugees. In France the latter were liable to internment, while the former were treated with a bit more consideration—for the time being. But all over Europe, Jews now lived in daily fear—and with a sense that their fate and future had become irrelevant to the rest of the world.

From 1933 to 1941 some 250,000 German and Austrian Jews had been able to leave Europe: 90,000 had been admitted to North America, 83,000 to South America, 66,000 to Palestine, 20,000 to Shanghai, and smaller numbers to Africa and Australia. They faced incredible and various levels of difficulties as they had to make a new beginning; this was more difficult for older people and those who had at one time been prosperous or at least middle class, and was somewhat easier for youngsters. These émigrés were safe, but many feared for their loved ones trapped in Europe and tried to do their best to help.

Suzanne and Heinz "Henry" Bauer had been admitted to the United States in 1937 and 1940 (see page 70). In late 1940 the siblings, now ages twenty-one and twenty-three, respectively, learned from their parents, Ludwig and Irma, that they had been evicted on October 22 from their home in Mannheim, put on a train with thousands of other Jews from the Palatinate area of Germany, and dumped in the Free Zone of France. They were all interned in the Gurs camp near the Pyrenees. On that day the couple's youngest child, Werner Bauer, returned to Mannheim from Antwerp to find his parents gone. He was placed in a Jewish orphanage in nearby Frankfurt.

Desperate to provide help, Suzanne and Henry each obtained an affidavit to facilitate Ludwig and Irma's application for a US visa that, with luck, might allow for their release from Gurs. As the United States was still a neutral power, its consulates in Germany and France were open. The Bauer siblings also sent care packages purchased through the New World Trading Company and money via the American Friends Service Committee. Because of this support and the expectation that the Bauers would receive a visa, the French authorities transferred them to two transit camps: Irma was interned in Hotel Bompard in Marseille, Ludwig in a former tile factory in the village of Le Mille. In the summer of 1942, communication ceased between parents and children. Only after the end of World War II did Suzanne and Henry learn that, in August 1942, the Vichy government had handed the Bauers and thousands of other German Jews held in French internment camps to Adolf Eichmann's men, who dispatched them to Auschwitz. As for Werner, he and the other children in the orphanage were deported in September 1942 to the Theresienstadt ghetto in Czechoslovakia and from there, most likely, to Auschwitz.

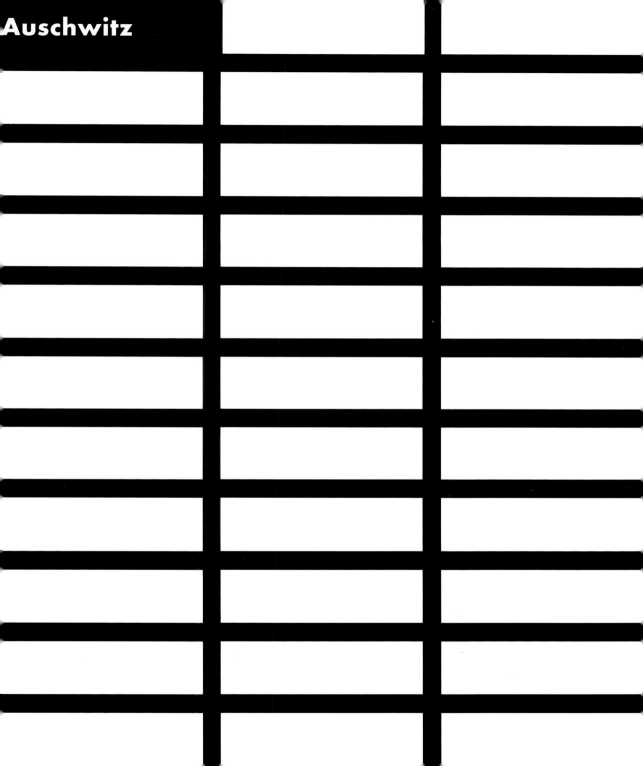

Auschwitz

A German Concentration Camp in Auschwitz

The tool kit the Germans used to dismantle the Polish state, destroy Polish civic society, and break the Polish spirit of resistance included not only summary executions and mass expulsions but also concentration camps. Initially, established camps in Germany such as Sachsenhausen were used, but in April 1940, SS chief Heinrich Himmler decided to create a concentration camp in the former Polish cavalry barracks at Auschwitz. Like the concentration camps in Germany, Auschwitz was to exist outside of the law.

Auschwitz was organized in the same way as the other camps. A commandant was in charge of the camp. The commandant's office provided general management. The Political Office, popularly known as the Camp Gestapo, was in charge of admissions, interrogations, and executions; the Protective Custody Department ran the prisoner compound; the Labor Department deployed inmates as slave laborers. The administration arranged for housing, food, and clothing of both the prisoners and the SS garrison, and also paid the wages of the SS men. The Medical Department oversaw hygiene in the camp and ran the sick bays for both SS men and inmates. Then there were minor departments, such as the Staff Welfare Section, which provided political training of the SS men and took care of their entertainment, and

Entrance to the Auschwitz display, showing the camp fence in fog (left), the desk of Commandant Rudolf Höss with objects that belonged to him (middle), and the Höss family garden (right). Desk and objects from Auschwitz-Birkenau State Museum, Oświęcim, Poland. Exhibition installation, Centro de Exposiciones Arte Canal, Madrid, 2017.

Photo montage showing senior SS officers at Solahütte, 1944. Having a relaxed conversation at Solahütte, a mountain retreat for the Auschwitz SS located half an hour's drive from the camp, are (left to right): Auschwitz commandant Richard Baer; Dr. Josef Mengele; former Auschwitz commandant Rudolf Höss; Josef Kramer, who was responsible for Auschwitz-Birkenau; Anton Thumann, who ran the prisoner compound of the Neuengamme camp; Baer's adjutant Karl Höcker; and Franz Hössler, responsible for the prisoner compound of the Auschwitz Stammlager *(main camp). United States Holocaust Memorial Museum, Washington, DC.*

SS men of the Auschwitz garrison enjoying themselves, 1940. Collection of Miroslav Ganobis, Poland.

the Central Construction Office, which planned and oversaw construction and maintenance.

Himmler appointed Rudolf Höss as commandant. A veteran of World War I, Höss had been imprisoned in the 1920s for a political murder. In 1933 he had joined the SS as a guard in the Dachau concentration camp, and in 1939 he was the second in command at the Sachsenhausen camp. Höss welcomed the opportunity to build his own camp; he chose twenty SS men to run the camp, thirty common criminals imprisoned in Sachsenhausen as prisoner function- aries to supervise the inmate population, and forty Polish inmates from Dachau as a construction crew. And he decided to make a home for his family in Auschwitz. "My family had it good in Auschwitz, every wish that my wife or my children had was ful- filled," he recalled six years later while awaiting his execution in a Polish prison. "The children could live free and easy. My wife had her flower paradise."[29]

Refurbishing the former military base as a con- centration camp proved laborious. The barracks were in poor condition, and Höss had great difficulty obtaining barbed wire for fences and building

Arbeit Macht Frei *(Work sets you free) gate, Auschwitz, 2017.*

materials for repairs and construction. The camp was not ready when, on June 14, a first transport of 728 Polish prisoners arrived from a jail in Tarnów. The group, which included scouts, students, educators, members of the underground, and soldiers of the September 1939 campaign, was temporarily housed in a nearby building. The prisoners were employed mainly in construction activities. One of them was the master blacksmith Jan Liwacz, who was given the task to forge the metal gate. Höss had instructed him to inscribe it with the motto *Arbeit Macht Frei* (Work sets you free). In 1933 in Dachau these words had referred to the idea that the purpose of the camp was to bring the "politically misguided" back into the national community. In Auschwitz this ideology did not apply, as the prisoners were Poles, who according to Nazi doctrine could never be part of the German national community. Liwacz realized this, and he welded the letter *B* in *ARBEIT* upside down. Many prisoners interpreted this as an act of resistance. Liwacz was punished but survived his imprisonment; he died in 1980.

Once the gate was made and the fence closed, Höss began to fill the camp: at the beginning of 1941 some 7,879 inmates had been registered—yet of these almost 1,900 had died. The first death occurred on July 7, when a Polish Jew, Dawid Wingoczewski, died after a long roll call. Exhaustion, deprivation, and arbitrary beatings were a main cause of death. A particularly lethal day occurred in early December, when a prisoner went missing. The SS found him asleep in the camp storehouse, the place of his work. They beat him to death and then, with the help of the prisoner functionaries, murdered another two hundred men.

In Auschwitz, individual SS men had a greater latitude in their actions than those in other camps. "Throughout Auschwitz military discipline was actually very loose," former SS man Oskar Gröning recalled sixty years later. "The lack of discipline meant that we went to bed completely pissed [drunk] and we had our pistols in their holsters hanging off the bed frame, and when somebody was too lazy to turn off the light, we just shot it out."[30] The enormous wealth that, from 1942 onward, became available to individual SS men, as many Jewish deportees brought valuables with them hidden in their clothing, added a layer of corruption to the life of the SS garrison. In 1943, after German postal authorities had intercepted a package containing at least seventy-five ounces of dental gold sent by an SS medic to his wife, an SS judge initiated an investigation into corruption that was to reveal lockers of individual SS men stashed full of gold, pearls, jewelry, and currency of all countries. It led, in November 1943, to the transfer of Höss to a desk job in Berlin.

Because the prisoners in Auschwitz were almost all non-Germans, and because of the lack of SS discipline, Auschwitz was from the outset the most violent and deadly concentration camp in Himmler's empire. The SS were prepared for this: in the summer of 1940 the Topf company of Erfurt had installed in a former ammunition depot a crematorium oven with a double muffle (a muffle is the receptacle, in this case for one or more corpses). Soon the oven's incineration capacity proved insufficient to deal with the mortality in the camp, and the SS ordered a second one that fall and a third one in the summer of 1941.

Until the fall of 1941 murder in Auschwitz remained artisanal—that is, murderer and victim were in each other's presence—and the camp authorities were not yet ready for industrialized killing, in which killer and victim were separated. When in July 1941 the camp authorities decided that 573 invalid or chronically ill inmates were a burden, they transported them by train to the Sonnenstein asylum, located five miles east of Dresden. This asylum was affiliated with the T4 program. However, shipping inmates to a distant T4 facility was inefficient, and SS doctor Friedrich Entress investigated ways to murder by means of injection. He settled on phenol, a compound known for its antiseptic properties. From September 1941 to April 1943, a phenol injection in the heart became the preferred way of murdering sick inmates who did not die quickly enough or liquidating those who were to be killed on orders of the so-called Political Department.

The interior of Auschwitz Crematorium 1, with double-muffle brick oven, 2017.

Mug Shots

Between 1940 and late 1944, the Germans deported 1.3 million people to Auschwitz. Of those 1.3 million deportees, some nine hundred thousand were killed immediately after their arrival. But four hundred thousand were admitted to the camp—of those, at least half were not to survive their imprisonment. These four hundred thousand human beings—men and women—were stripped naked, shaved bald, and given a striped uniform. They were numbered and classified according to their nationality or ethnicity and their reason for imprisonment. They were given a number printed on a cotton strip and an appropriate triangular mark designating their status (green for ordinary criminals, red for political prisoners, yellow for Jews, purple for Jehovah's Witnesses, black for "asocials," pink for homosexuals). Both were to be sewn on their uniform. At least fifty thousand of those admitted to the camp were sent to the Erkennungsdienst (Identification Department), put in front of a large camera, and photographed: one picture *en face*, one *en profile*, and one at half profile. The mug shot also included a few labels: a letter code indicating the prisoner category and/or nationality (which was also denoted on the triangle sewn on the camp uniform), the prisoner number (no name appended), and the name of the camp: K. L. (Konzentrationslager) Auschwitz. Overseen by two SS men, the work was done by about ten prisoners, including the twenty-three-year-old Polish professional photographer Wilhelm Brasse (prisoner 3444).

The practice of photographing registered prisoners ended in 1943, which means that the majority of the collection shows the faces of Polish prisoners who arrived in Auschwitz before it became the destination of Eichmann's deportation trains carrying Europe's Jews. But as the women's compound was opened in the spring of 1942, the collection also includes the faces of female inmates. The children are mostly Polish youngsters who were deported to the camp in the fall of 1942 as part of ethnic cleansing in the Zamość area.

Of the fifty thousand sets of mug shots, some thirty thousand survived the attempt made by SS men to destroy the camp records in January 1945. Preserved by the conservation team of the Auschwitz-Birkenau State Museum, today the enlargements of some two thousand mug shots are on display in Block 6. The mug shots reveal the tension between the constraint of a crude taxonomy that organizes human beings into a limited number of categories and the individuality of each person. French philosopher Emmanuel Levinas observed that in a face that is turned to another, a human being appears totally naked. "The face is present in its refusal to be contained," he wrote. Levinas noted that in its nudity and defenselessness the face issued a single command: "You shall not commit murder."[31] Significantly, in Auschwitz, as in all the other German concentration camps, prisoners were not allowed to look into the eyes of an SS man.

On these pages are twelve faces (pages 92–93) and what we know about them—which is at times little or even less.

German-born Otto Küsel had been imprisoned in Sachsenhausen for theft before being chosen by Rudolf Höss to become a prisoner functionary in Auschwitz in April 1940. Known for his kindness to other inmates, Küsel escaped Auschwitz but was recaptured. He survived, returned to live in Germany, and testified as a witness in the Frankfurt Auschwitz trials.

Polish school administrator Jan Paradysz was arrested by the Germans and deported to Auschwitz on June 14, 1940, in the first group of Polish prisoners. The SS murdered the fifty-six-year-old Paradysz in June 1941.

Army officer Eugeniusz Siewierski was a soccer player with Club Resovia. The twenty-three-year-old was murdered in Auschwitz in 1940.

Władysław Bartoszewski was working for the Red Cross in Warsaw when he was arrested and sent to Auschwitz in September 1940. Thanks to the intervention of the Red Cross, the nineteen-year-old was released in April 1941. He joined the underground Polish army and became a member of Żegota, an organization under the auspices of the Polish government-in-exile that was dedicated to helping Jews. After the war Bartoszewski went on to become a writer, politician, and diplomat serving Poland. He received the Righteous Among the Nations medal for his role in Żegota.

Eighteen-year-old Dawid Kaufmann was born in Zawiercie in Upper Silesia. In late 1939 Germany annexed Zawiercie and renamed it Warthenau. Dawid was arrested, sent to a prison in the provincial capital, Oppeln, and from there was sent to Auschwitz, on July 14, 1941. He was murdered five months later.

Stanisław Watycha was deported to Auschwitz in August 1941. On November 11 of that year, Polish independence day, the SS executed the thirty-five-year-old Watycha among 150 other prisoners in the courtyard of Block 11.

August Pfeiffer, a German national, had been arrested as a homosexual under Paragraph 175 of the penal code. He was sent to Auschwitz in November 1941 as part of a small transport of inmates rounded up from prisons in the Reich. He was given not the pink triangle but the red one of a political prisoner. The SS murdered him six weeks after his arrival.

We don't know the name of the Russian prisoner registered under number 60287 in August 1942. Nothing is known about his background or his fate, as is the case for most Russian prisoners.

Charlotte (Lotte) Frankl was seventeen when she and her sisters, Lilly and Erika, were transported from Slovakia to Auschwitz in March 1942. When her sisters became ill they were sent to the gas chambers. Subsequently Lotte attempted suicide but was stopped by a prisoner overseer, or *Kapo*, who put her to work sorting the goods of the deported. She survived a death march and was liberated by the Red Army in Theresienstadt.

Along with her mother, fourteen-year-old Czesława Kwoka was deported from Zamość to Auschwitz in December 1942 as part of the German policy to ethnically cleanse the Zamość region. "She was so young and so terrified," Wilhelm Brasse remembered decades later. "The girl didn't understand why she was there and she couldn't understand what was being said to her. So this woman Kapo (a prisoner overseer) took a stick and beat her about the face. . . . Such a beautiful young girl, so innocent. . . . Before the photograph was taken, the girl dried her tears and the blood from the cut on her lip."[32] In February 1943 Czesława's mother died, and a month later Czesława died as well. The circumstances of her death are not recorded.

On January 23, 1943, Charlotte Delbo and 229 other Frenchwomen, arrested for their resistance activities, were put on a train to Auschwitz. It was one of just a few transports of non-Jewish prisoners from France to that camp and the only one carrying only women. The group entered Auschwitz-Birkenau singing "La Marseillaise." After one year, the survivors of the group were sent to Ravensbrück, to be released to the custody of the Red Cross in 1945 as the war drew to a close. Only forty-nine of the women, including Charlotte, survived.

Anna Kreutz was born in Germany to a Roma family. In September 1943 the seventeen-year-old arrived in Auschwitz. She was registered not as a *Zigeuner* (Gypsy) but as an *Asoziale* (asocial). In August 1944 she was sent to the Ravensbrück camp and was later liberated by the American army during a death march to Dachau. Anna became a vocal advocate for Roma rights.

The purpose of the Auschwitz mug shots was to allow the SS to match a number with a face—or, to put it differently, to match a registration number and a prisoner's category and nationality with a

Mug shots, taken by the Auschwitz Identification
Department, 1940–42. Auschwitz-Birkenau State
Museum, Oświęcim, Poland.

Otto Küsel, Auschwitz #2, BV (Berufsverbrecher,
or professional criminal).

Jan Paradysz, Auschwitz #128, Pole (Pole).

Eugeniusz Siewierski, Auschwitz #630, PPole (political Pole).

Władysław Bartoszewski, Auschwitz #4427, PPole
(political Pole).

Dawid Kaufmann, Auschwitz #18145, Pole J (Pole Jew).

Stalisław Watycha, Auschwitz #20107, PPole (political Pole).

August Pfeiffer, Auschwitz #22512, Pol (political).

Unknown man, Auschwitz #60287, Pol R (political Russian).

Charlotte (Lotte) Frankl, Auschwitz Women's Camp #2065 Jude (Jew).

Czesława Kwoka, Auschwitz Women's Camp #26947, Pole (Pole).

Charlotte Delbo, Auschwitz Women's Camp #31661, Pol F (political French).

Anna Kreutz, Auschwitz Women's Camp #41263, ASo (asocial).

body. When in 1942 the SS introduced the practice of tattooing the registration number on the body of the prisoner, the mug shot lost much of its rationale. Also, the number of new arrivals overwhelmed the resources of the Erkennungsdienst. In addition, the possibilities of escape had been largely removed through the enlargement of the SS-controlled territory around the camp. Finally, and perhaps most important, the great majority of newly registered inmates had been admitted to Auschwitz not on the basis of having violated, by means of an act, some Nazi law or decree, which made them into "criminals," but because they had been born as Jews. In Auschwitz this meant they had no status whatsoever. They were there to be worked to death, to be murdered sooner rather than later. With the term *Vernichtung durch Arbeit* (annihilation through labor), the SS summarized the reason for their presence in the camp. As the SS admitted that the only possible future for these inmates was death, they ceased to record their presence through mug shots.

Prisoner Functionaries

"Perhaps for reasons that go back to our origins as social animals, the need to divide the field into 'we' and 'they' is so strong that this pattern, this bipartition—friend/enemy—prevails over all others," Primo Levi observed thirty years after his liberation from Auschwitz. He recalled that when he realized that he was to be admitted to a concentration camp he had expected to find "a terrible but decipherable world, in conformity with that simple model which we atavistically carry within us—'we' inside and the enemy outside, separated by a sharply defined geographic frontier." Yet this did not happen. "The world into which one was precipitated was terrible, yes, but also indecipher-

Jan Komski (1915–2002), Kapo Forcing Prisoners to Crouch, 1970–97. Pencil on paper. The Polish artist Jan Komski was imprisoned in Auschwitz in June 1940, escaped in December 1942, and was reimprisoned in Auschwitz in 1943. The many drawings that he created both immediately after the war and between 1970 and 1997 provide important visual testimony of life in the camp. Auschwitz-Birkenau State Museum, Oświęcim, Poland.

able: it did not conform to any model; the enemy was all around but also inside, the 'we' lost its limits, the contenders were not two, one could not discern a single frontier but rather many confused, perhaps innumerable frontiers, which stretched between each of us." On his arrival in Auschwitz, Levi did not encounter solidarity among inmates. There was no sense that they were bound to each other as "companions in misfortune." Instead, the prisoners had to struggle against one another. "This brusque revelation, which became manifest from the very first hours of imprisonment . . . was so harsh as to cause the immediate collapse of one's capacity to resist."[33]

Bellum omnium contra omnes (the war of each against all): thus the English political philosopher Thomas Hobbes described human life without civil society, and in many ways Auschwitz provided an example of this, because the paucity of resources—shelter, clothing, food, medicine, and so on—resulted in a zero-sum situation in which the survival of some depended on the death of others. Yet, if the prisoners had been left to themselves, they might have found a way to collectively develop an ethics of survival that would, as a necessary component, have included both acts of altruism and acts of self-sacrifice, and these would have allowed for a reconstruction of community. But the prisoners were never given such a chance except at the individual level. The SS ensured that all the prisoners would remain in Hobbes's state of nature by creating a class of prisoner functionaries, men and women who enjoyed, at the pleasure of the SS, absolute power over ordinary prisoners and who could, if they so desired, help a few favorites but always had to maintain an environment of absolute terror for all.

The *Lagerälteste* (camp elder), the many *Blockältester* (barrack elders), the *Rapportschreibers* (roll-call secretaries), and the *Kapos* who oversaw

Whip, 1940s. Auschwitz-Birkenau State Museum, Oświęcim, Poland.

work details enjoyed many privileges: a separate bunk, more and better food, boots that fit, a uniform in good repair, underwear, a coat, socks, boots, and—perhaps the most valuable item—cigarettes, the universal and only currency in the camp. But they knew that at a moment's notice they could lose everything and that they could be thrown back into the general prisoner population if they did not please their German masters. And they also knew that the SS did not care if they arbitrarily humiliated those below them, arbitrarily withheld food, arbitrarily extended the roll calls, arbitrarily forced prisoners to remain crouched for hours, arbitrarily whipped them, arbitrarily choked them, arbitrarily killed them.

Initially most of these functions were filled by ordinary German criminals who, after serving their sentences in ordinary prisons, had been committed indefinitely to a concentration camp. They identified with the SS, not with their Polish prisoners. As the camp grew, Polish prisoners and, in Auschwitz-Birkenau, even Jewish prisoners were able to assume such positions of power—sometimes out of ambition, sometimes because it appeared to be the only way to survive, sometimes because they just happened to be at a certain place at a certain time. Many of them were from the outset ruthless, though fewer were born sadists. But most of them, once they acquired a position in the camp that depended on maintaining the regime of terror, taught themselves to despise and even hate those below them.

The Common Prisoners

If the situation for German prisoners in the concentration camps in the 1930s had been bad, that of the Polish prisoners in Auschwitz was worse. To their captors, their lives had no value whatsoever; separated from their charges by language and racial ideology, the SS considered the prisoner only from a perspective of pure utility—if at all. Both SS men and *Kapos* had the power to kill a common prisoner on a whim, and they made use of the opportunity when they felt like it. For a perceived infraction of the camp rules, a prisoner could end up for a few nights crammed with three or more other prisoners upright in one of the notorious standing cells, which often led to death, if not while in the cell then after the day of release. And the penal colony, which was proving

to be a death trap, was always greedy for men and women to replace the ones that had died. The result was that those great masses of prisoners lived in a state of radical uncertainty. Obedience to the camp rules and utter submissiveness did not provide safety, as many rules contradicted one another, and prisoners who happened to be at the wrong place at the wrong time could be included in a collective punishment.

Every situation could quickly become one of life and death. This uncertainty shattered prisoners' normal sense of time: no one could be sure he or she would be alive the next month, the next week, the next day. Time became of endless duration, constantly interrupted by sudden attacks and

Prisoner uniform, 1940–44. The striped uniform was used throughout the concentration camp system. The Ravensbrück camp for women produced bolts of the striped linen material, and the uniforms were cut and sewn in tailor workshops in each of the larger camps. In Auschwitz, prisoners often received used uniforms of inmates who had died or, when these were in short supply, civilian clothes marked with paint and badges. Auschwitz-Birkenau State Museum, Oświęcim, Poland. Exhibition installation, Centro de Exposiciones Arte Canal, Madrid, 2017.

Jan Komski (1915–2002), Work Sets You Free, 1970–97.
Pencil on paper. Auschwitz-Birkenau State Museum,
Oświęcim, Poland.

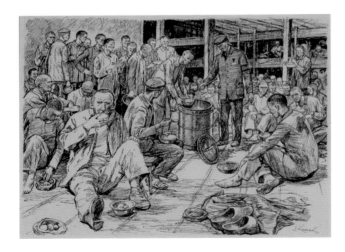

Jan Komski (1915–2002), Dinner Time, 1970–97.
Pencil on paper. Auschwitz-Birkenau State Museum,
Oświęcim, Poland.

Bunks from an Auschwitz prisoner barrack, 1941. Prisoners
slept on the floors of the barracks for the first year of the
camp. Triple bunk beds were introduced at the end of 1941.
Auschwitz-Birkenau State Museum, Oświęcim, Poland.
Exhibition installation, Centro de Exposiciones Arte Canal,
Madrid, 2017.

Spoon, 1940s. In Auschwitz, a spoon was very valuable. This spoon was owned by Stanisław Śitaj, who was admitted to the camp on April 17, 1942. His nickname, Zośka, appears on the upper side, his registration number, 30921, on the underside. Auschwitz-Birkenau State Museum, Oświęcim, Poland. Exhibition installation, Centro de Exposiciones Arte Canal, Madrid, 2017.

incursions; a single day was experienced as a year. The German sociologist Wolfgang Sofsky, who has produced the most incisive analysis of life in German concentration camps, speculated that this constant state of terror radically undermined the agency of prisoners, and this prevented the formation of mutual trust and aid.[34]

The impossible living conditions thus prevented the formation of a viable prisoner society. No one could escape the suffocating presence of others, a closeness that made it impossible to gather oneself. Few prisoners knew one another's names, and many prisoners even forgot their own. There was no relief at night: jammed together in overcrowded barracks, inmates had to share a bunk—if they were lucky enough to have one—with two or three others. The body of each inmate was in the way of the body of his neighbor, and this proximity led, strangely, to a situation of utter isolation. In such conditions, a prisoner did not mourn the death of his neighbor but welcomed it, as it provided, if only for a moment, a bit of extra space or a bit of extra bread.

Prisoner-made chess set, with storage box for chess pieces made out of a sardine tin, engraved with "Auschwitz 1943," 1943. Collection of Miroslav Ganobis, Poland.

Prisoners' clogs, 1940–44. The image in the right background is the mug shot of Polish artist Jan Komski. Clogs and mug shot from Auschwitz-Birkenau State Museum, Oświęcim, Poland. Exhibition installation, Centro de Exposiciones Arte Canal, Madrid, 2017.

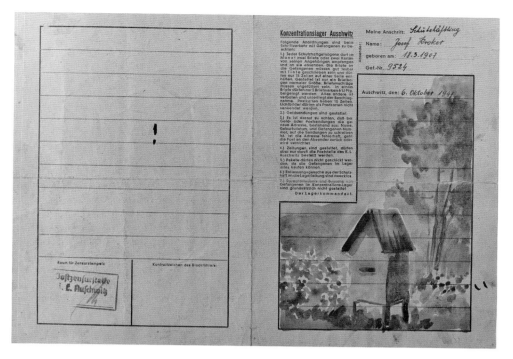

Reverse of letter written by camp prisoner Josef Kroker on Auschwitz stationery decorated with a watercolor scene, 1941. A teacher from Chorzów in Upper Silesia, Kroker was imprisoned in the Auschwitz camp from January 1941 until May 1942, when he was transferred to Flossenbürg. He survived the war and testified in the 1947 trial of Auschwitz personnel held in Kraków. Florence and Laurence Spungen Family Foundation, Santa Barbara, California.

The result was a coerced mass that was structured on animosity and that lacked the fabric of reciprocity. And there was only so much any one person could do for the other. Yes, the lucky ones who received a bit of extra food because they had a job could share some of it with a less fortunate neighbor. But there were too many situations—of the kind that in civilian life are at worst a small irritation—that in the camp quickly turned into life-threatening crises. "Death begins with the shoes," Auschwitz survivor Primo Levi observed.[35] In Auschwitz "shoes" were often wooden clogs, which caused sores that, in turn, caused infections and swelling that triggered a physical decline in which the inmate became a so-called *Muselmann*: a man unable to keep himself clean, indifferent to his surroundings, only dreaming about food—a man whose life had become a burden, a man who,

himself, had become a burden on the lives of other inmates.

There were, however, cracks in the edifice of terror and torture. An hour or two spent in a game of chess, played with homemade pieces, could provide an anchor in a more reasonable and predictable reality. And Polish inmates had the opportunity, once a month, to write a letter home. The letter, which was censored, had to be written in German, could contain only personal information, and could be sent only to relatives. Occasionally, a prisoner with graphic skills and access to watercolors and brushes might be persuaded, in exchange for a piece of bread, to paint a peaceful and uplifting scene on one's letter. Such scenes provide a clue as to why these letters were important: they could make each prisoner who wrote one remember that another and better world existed outside the camp.

Prisoners with a "Good" Job

Besides the camp elite of prisoner functionaries and the larger mass of common prisoners, there existed a special group of prisoners who occupied a stratum in between. They had no power over others but possessed a particular skill that was valued by the SS or the prisoner functionaries. An inmate with a medical degree could find work in the sick bay; an architect could be employed as a draftsman in the Central Construction Office; a seamstress could be put to work repairing SS uniforms and sewing dresses for the wives of SS officers; a locksmith could find employment in the metal workshop; a person who spoke many languages was useful as an interpreter, and so on. Typically such jobs were done indoors, and this made all the difference in the winter. Of course, an electrician who ensured that the fence remained electrified or a roofer who kept the tar paper that covered the barracks in good repair had to work outside. But typically such workers got some extra clothing to protect against the elements. Having a skill could make one, if not indispensable—as almost every day new people arrived with similar

skills—at least somewhat useful, and once the SS had identified a prisoner as useful, his or her survival chances increased.

Born in the Tatra Mountains, Bronisław Czech had learned the traditional craft of woodworking. An accomplished mountaineer and skier, he competed for Poland in the 1928, 1932, and 1936 Olympic Winter Games. After the German conquest of Poland, Czech joined the resistance, guiding refugees over the Tatras into Slovakia. Arrested in 1940, he was given the opportunity to buy his freedom by becoming a ski instructor for the German mountain troops. He refused the offer and was sent to Auschwitz. The SS appreciated Czech's carpentry skills. Employing him in the camp woodworking shop, they ordered him to make items for their use. They knew who he was—and that was an incredible advantage in a place in which prisoners were anonymous. In 1941 Czech was assigned to attend to the fledgling art gallery the SS had established as part of the camp headquarters. However, he lost the relative protection afforded by this job when, in February 1944, he was reassigned

Bronisław Czech, Olympic skier and woodworker (and, later, Auschwitz prisoner), 1930s. Auschwitz-Birkenau State Museum, Oświęcim, Poland.

Detail of a box (page 103) made by Bronisław Czech, showing his signature, CZECH, in the form of a ski jumper, 1941–44. Auschwitz-Birkenau State Museum, Oświęcim, Poland.

Decorative box made by Bronisław Czech, 1941–44.
Auschwitz-Birkenau State Museum, Oświęcim, Poland.

as a cleaner—nothing in Auschwitz was ever permanent. Having fallen back into anonymity, Czech now had to struggle, like all the common prisoners, against everyone else. After a few months at the bottom he caught typhus and died.

Nevertheless, a good job might mean an increased possibility of survival. In the fall of 1944, after Primo Levi had lived and suffered at the bottom for many months, someone recognized his skills in chemistry and decided he might be useful in a laboratory in the IG Farben synthetic rubber and gasoline factory,

which had been under construction just east of Auschwitz since 1941. This inside job helped Levi survive.

A few hundred musicians played in marching bands and orchestras. Bands played at the prisoners' departure for work and at their return. "They played in the morning when the columns were leaving for work," French prisoner Charlotte Delbo (page 93) recalled after the war. "When we passed by, we had to keep in step to the music. Later they played waltzes. Waltzes we had heard elsewhere, back in an abolished past. To hear them was intolerable."[36] Music attended special occasions, such as executions, or visits by important personalities. When Himmler visited Auschwitz, he entered the camp accompanied by the "Marcia Trionfale" from Giuseppe Verdi's *Aida*, played by the full camp orchestra.

Before the war, jazz musician Louis Bannet was well known as the Dutch Louis Armstrong. When in the summer of 1942 the deportations began of Dutch Jews to Auschwitz, Bannet went into hiding. One day he decided to go out and was recognized by a Dutch Nazi who happened to be one of his fans—but not fan enough. The Nazi betrayed Bannet to the police, and a month later the musician was on his way to Auschwitz. Bannet survived selection, was registered as prisoner 93626, and attended an audition for the camp orchestra, before which he was told that he would be playing for his life. Bannet played W. C. Handy's *Saint Louis Blues*, a Louis Armstrong standard, and passed the test. He played the trumpet in Auschwitz until his departure by freight train for the Ohrdruf camp in November 1944. Having smuggled the trumpet onto the train, he held on to it until his liberation in May 1945.

Promotional photograph of Dutch jazz musician Louis Bannet, 1938. Museum of Jewish Heritage—A Living Memorial to the Holocaust, New York.

Business

The primary purpose of the concentration camp system was the incarceration of real or perceived opponents to the Nazi regime, the removal of people deemed superfluous to the needs of society, and the establishment of an atmosphere of fear among the general population. In addition, Himmler's oversight of the concentration camps from 1934 onward had helped him in acquiring control of both the law enforcement and state security apparatuses. In late 1939 Himmler had acquired responsibility for the Germanization of the New East, the German-annexed part of Poland; a year later he decided that the

Auschwitz camp was to have a vital role in the policy of ethnic cleansing that led to the expulsion of Poles into the German-occupied part of Poland known as the General Government, and the immigration of ethnic Germans into the New East. He ordered Commandant Rudolf Höss to create a fifteen-square-mile agricultural estate around the camp that was to support the settlement of some one hundred thousand ethnic Germans from the Bukovina area (today split between Romania and Ukraine) in the area of the one-time duchy of Auschwitz. By the summer of 1941, the SS-controlled *Interessengebiet*, or "zone

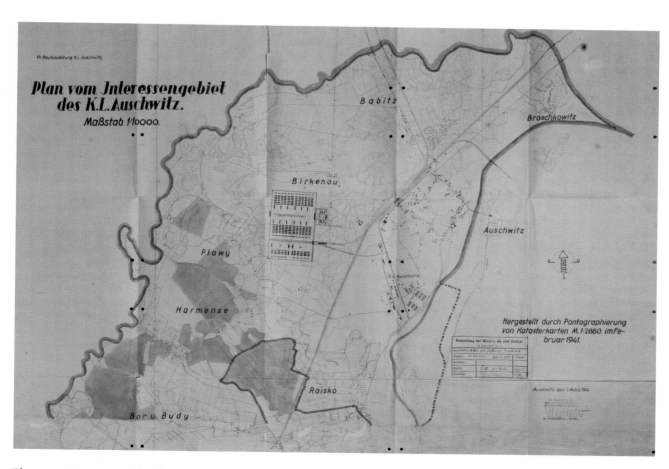

Plan vom Interessengebiet des K.L. Auschwitz *(Plan of the zone of interest around Auschwitz), 1941. The concentration camp is marked on this plan as "K.L. [for* Konzentrationslager*] Auschwitz." Yad Vashem: The World Holocaust Remembrance Center, Jerusalem.*

Landscape in the "zone of interest," 2012. The zone of interest included idyllic landscapes with picturesque fishponds. To the prisoners who were forced to work for twelve hours daily in those ponds, cleaning the accumulated muck from the bottom, these sites were places of torture.

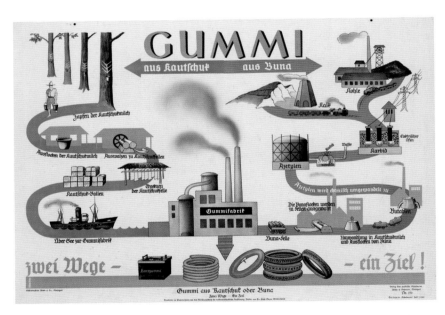

Gummi aus Kautschuk / aus Buna: zwei Wege, ein Ziel! *(Rubber from natural rubber / from Buna: Two roads, one goal!), 1940. Collection of Robert Jan van Pelt, Canada.*

of interest," included the Auschwitz concentration camp, villages such as Birkenau (Brzezinka), Harmense (Harmęże), and Raisko (Rajsko), and hundreds of confiscated farms. All Polish inhabitants had been expelled, and thousands of inmates were employed as slave laborers, digging drainage canals, building dikes along the Vistula River, and cleaning the huge fishponds that had existed since medieval times. It was backbreaking work, and many died or were killed in the fields and meadows of the zone of interest.

Since the late 1930s the German concentration camps had also served as business opportunities for the SS, which operated brick factories in Sachsenhausen and Neuengamme, and granite quarries in Mauthausen and Flossenbürg. Big business entered Auschwitz in 1941, when the Interessen-Gemeinschaft Farbenindustrie (Dye-industry syndicate), or IG Farben, the conglomerate of all of Germany's major chemical and pharmaceutical companies, became interested in the town. The largest company in Europe by the mid-1930s, IG Farben had become central to Germany's rearmament, due to its ability to produce synthetic gasoline on an industrial scale, lessening the empire's dependency on foreign crude oil. Even more important was Farben's capacity to produce synthetic rubber, enabling Germany to be independent of the natural rubber supply from the British colony of Malaya. The raw materials for IG Farben's synthetic rubber, known as Buna, were coal, lime, and water—and all three were in ample supply near Auschwitz, which was located close to coal mines and large lime deposits and at the confluence of three rivers. In addition, just east of Auschwitz stretched a large, geologically stable plateau that allowed for the construction of a big manufacturing plant. Construction of the massive IG Farben Buna plant began in late 1941 and continued until the end of the war. Civilian laborers from Germany and forced laborers from all over Europe were involved with the construction, as were many thousands of prisoners from the Auschwitz concentration camp.

Collaboration between IG Farben and the SS meant that the Auschwitz concentration camp obtained both financial and material resources to begin a large program of construction to expand the prisoner capacity of the main camp from ten thousand to thirty thousand. This project involved the construction of an additional sixty-seven two-story barracks, five interconnected workshops, a kitchen building, a delousing facility and laundry, a camp hospital, and a camp prison—all huge in size. The SS also took care of its own, constructing a monumental office building for the commandant and his staff, spacious quarters for SS officers and men, a village for married SS personnel, and even a little museum to preserve, for future generations, the history of the camp itself. The project also involved the construction of

Photograph of the construction of the IG Farben plant at Auschwitz, 1943. Bundesarchiv, Berlin.

Partly completed model of the planned expansion of the Auschwitz concentration camp created by the Auschwitz Central Construction Office, 1942. Auschwitz-Birkenau State Museum, Oświęcim, Poland.

Courtyard of Block 11 of the Auschwitz concentration camp, 2012. This courtyard was a place of many executions by means of firing squads or neck shots.

a massive crematorium that was to take the place of the existing one put in operation in 1940 in the former ammunition depot. It was to serve the needs of both the main camp and a satellite camp holding 125,000 inmates on the other side of the railroad tracks (discussed more in the next chapter). With fifteen muffles, organized in five triple-muffle ovens, the crematorium was to have an incineration capacity of 1,440 corpses per day—an enormous capacity to be sure, but taking into account the 155,000 inmates to be assembled at Auschwitz, it

was within the incineration capacity deemed appropriate by the Concentration Camps Inspectorate in Oranienburg.

Auschwitz also provided a much-needed service to the regional Gestapo summary court, officially located in the nearby city of Kattowitz. This court regularly convicted Polish patriots, sentencing them to death. In Germany itself, executions of civilians were carried out by beheading, with guillotines located in either selected courthouses or prisons—hanging was only introduced in 1942. Military

Jan Komski (1915–2002), Execution in the Courtyard of Block 11, *1970–97. Pencil on paper. Auschwitz-Birkenau State Museum, Oświęcim, Poland.*

offenders were executed by firing squad. No guillotine was available in Kattowitz, and with a concentration camp nearby, the president of the Kattowitz Gestapo Summary Court realized that he could have the Auschwitz SS do the dirty work. Thus in 1942 he made an arrangement with Höss in which those who had been tried and sentenced were to be brought to Auschwitz to be executed in the courtyard of the camp's prison, Block 11. In 1943 the agreement was modified: now the summary court also convened in Block 11. The accused were brought to the camp and held until their trial, without being registered as prisoners. After a trial that typically lasted a only matter of minutes, 95 percent of defendants were sentenced to death and shot immediately afterward in the adjacent courtyard. Between three thousand and forty-five hundred people were thus killed in Auschwitz. The 5 percent who escaped immediate death were imprisoned in the camp. Not a single accused person was acquitted.

The Invasion of the Soviet Union and

the Construction of Auschwitz-Birkenau

Map of the German attack on the Soviet Union in 1941. Collection of Robert Jan van Pelt, Canada.

When Reichsführer-SS Heinrich Himmler decided in the spring of 1940 to establish a concentration camp in Auschwitz, his ambition had been modest: the camp was to create terror among Poles. The inclusion of the camp into his Germanization program for the annexed territories and the collaboration agreement between IG Farben and the SS had increased the scope of the camp's operation. Yet its significance remained regional. Two other developments were to turn Auschwitz into a place of first European and ultimately global importance. The first was the German invasion of the Soviet Union in June 1941. Germany and the Soviet Union had been allies of a sort since August 1939, but driven by his hatred for Communism and his promise to the German people of more living space, Hitler had never wavered in his conviction that the German-Soviet nonaggression pact that had resulted in the partition of Poland was only a temporary expedient.

The combination of the largest mobilization in world history, an annihilatory assault, and a propaganda campaign skillfully managed by Joseph Goebbels made most Germans believe that the invasion of the Soviet Union was not a conventional war but a true crusade in which none of the customary laws of war applied. A notorious propaganda pamphlet was *Der Untermensch* (The Subhuman), published in 1942 by the SS. Sold at German newsstands, it was to justify the war against the Soviet Union as an ideological and racial crusade against Judeo-Bolshevism, an antisemitic canard. Only through a full destruction of "the Subhuman"—which was humanity in the clutches of "the Jew," embodied, in the case of the Soviet Union, by the Communist commissars—could civilization be preserved.

110

In their fight against *Der Untermensch*, the Germans decided to ignore the international conventions that had established minimal standards of prisoner-of-war maintenance. For most of the summer and fall of 1941, Soviet prisoners of war were left to themselves, without food, without shelter, often without clothing, and without medical care. Hundreds of thousands died in the most atrocious conditions. In October 1941 construction of a very large prisoner-of-war camp began within the Auschwitz zone of interest, close to the existing concentration camp but on the other side of the railroad tracks, on the site of the village of Birkenau (Brzezinka). This camp, respectively known as Kriegsgefangenenlager (prisoner-of-war camp) Auschwitz, Auschwitz-Birkenau, and Auschwitz II, was conceived and initially constructed to house 100,000 prisoners of war. Even before the ground had been broken for its construction, Berlin ordered a capacity of 125,000.

Only fifteen thousand Soviet prisoners of war ever arrived at Auschwitz; only a few dozen survived the camp. "We knew our place, a grave," Pavel Stenkin recalled sixty years later. "I'm alive now and in a minute I'm finished. This was a constant feeling. . . . Death, death, death. Death at night, death in the morning, death in the afternoon. Death. We lived with death."[37]

Cover of Der Untermensch *(The Subhuman), a pamphlet published by the SS, 1942. Collection of Robert Jan van Pelt, Canada.*

The exact reason Himmler sought to gather so many prisoners in a new camp adjacent to the existing concentration camp remains an object of debate. In his postwar memoir, Rudolf Höss suggested that Himmler decided in March 1941 to build a large camp to house captured Red Army soldiers as part of the Auschwitz camp. That March, the IG Farben company was deciding whether to build the large Buna factory, which would shape the future of the town of Auschwitz. Were the Red Army prisoners in the new Birkenau camp, who were to be used as slave labor to transform the town of Auschwitz into a model city, acceptable to the IG Farben management? Or was the decision to construct the Auschwitz-Birkenau camp more ad hoc in nature and made only in late September 1941?

What is clear is the identity of the architect who designed the camp: Fritz Ertl. A native of Linz, Austria, Ertl was a graduate of the Bauhaus—the most innovative design school in Weimar Germany. Unlike the main Auschwitz camp, which was based

A German soldier approaches a Red Army casualty and a burning Soviet tank, 1941. Bundesarchiv, Berlin.

Horse-stable barracks in Auschwitz-Birkenau, 1943.
Auschwitz-Birkenau State Museum, Oświęcim, Poland.

on preexisting buildings, Auschwitz-Birkenau was designed from scratch. Its basic structure consisted of a series of identical fenced compounds that could function as independent camps. A railway spur, which was to enter Auschwitz-Birkenau through an asymmetrical (originally) gate building that also included a watchtower, was located in a zone separating the main camp (to the north) from a quarantine camp (to the south). In late 1943, the building was extended on the northern side, creating the largely symmetrical structure that exists today. Popularly known as the Gate of Death, it has become *the* symbol of Auschwitz as a death camp, a symbol of the Holocaust of the Jews and the Porajmos of the Roma, and as such one of the most recognizable buildings in the world (see pages 9, 143, and 213).

The camp was designed to be constructed in brick. Each barrack was to crowd as many people into as little space as possible—the Germans did not consider the Soviet prisoners of war fully human and hence believed they did not deserve shelter that allowed

them to maintain the minimal conditions of human existence. The basic structure of a barrack consisted of sixty-two bays, each bay measuring six by six feet and holding three superimposed sleeping platforms, the bottom one located on bare soil. Originally each platform was supposed to hold three men, providing each barrack with the capacity for roughly 550 men. The Birkenau barracks did not offer much space beyond that of the sleeping platforms and did not provide sanitary facilities or water. Shoddily built, without decent flooring or insulation, and equipped with only two small stoves each, the barracks were impossible to heat.

The Subhuman imprisoned in Auschwitz-Birkenau deserved only the most minimal and basic form of food, cooked in sheds that accommodated forty-eight cauldrons. Each cauldron, with a capacity of sixty-six gallons, was used to cook gruel for more than two hundred prisoners. This capacity matched the food allowance of about one quart of turnip soup per person per day, in addition to one and a quarter

Auschwitz-Birkenau landscape, 2008. This photograph shows the same site as the photograph on page 112, after the horse-stable barracks were removed, leaving the chimneys, which could not be dismantled.

Cauldron and big wooden spoon from a kitchen at Auschwitz-Birkenau, 1941–42. Auschwitz-Birkenau State Museum, Oświęcim, Poland. Exhibition installation, Centro de Exposiciones Arte Canal, Madrid, 2017.

ounces of bread. As for latrines, they were basically open sewers enclosed by a shed.

The brick barracks were constructed only in the quarantine camp, to the south of the railway siding. In early 1942, seeking to speed up construction of Auschwitz-Birkenau, the government of the Reich in Berlin assigned 253 prefabricated wooden horse stables to be constructed to the north of the siding. A crew of thirty could assemble one stable in less than a day. As the horse-stable barracks held fewer prisoners than the brick ones, the number of barracks was almost doubled, increasing the size of the camp.

Most of the wooden barracks were heated by two small stoves, each connected to a brick chimney. When the camp was empty, in the summer of 1945, the Polish authorities decided to disassemble the prefabricated wooden barracks and rebuild them elsewhere—shelter was in short supply in postwar Poland. But the brick chimneys could not be removed and thus remained in place, memorials of the barracks that once stood there. Some see the chimneys as tombstones, others as the fingers of corpses gesturing to the living.

The Beginning of the Holocaust

Before June 1941, Germans had persecuted Jews in many different ways, and from time to time this persecution ended in murder. But the German government that carried responsibility for the persecution had not yet formulated the concept that the so-called Final Solution to the Jewish Question was to be genocide. First emigration, then forced emigration and expulsion, and finally deportation to Madagascar had been the methods of choice to make first Germany and then, from the summer of 1940 onward, Europe *Judenfrei* (free of Jews).

The invasion of the Soviet Union brought millions more Jews under German control. In the spring of 1941, Reinhard Heydrich and Heinrich Himmler had organized special mobile killing units to accompany the German army into the Soviet Union. These *Einsatzgruppen* (deployment groups) were to be used to execute Communist officials. For the first weeks of July the Einsatzgruppen focused on murdering those original targets. However, later that month, Heydrich ordered the Einsatzgruppen to begin massacring Jewish men, and soon women and then children as well.

One of the early massacres occurred in Zhitomir (or Zhytomyr), Ukraine. "The earth that had been dug out was piled up to one side of [the hole]," German army major Karl Rösler reported in July to a superior officer. "The pit itself was filled with innumerable human bodies of all types, both male and female." Rösler was shocked not only by the massacre, conducted by Himmler's men, but also by the attitude of ordinary German soldiers, "some of them in bathing trunks." Obviously, the massacre was a spectacle of interest to these men—and also to others: "There were also an equal number of civilians, including women and children."[38]

From then on German policy in the occupied Soviet Union, which at that time included also the part of Poland the Soviets had annexed in 1939 and the Baltic countries, was either instant massacre of a village or town's Jewish population by means of rifles and machine guns or a delayed massacre following a period of ghettoization. In both cases the massacres left few traces. When victims were brought to the sites where they were to be shot, they typically were ordered to undress, and they were slaughtered naked. And, typically, the mass graves were cleared by the Germans themselves. This was done within

Jews from Lubny, Ukraine, shortly before their murder by an Einsatzgruppe, *1941. Hamburger Institut für Sozialforschung, Hamburg.*

the context of the *Enterdungsaktion* (exhumation operation) that carried Gestapo reference number 1005 and hence became known as Aktion 1005. The Aktion 1005 unit had begun work in the summer of 1942, clearing the mass graves of those murdered in gas vans near the village of Kulmhof (Chełmno), in western Poland. It moved on to clearing the mass graves of Jews killed by bullets, for which it perfected its disposal methods. After many experiments, which included the use of flamethrowers and incendiary bombs, the commander of the operation, Paul Blobel, consulted a specialist in the disposal by fire of animal carcasses, and they settled on the construction of large fire pits, thirteen feet deep, lined with firebrick cement, with a grate at the bottom. The pits were filled with bullet-ridden corpses and firewood in alternating layers with space in between. The men of Aktion 1005 then systematically emptied the corpses from mass graves into the pits and set them alight. With no bodies, the most important artifacts left to testify to what has been called "the Holocaust by bullets" are bullet casings.

Occasionally one encounters an artifact and a story that, miraculously, escaped the German cleaning-up effort. One of these is the blouse made by Chaya Porus for her sister Rachel. Chaya and Rachel Porus's hometown of Swieciany (today in Lithuania) came under German rule on June 24, 1941. For twenty-two months the sisters lived with their family in the Swieciany ghetto. In the ghetto Chaya made Rachel a blouse. In April 1943 the Germans liquidated the ghetto and massacred its inhabitants in the Ponary forest—the site where, in a three-year period, the Germans killed an estimated seventy thousand Jews, twenty thousand non-Jewish Poles, and eight thousand Soviet prisoners of war. Miraculously Chaya escaped this fate and ended up in the Vilna ghetto. There she received a package sent by a friend who had been forced to sort the victims' belongings at the Ponary pits. The friend had recognized Rachel's blouse and made sure Chaya received it. Later that year Chaya joined a Jewish partisan unit in

Blouse made by Chaya Porus for her sister Rachel, early 1940s. Museum of Jewish Heritage—A Living Memorial to the Holocaust, New York.

the Naroch forest. In memory of Rachel she wore her sister's blouse for the year that she participated in the military struggle against the German army.

The genocide of the Jews living in the occupied Soviet territories began in August 1941; at that time the conditions under which Jews lived in Germany and German-occupied western Europe worsened rapidly: expropriation, forced labor, social isolation. In Germany the government further marginalized the Jews, physically and socially, by marking them with yellow stars; this policy was applied to Jews in the occupied Netherlands, Belgium, Luxembourg, and France in the spring of 1942. And Jews were now also formally forbidden to emigrate abroad—something that had already become practically impossible. The German leadership had concluded that a powerful reason not to kill Jews—their value as hostages—had failed to pay off. By the middle of August 1941, the United States and Britain had effectively become allies, and in a joint declaration, Franklin D. Roosevelt and Winston Churchill called for "the final destruction of Nazi tyranny." With the Madagascar option dead because of the continuing war in the

Felix Nussbaum (1904–1944), Self-Portrait with Jewish Identity Card, *1943. Oil on canvas. Nussbaum depicted himself wearing the yellow star with the J assigned to Jews living in Belgium. This painting is the last self-portrait Nussbaum made. On June 20, 1944, the painter was arrested in Brussels, and on July 31 he was deported from the Mechelen transit camp to Auschwitz. There he was murdered. Museumsquartier Osnabrück, Felix-Nussbaum-Haus, loan from the Niedersächsische Sparkassenstiftung, Osnabrück, Germany.*

West, deportation of Jews to a territory outside Europe had ceased to be an option. Thus the German leadership slowly but certainly moved to the decision to kill all European Jews.

In parts of Poland annexed by Germany, genocidal practices became part and parcel of the program to ethnically cleanse the area and prepare it for settlement by ethnic Germans. Non-Jewish Poles were expelled, but Jews had been concentrated in ghettos, the largest of which was the one at Litzmannstadt (Łódź). In the fall of 1941 the German government began to send Jews from Berlin, Vienna, and other major cities in Greater Germany to the Litzmannstadt ghetto. The senior official in the region, Arthur Greiser, was appalled. Since 1939 he had wanted to make his province *Judenfrei* (free of Jews), and now it had become a dumping ground for Jews from other parts of Germany. As the trains with Jewish deportees arrived in Litzmannstadt, Greiser made the decision to murder Polish Jews incarcerated in that ghetto who could not work. It proved a decisive step in the history of the Holocaust: it was the first time Jews outside the occupied Soviet territories were included as a matter of principle in the unfolding genocide. Greiser entrusted the operation to regional police chief Wilhelm Koppe, who ordered his subaltern Herbert Lange to set up a killing installation.

Lange, as part of the Aktion T4 program, had commanded a roving, gas-van-equipped unit that had been killing inmates of mental asylums since early 1941. Now Lange was to make a decisive and historic contribution to the Final Solution. He conceived of a three-part extermination facility. The first part was a waiting facility. A synagogue in the town of Warthbrücken (formerly, and currently, Koło), located some forty-five miles from Litzmannstadt, functioned as a holding pen for Jews arriving in Warthbrücken by train. The second part, a loading station for gas vans, was located in a partly ruined manor house in the village of Kulmhof. Once the van was filled with people and the doors were closed, the van pulled away from the manor house, and exhaust, piped into the hold, did its lethal work. The Rzuchów forest was the third part of the facility: it was the site of the mass graves. On December 8, 1941, Lange engaged in a first trial of the unprecedented facility, the first of the *Vernichtungslager* (death camps). The guinea pigs were Jews from the surrounding area. The production of death proved satisfactory. In the next year the Germans murdered some 150,000 Jews and thousands of Roma in the Kulmhof factory of death.

One day before Lange's first experiment at Kulmhof, on December 7, 1941, Japan attacked the American fleet in Pearl Harbor. The United States declared war on Japan. In support of its ally, Ger-

Land	Zahl
A. Altreich	131.800
Ostmark	43.700
Ostgebiete	420.000
Generalgouvernement	2.284.000
Bialystok	400.000
Protektorat Böhmen und Mähren	74.200
Estland - Judenfrei -	
Lettland	3.500
Litauen	34.000
Belgien	43.000
Dänemark	5.600
Frankreich / Besetztes Gebiet	165.000
Unbesetztes Gebiet	700.000
Griechenland	69.600
Niederlande	160.800
Norwegen	1.300
B. Bulgarien	48.000
England	330.000
Finnland	2.300
Irland	4.000
Italien einschl. Sardinien	58.000
Albanien	200
Kroatien	40.000
Portugal	3.000
Rumänien einschl. Bessarabien	342.000
Schweden	8.000
Schweiz	18.000
Serbien	10.000
Slowakei	88.000
Spanien	6.000
Türkei (europ. Teil)	55.500
Ungarn	742.800
UdSSR	5.000.000
Ukraine 2.994.684	
Weißrußland aus-schl. Bialystok 446.484	
Zusammen: über	11.000.000

K210405   372029

Page of the minutes of the Wannsee Conference showing the numbers of Jews targeted in each European country, 1942. Haus der Wannsee-Konferenz, Berlin.

Dreidels and bullets (ca. 1940). These dreidels (children's toys associated with the Jewish festival of Hanukkah) and bullets were found in a mass grave identified and excavated by Yahad-In Unum (Hebrew and Latin for "together"), an organization, established by the French priest Patrick Desbois, dedicated to tracing mass graves of the Einsatzgruppen and police-battalion killings in the German-occupied Soviet Union. Museum of Jewish Heritage—A Living Memorial to the Holocaust, New York.

many declared war on the United States. The European war had become a world war. Hitler responded immediately in a speech to the Nazi leadership. He announced "a clean sweep" to solve the "Jewish Question." Recording this event in his diary, Joseph Goebbels noted that in his speech of January 30, 1939, Hitler "had warned the Jews that if they again unleashed a world war, they would be destroyed. That has proved no empty threat." Paraphrasing Hitler, Goebbels continued, "The world war has arrived, and the destruction of Jewry must follow. This matter is to be considered without any sentimentality. It is not for us to have pity on the Jews, but on the German people."[39] Now all of European Jewry was condemned to death.

Once Hitler had decided that the so-called Final Solution would be enacted, one important question remained: Who was to be in charge of the genocide of the Jews? Himmler sought this responsibility, as he believed it would help him consolidate his power. He instructed Heydrich to invite top bureaucrats to a meeting in a villa in the Berlin borough of Wannsee. The meeting took place on January 20, 1942. Heydrich quickly proceeded to his central objective: to establish exclusive authority over the Final Solution. No one protested. Heydrich wrapped up the conference in ninety minutes.

By the time the conference closed, eight hundred thousand Jews had already been slaughtered, mostly in the German-occupied Soviet Union. One country, Estonia, was officially *Judenfrei*. Now an estimated eleven million Jews were to be massacred or worked to death as slave laborers. Six days after the meeting, Himmler decided Jews would replace Soviet prisoners of war in Auschwitz-Birkenau and in Majdanek, a second concentration camp in the General Government, near Lublin. Auschwitz-Birkenau had been designed to house first 100,000 and later 125,000 captured Red Army prisoners. Only 15,000 had arrived by mid-January 1942, and most of them had been worked to death. Now it was to become a destination for Jews from all over Europe.

Genocidal Ingenuity

"In all of my work I have never begun by asking the big questions, because I was always afraid that I would come up with small answers; and I have preferred to address . . . details in order that I might then be able to put together . . . at least a description . . . of what transpired," Holocaust historian Raul Hilberg told filmmaker Claude Lanzmann in January 1979. He added that he believed his method of asking "small" questions fitted the German bureaucratic process that laid the groundwork for the Holocaust, which Hilberg described as "a series of minute steps taken in logical order and relying above all as much as possible on experience." Yet in the late fall of 1941 the Germans moved in their treatment of the Jews

beyond precedent, when they began to gas them on a large scale. As Hilberg put it, "Then, these bureaucrats became inventors."[40] Hilberg focused on the bureaucrats in Berlin. In this story of Auschwitz we focus on six inventors "in the field": policemen Odilo Globocnik and Christian Wirth, Auschwitz SS men Karl Fritzsch and Walther Dejaco, and Topf and Sons engineers Kurt Prüfer and Fritz Sander.

Odilo Globocnik was Himmler's immediate subordinate in Lublin, on the eastern border of the General Government. He orchestrated Operation Reinhard, named in memory of Reinhard Heydrich, the mastermind of the Final Solution, who was assassinated in May 1942 by British-trained Czech agents. Operation

MAP OF OCCUPIED POLAND
SHOWING KILLING CENTERS (1942)

The Grünbaum family, Kraków, ca. 1937. In 1941 the men in the photo—Leser, Sol, Aron, Sholem, and Jakob—were sent to the Stalowa Wola slave labor camp in German-occupied Poland. Except for Jakob, all were shot in the fall of 1942, together with 296 other Jewish men, in the forest of Rozwadów by camp commandant Josef Schwammberger. The women of the family seen in the picture—Maria and her married daughters, Gela and Sara—and their children, were murdered in 1942 in the Belzec death camp. Collection of Miriam Greenbaum, Canada.

Reinhard provided an assembly-line murder operation in which Jews, and occasionally also Roma, from the General Government were transported to three specially constructed camps: Belzec in the south, Sobibor in the center, and Treblinka in the north. Each of these smallish camps was built on undeveloped rural land, next to small villages with railway spurs. The camps were equipped with gas chambers, which were the brainchild of Christian Wirth, who had constructed the carbon monoxide chambers disguised as shower rooms used in the Aktion T4 program. Globocnik had organized the transfer of Wirth and some of his assistants from Berlin to Lublin to develop killing installations capable of exterminating more than a thousand people at a time. Unable to obtain bottled carbon monoxide, Wirth decided on the use of engine exhaust as the killing agent.

David Olère (1902–1985), drawing showing Bunker 2 (labeled DEZINFEKTION), *Auschwitz, 1945. Ink and watercolor. Marc Oler, France, and Yad Vashem: The World Holocaust Remembrance Center, Jerusalem.*

Model (scale 1:100) of Crematorium 2, Auschwitz. In the fore-ground is the underground gas chamber with its wire-mesh gas columns. Musealia, San Sebastián, Spain. Exhibition installation, Centro de Exposiciones Arte Canal, Madrid, 2017.

Photograph taken at Auschwitz during construction of Crematorium 2, early 1943. The underground gas chamber is clearly visible immediately to the right of the locomotive's chimney. The roof of this room, after its construction, was covered with dirt. Auschwitz-Birkenau State Museum, Oświęcim, Poland.

In terms of manpower, Belzec, Sobibor, and Treblinka were small operations: twenty SS officers, aided by a company of mostly ethnic Germans and Ukrainian guards recruited from among the Soviet prisoners of war and trained in the Trawniki concentration camp near Lublin, ran each of the camps, while a group of a few hundred Jewish slave workers, selected from early transports, undertook the gruesome task of emptying the gas chambers, burying and later burning the corpses, and sorting and packing the murdered prisoners' belongings for dispatch to the Reich.

While Wirth used the expertise he had obtained in Aktion T4 to murder the Jews of Poland, the Concentration Camps Inspectorate in Oranienburg, which as early as September 1941 had decided to find ways to create efficient methods of the mass murder of prisoners who had ceased to be useful, relied on

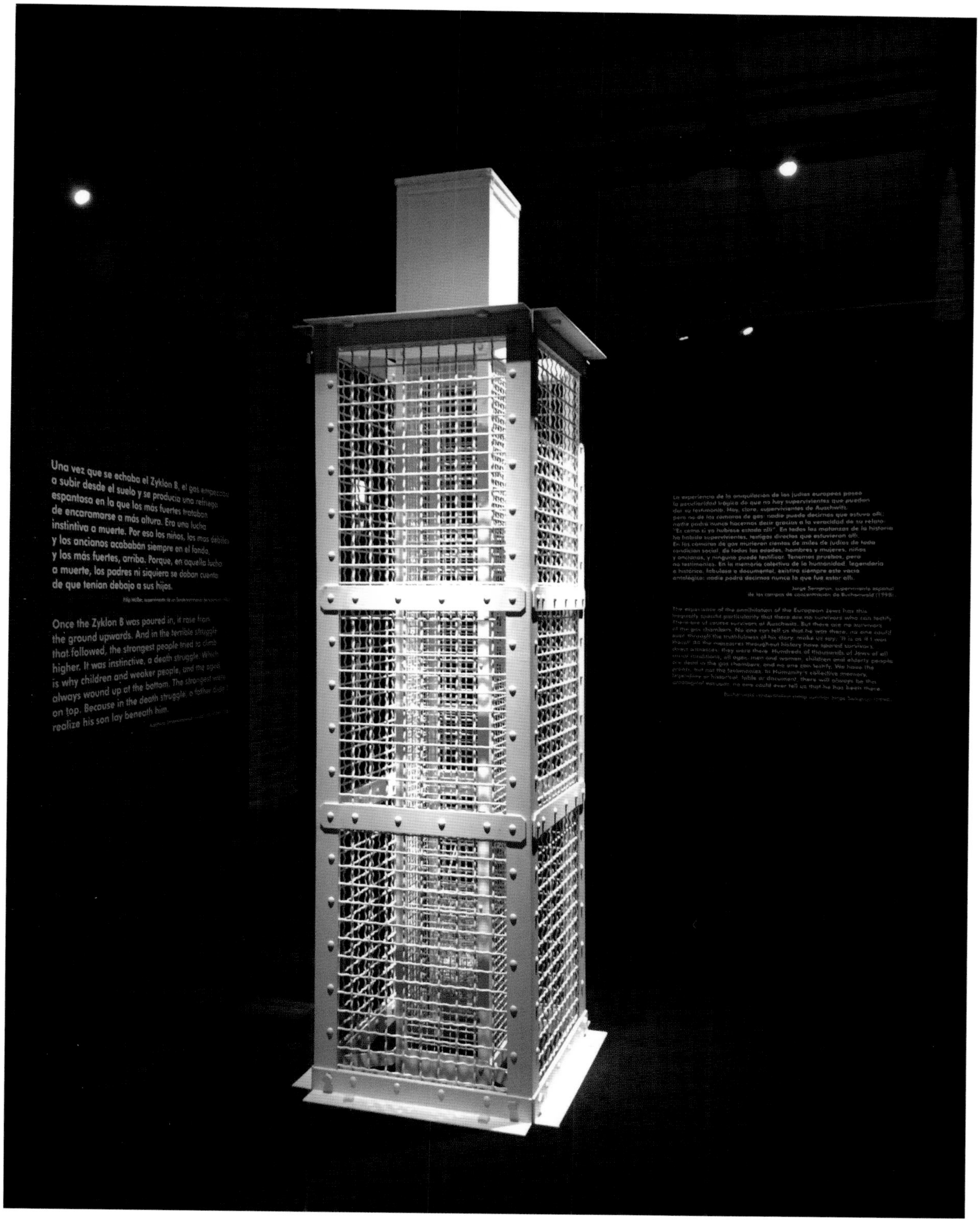
Una vez que se echaba el Zyklon B, el gas empezaba
a subir desde el suelo y se producía una refriega
espantosa en la que los más fuertes trataban
de encaramarse a más altura. Era una lucha
instintiva a muerte. Por eso los niños, los más débiles
y los ancianos acababan siempre en el fondo,
y los más fuertes, arriba. Porque, en aquella lucha
a muerte, los padres ni siquiera se daban cuenta
de que tenían debajo a sus hijos.
Once the Zyklon B was poured in, it rose from
the ground upwards. And in the terrible struggle
that followed, the strongest people tried to climb
higher. It was instinctive, a death struggle. Which
is why children and weaker people, and the aged
always wound up at the bottom. The strongest were
on top. Because in the death struggle, a father didn't
realize his son lay beneath him.

Model (scale 1:1) of wire-mesh gas column used to lower poison gas into Crematoria 2 and 3 at Auschwitz. Musealia, San Sebastián, Spain. Exhibition installation, Centro de Exposiciones Arte Canal, Madrid, 2017.

Crematorium 4, Auschwitz, 1943. Auschwitz-Birkenau State Museum, Oświęcim, Poland.

the inventiveness of its own personnel. The SS of the Sachsenhausen concentration camp developed and constructed a neck-shot facility, in which a gun would be fired from behind a wall into the back of the neck of the unsuspecting victim. In Auschwitz, in September 1941, Rudolf Höss's deputy Karl Fritzsch conducted a successful killing experiment in the basement of Block 11. He used the commercially available cyanide-based fumigant Zyklon-B, which came in airtight tins that contained paper disks or silicon dioxide or calcium sulfate pellets soaked with liquid cyanide. These tins were safe to transport and easy to use. When the container was opened and the contents were exposed to air, the hydrogen cyanide was degassed.

Höss attended the second gassing of some 600 Soviet prisoners of war and 250 sick prisoners. Satisfied with the results, Höss adopted cyanide gassing as the method of mass killing to be used in Auschwitz. However, the facility used was not to be Block 11; its basement was ordinarily used as a prison, and the building was at some distance from the crematorium, which would necessitate the transport of many corpses through the camp. Therefore Höss moved the murder operation directly to the crematorium by transforming the morgue into a Zyklon-B gas chamber. As the morgue had a flat roof, it was not difficult to create holes that allowed camp personnel to drop Zyklon-B canisters into the gas chamber below. In early 1942 the gas chamber in the

just under the roofline for the insertion of Zyklon-B. In these crematoria, there was no mechanism for removing the degassing pellets after the people in the gas chambers had been murdered, and therefore the design assumed a delay of up to a day between the gassing and the beginning of the disposal of the corpses. In each crematorium, a large central hall served as both an undressing room and a morgue, while the incineration room accommodated eight ovens arranged in two units.

These four crematoria, which had, according to the builders, a combined daily incineration capacity of 4,416 corpses, came into operation between mid-March and July 1943. By that time the bunkers had killed close to three hundred thousand Jews.

The collaboration between the Auschwitz SS and the Topf firm was close and, as Topf engineer Fritz Sander testified after the war, did not raise any moral questions. "I was a German engineer and a key member of the Topf works, and I saw it as my duty to apply my specialist knowledge in [the construction of crematoria] to help Germany win the war, just as in wartime an aircraft construction engineer builds airplanes, which also kill human beings."[42]

Between late 1941 and 1943, men like Globocnik, Wirth, Fritzsch, Höss, Dejaco, Prüfer, and Sander had been extraordinarily inventive in seeking to find ways to murder civilians in a procedure that gave the SS total control over the killing process and that ensured that no traces remained of the murdered. Inventiveness was paired with rivalry. "I visited Treblinka to find out how they carried out their exterminations," Höss recalled in 1946 while in Polish captivity. "I did not think his [Globocnik's] methods were very efficient." In turn, Globocnik visited Auschwitz after the four crematoria had come into operation, and "didn't think anything was special," Höss remembered. "According to him, his extermination centers worked much more quickly. . . . His bragging was incredible on every occasion."[43]

Hiding

While the violation and abrogation of the rights of Jews and those who opposed the Nazis happened at first incrementally in Germany, the German conquests after 1939 meant that Jews in many European countries experienced a quickened pace of the terror and increasingly few options for escape. By 1941 departure from Nazi-ruled Europe was practically impossible. Jews were physically trapped when, in 1942, the deportations began to destinations thought to be work camps that turned out to be factories of death. They were also socially trapped. Sociologist Zygmunt Bauman, who avoided the Holocaust through a timely escape to the Soviet Union, observed that the key to the success of the Final Solution was the practice to make the victims "part of that social arrangement that was to destroy them." In all the phases of the persecution that preceded the massacres by the mobile killing squads and the deportations to the death camps, the perpetrators first isolated the Jewish minority from the non-

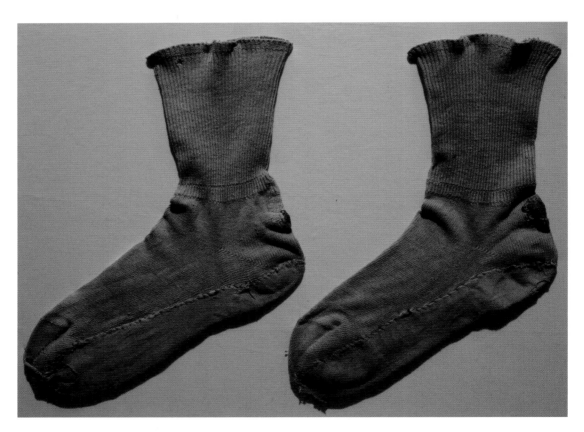

Aurelia Gamzer's socks, 1941. While eight-year-old Aurelia was in hiding in Lwów (then Poland), she wore these socks, specially made by her mother to muffle the sound of her footsteps. Museum of Jewish Heritage—A Living Memorial to the Holocaust, New York.

Jenny Bunge-Hanf and her husband, Hans Bunge, in their garden in Aerdenhout, the Netherlands, 1941. Collection of Robert Jan van Pelt, Canada.

Yellow badge issued to Jenny Bunge-Hanf, 1942. Collection of Robert Jan van Pelt, Canada.

Jewish majority. They then reinforced the communal structure that gave both Jewish leaders and individual Jews a sense that rational action—which meant some form of cooperation with the Germans—would allow them to save, if not everything and everyone, then at least much and many, including of course themselves. This created a situation that placed "individual rationality in the service of collective destruction."[44] The German strategy proved immensely successful: by January 20, 1942, the day of the Wannsee Conference, approximately one and a half million Jews had already been murdered by the Germans, but nine million were alive. Three years and four months later, half of those alive had been murdered also.

How did the other four and a half million escape the fate of the six million? Three million of them survived because the Germans never got to them, either because they lived in neutral countries (ninety-four thousand) or because they were sheltered by the British and Soviet armies (two and a half million) or because their governments, although allied to Germany, were unwilling to hand Jewish citizens over to the Germans (fifty thousand Bulgarian Jews) or because their government, after an initial period of happy collaboration with the Germans in murder-

ing Jews, lost its appetite to do so in 1943 (330,000 Romanian Jews).

But one and a half million Jews survived while experiencing at one time or another the direct threat of massacre or deportation, and they did so because they resisted believing that they might be the exception to the rule and playing into the hands of their oppressors. In eastern Europe between twenty thousand and thirty thousand Jews survived as partisans, and in western Europe tens of thousands fled to Spain, Sweden, or Switzerland, or survived in German-ruled Europe in some state of legal and economic limbo in places where local authorities were unwilling to fully participate in the Germans' Final Solution. And then there were many—perhaps as many as a million—who spent time in hiding, either by successfully adopting a non-Jewish identity or by literally finding a shelter in a basement, spare room, or attic of a house; in a barn or chicken coop of a farm; or in a shelter constructed in a forest or a marsh.

Jews seeking safety had to become active agents of their own survival. They had to make the all-important judgment call that made the difference between life and death. How could one adopt a non-Jewish identity, or, on whose door could one

Frank family, 1941. From left to right: Margot, Otto, Anne, and Edith. Anne Frank House, Amsterdam

Peter van Pels, 1942. Anne Frank House, Amsterdam.

Bookcase covering the entrance to the secret annex that housed the Frank and van Pels families, Prinsengracht 263, Amsterdam, 1960s. Anne Frank House, Amsterdam.

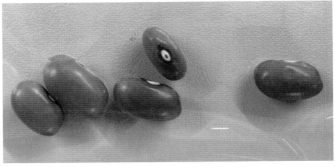

Dried beans spilled by Peter van Pels in the annex on November 9, 1942, and retrieved by Otto Frank after the war. Anne Frank House, Amsterdam.

knock? In most cases hiding meant, of course, that non-Jews who were not targeted by the Germans had to be willing to aid those who were. Rescuers came from all walks of life and all faiths, and many were strangers to the people to whom they offered shelter at great personal risk. In Poland to help Jews meant death; in the Netherlands the penalty for helping Jews was confinement in concentration camps from which many did not return. Most rescuers acted with only immediate friends and family to support them, but others operated as part of a network. Being in hiding, either literally or with an assumed identity, or hiding someone took ingenuity, creativity, patience, sometimes money, and always simple luck.

In the summer of 1941 the Germans forced the Jews of Lwów, in the General Government area of Poland (now Lviv, Ukraine), into a ghetto. Seeking to protect their eight-year-old daughter, Aurelia, Barbara and Isaac Gamzer searched for a hiding place. The Szczygiels, a Catholic family, agreed to take in the girl. For eight months Aurelia hid in the bedroom of the Szczygiels' daughter, Joanna. The Gamzers were reunited when the Ojak family offered to shelter the whole family. In hiding, Aurelia wore special socks, made by her mother, to keep warm and to muffle the sound of her footsteps.

When in late 1940 the German occupational authorities in the Netherlands initiated the persecution of Jews by ordering all people with one or more Jewish grandparents to register with the government, my own grandmother, Jenny Bunge-Hanf, complied by filling in the proper form. A civil servant in the Bloemendaal municipality in charge of the population registry then made the card that included her picture, her fingerprint, and a printed *J*, to which is added the handwritten number *4*, indicating that all four of her grandparents were Jewish. In the spring of 1942, Adolf Eichmann, the head of the Jewish desk of the Gestapo, decided to deport Dutch Jews to Auschwitz. Now the German occupational authorities in the Netherlands decreed that all Jews had to wear a yellow star on coats,

jackets, shirts, dresses, and sweaters. Initially, Jenny Bunge-Hanf complied. Yet, when the deportations to "the East" began, Jenny Bunge-Hanf found a way to adopt another identity. Through a resistance group, she obtained the identity card of Fenna Anna Deekens. Trained forgers replaced Fenna's picture with Jenny's. This card saved Jenny twice from arrest during a roundup—and the likelihood of deportation to Westerbork, the Dutch transit camp, despite being married to a non-Jew, Hans Bunge. Her brother, Robert Hanf, known as Bob (page 14), was not so lucky. He went into hiding in the fall of 1942 but was betrayed in the spring of 1944 and deported to Auschwitz.

While in hiding, Jenny and Bob lived on the Prinsengracht in Amsterdam, close to the house where the Frank family—father Otto, mother Edith, and daughters Margot and Anne—was hiding in the secret annex from July 1942 until August 1944. Realizing that as German Jewish refugees to the Netherlands they would face deportation before native Dutch Jews, businessman Otto Frank had organized with unusual foresight a hiding place for his family, in the annex of his office at Prinsengracht 263, and had created a small network of his employees to help him: Jan and Miep Gies, Victor Kugler, Johannes Kleiman, and Bep Voskuijl. They loyally supported the Frank and van Pels families, who shared the annex, by supplying them with food, newspapers, books, and moral support. In conditions in which all food was both rationed and limited in supply, it was very difficult to provide nutrition for people in hiding, as they had ceased to exist from an administrative point of view. In the fall of 1942 the main stock in the secret annex was 150 tins of vegetables. At the beginning of November the helpers delivered six bags of dried peas and beans, totaling 270 pounds. Peter van Pels safely hoisted five of the sacks up to the attic of the annex, but when he moved the last bag the bottom seam split. "A shower—no a positive hailstorm of brown beans came pouring down and rattled down the stairs," Anne wrote in her diary that

Group portrait of Jewish and non-Jewish refugee children sheltered in various public and private homes in Le Chambon-sur-Lignon during World War II, with some of the French men and women who cared for them, 1943. Pastor André Trocmé is in the center of the top row, wearing glasses; Daniel Trocmé is in the top row, right, partially hidden; Edouard Theis is to the left of André Trocmé. United States Holocaust Memorial Museum, Washington, DC.

day. "Quickly we started to pick them up. But beans are so slippery and small that they seemed to roll into all the possible and impossible corners and holes."[45]

Discovered by the authorities in August 1944, the Frank and van Pels families were deported to Auschwitz in September. In late October, Margot and Anne were transferred to Bergen-Belsen, where they died in March 1945. By that time Edith had died in Auschwitz, and Otto had been liberated there by the Red Army. Peter van Pels was to die in Mauthausen on or close to the day of the camp's liberation, May 5, 1945. Otto returned to Amsterdam in the summer of 1945, where Miep Gies handed him Anne's diary, which she had found after the family's arrest. Some

time later, Otto noticed in the cracks of the stairs some of the beans that Peter van Pels had spilled in November 1942. He carefully collected them—modest but unique reminders of the daily struggle for survival while in hiding.

The Frank and van Pels families depended on five people. Only in very rare cases did whole communities get involved. A notable case is the French town of Le Chambon-sur-Lignon, which sheltered more than thirty-five hundred Jews and fifteen hundred non-Jews in need. Le Chambon was home to Protestants whose history had included years of religious persecution. They were known for their pacifism and their belief that the Jews were God's chosen people. In 1940 Le Chambon became a destination for Spanish Republicans, anti-Nazi Germans, young Frenchmen seeking to avoid forced labor in Germany, and Jews. Led by pastor André Trocmé, his wife, Magda, and his colleague Edouard Theis, the village provided a safe environment from which rescue organizations could operate.

In 1941 the people of Le Chambon offered their

Poster issued by a French railway company (Compagnie des chemins de fer de Paris à Lyon et à la Méditerranée PLM) advertising Le Chambon-sur-Lignon as a destination for hiking, fishing, and forests, 1920s. The image was drawn by well-known landscape painter Pierre Commarmond. Lithograph. Collection of Robert Jan van Pelt, Canada.

A French policeman at Rivesaltes directs a group of children, including Hilda and Hannah Krieser (center right), as they depart from the camp, 1941. United States Holocaust Memorial Museum, Washington, DC.

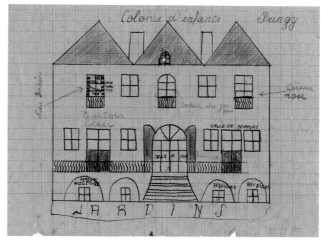

Hannah Krieser's drawing of the Pringy children's home, the Swiss-run orphanage to which she and her sister were taken, 1941–44. United States Holocaust Memorial Museum, Washington, DC.

village as shelter for Spanish, Roma, and Jewish children, when they learned that the American Friends Service Committee and the Secours Suisse aux Enfants (Swiss Aid to Children) had negotiated a deal with the Vichy government to take these children from French internment camps such as Gurs and Rivesaltes. Two of these children were Hilda and Hannah (or Anny) Krieser, who, after escaping Belgium for France, were interned in Rivesaltes

with their parents, Solomon and Perla (pages 38 and 39). A nurse with the Secours Suisse, Friedel Reiter, arranged for the girls' release. They found a haven in an orphanage run by August Bohny, a Swiss citizen who, in collaboration with Trocmé and Secours Suisse, set up such facilities in Le Chambon and the surrounding area.

When deportations began from the French internment camps to Auschwitz, Le Chambon

Ángel Sanz-Briz in his office in the Spanish embassy in Budapest, ca. 1943. Collection of the Sanz-Briz family, Spain.

Letter of protection for Mr. Dezsö Grósz, his wife, and a relative, issued by the legation of Spain in Budapest and signed by Ángel Sanz-Briz, November 1944. Collection of the Sanz-Briz family, Spain.

became an important assembly point for escape to the safety of neutral Switzerland and the center of a hiding network that involved the surrounding region. The Krieser girls were among the thirty-five hundred Jews saved. Their parents, however, never made it out of Rivesaltes—except to be deported to Auschwitz, where they were murdered upon their arrival. Just before their deportation, Solomon proved able to send his daughters a parcel containing letters, a last postcard, and his tallit (page 39). Perla tossed a last letter from their train as it passed Toulouse.

In June 1943 the Germans raided the secondary school of Le Chambon and arrested nineteen Jewish youngsters and deported them to Auschwitz. In addition, they arrested their teacher, André Trocmé's nephew, Daniel Trocmé. He was murdered in the Majdanek concentration camp in early 1944. On September 3, 1944, the Free French First Army liberated Le Chambon.

Many individuals provided protection in secret, but some did so openly—and could do so because they enjoyed diplomatic immunity (but not necessarily support of their own government back home). In 1944, when the persecution of Hungary's Jews intensified, the Spanish diplomat Ángel Sanz-Briz offered to give Jews of Sephardic origin Spanish passports. Initially the Hungarian authorities allowed him to issue Spanish passports to two hundred individuals, but Sanz-Briz discreetly changed that figure to two hundred families, continually increasing the number as the situation worsened. He also set up special apartment buildings in Budapest, marked with Spanish flags, to house "his" Jews, and provided them with food. Sanz-Briz also convinced the Red Cross representative to put Jewish hospitals, maternity clinics, and orphanages under Spanish protection. Through his various efforts, Sanz-Briz saved some five thousand Jews.

Sanz-Briz is recognized by Yad Vashem, Israel's Shoah-remembrance authority, as one of the Righteous Among the Nations, as are the Szczygiel and Ojak families, Friedel Reiter, August Bohny, and all the inhabitants of Le Chambon and nearby villages. Each of the Righteous received honorary citizenship of Israel and a medal that bears the Jewish saying, "Whosoever saves a single life, saves an entire universe" (Mishnah, Sanhedrin 4:5).

The Germans aimed not only to kill every last Jew but also to eradicate Jewish religious and cultural artifacts. Between the November pogrom of 1938 (Kristallnacht) and May 1945, the Germans and their allies destroyed countless synagogues and Jewish ritual objects and books. One Polish farmer risked his life by saving a Torah scroll—an act of faith that, after the war was over, there would be a new future in Poland not only for Jews but also for Judaism.

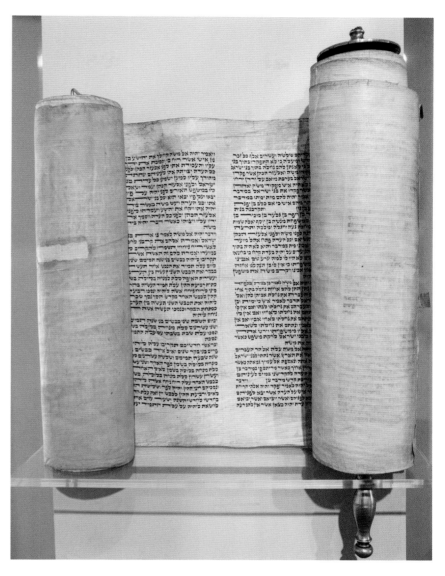

Torah scroll hidden by a Polish farmer during the war. Museum of Jewish Heritage—A Living Memorial to the Holocaust, New York.

Deportations

A young Jewish woman from the Greek town of Ioannina during the German roundup of the populace, 1944. Bundesarchiv, Berlin.

On Saturday, March 25, 1944, a German army detachment, accompanied by photographers of a propaganda unit, arrived in the town of Ioannina (or Janina), located in northern Greece. In Ottoman days the town was known for its beauty and quality of life, expressed in the Greek saying "to live like the pasha in Ioannina." The Romaniote Jews could attest to the truth of this piece of popular wisdom: for more than two millennia the town had been the center of their community. Speaking Judeao-Greek and maintaining unique traditions, they are distinct from the much more populous Ashkenazi, Sephardic, and Mizrachi Jewish communities. Their good fortune lasted even in the first years of the Holocaust; from 1941 to 1943 the Ioannina Jews were under the protection of the Italian army, which occupied most of Greece. However, after the fall of Benito Mussolini and the new Italian government's decision in September 1943 to switch sides in the war, the Germans took over. Six months later German soldiers rounded up 1,960 of the 2,000 Romaniotes, sending them in trucks to an assembly point, to ship them from there in freight cars to Auschwitz. Only 128 of them returned.

More than two years before that Saturday in 1944, the German authorities had gathered in Wannsee and aligned behind a policy to murder the remaining Jews in Europe, and security chief Reinhard Heydrich had set the genocide into high gear. Two million Jews were trapped in the ghettos of occupied Poland; the Germans needed only to order the ghetto authorities to call up so many Jews for each transport and organize freight trains to bring them to Kulmhof, Belzec, Sobibor, and Treblinka.

The Final Solution in the rest of Europe demanded more work. Jews had not been ghettoized; they needed to be motivated to voluntarily report for "labor deployment," or, if they did not show up, they

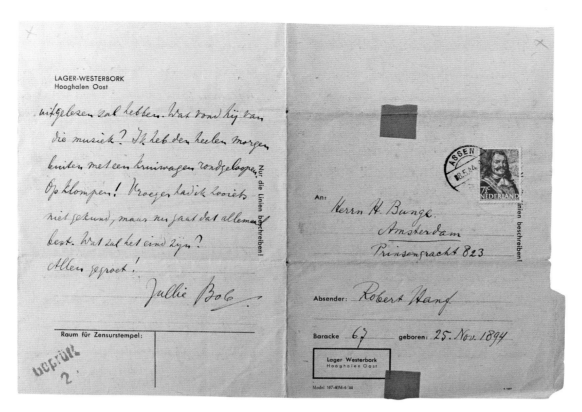

Bob Hanf's final letter, 1944. After hiding in Amsterdam for two years, the Dutch painter, poet, and composer Bob Hanf was betrayed in April 1944 and sent to the Westerbork transit camp. From there he mailed two letters, providing an account of his arrest, transport, and his new appearance as a convict, and wondering, "What will be the end?" On May 19, Hanf was deported to Auschwitz. Collection of Robert Jan van Pelt, Canada.

had to be rounded up from their homes—often by local police. From assembly points in cities they were brought, under guard, in ordinary passenger trains to transit camps located at some distance. These places—Westerbork in the Netherlands, Mechelen in Belgium, Drancy in France, Fossoli di Carpi in Italy, and others—camouflaged the ruthlessness of the deportation and destruction machine. In these camps the deportees could be enticed to give up whatever valuables and financial means they might have hidden with neighbors or friends in exchange for a promised stay of deportation, and they could be held until the necessary transport capacity was available and the death camps were ready for their arrival.

Journalist Philip Mechanicus, who spent more than a year at Westerbork before his deportation to first Bergen-Belsen and then to Auschwitz, kept a detailed diary of his time in the Dutch transit camp. On Tuesday, June 1, 1943—the day of the departure of a transport to the East—he provided an extensive description of the loading of a train. "The exiles have a bag of bread which is tied to their shoulder with a tape and dangles over their hips, and a rolled up blanket fastened to the other shoulder with string and hanging down their backs. Shabby emigrants who own nothing more than what they have on and what is hanging from them." The three thousand people were forced into forty-eight freight wagons. "They all go on the bare floor, in amongst the baggage and on top of it, crammed tightly together. There is a barrel, just one small barrel for all these people, in the corner of the wagon where they can relieve

Vacuum flasks taken by detainees to Auschwitz and notes thrown from deportation trains heading to that camp, 1940s. Auschwitz-Birkenau State Museum, Oświęcim, Poland. Exhibition installation, Centro de Exposiciones Arte Canal, Madrid, 2017.

themselves publicly. . . . In another corner there is a can of water with a tap for those who want to quench their thirst."[46]

Those who remained behind in Westerbork were left with their sorrows and their fears. "One more piece of our camp has been amputated," Etty Hillesum wrote, on Tuesday, August 24, 1943. "A hundred thousand Dutch members of our race are toiling away under an unknown sky or lie rotting in some unknown soil. We know nothing of their fate. It is only a short while, perhaps, before we find out, each one of us in his own time. For we are all marked down to share that fate, of that I have not a moment's doubt."[47]

Yet, despite the sorrow of the departure from the world that had been home, despite the horror of the conditions within the deportation trains, and despite the fear of the future, there was also hope among the deportees as they departed from transit camps like Westerbork or from assembly points in cities like Berlin—a faith in the future that was nurtured by the fact that husbands and wives, parents and children, brothers and sisters were still together, and after a life of supporting each other through difficult times, many tried to bring comfort to loved ones, speaking words of encouragement.

From Berlin, Norbert Wollheim had organized *Kindertransport* after the November 1938 pogrom. On March 8, 1943, Norbert; his wife, Rosa; their son, Peter Uriel; and Norbert's sister, Ruth, were arrested by the Gestapo, which was intent on making Berlin *Judenfrei* in one fell swoop. The Wollheims were brought to the Grosse Hamburger Strasse assembly point, located in a Jewish old-age home that had already been cleared of its residents. There they had to wait without provisions in bare rooms for four days. On Friday, March 12, they were forced on a freight train parked along a siding in the Moabit station. Rosa faced the inevitable with courage, saying "Well, we'll take it, we can take it," Wollheim told an interviewer in the 1990s. "And I remember that also, my wife also wrote some of these cards, which were received, because you could throw them through the hole and sometimes they were picked up, and people then mailed them."[48] Because Jews were not permitted to send a last letter to family and friends once informed about their upcoming journey, their only available means of communicating a goodbye or farewell was to throw letters or cards from the deportation trains, trusting that their messages would be found and mailed by a sympathetic person.

Transport 36 from Berlin, with the Wollheim family and 937 other people on board, began its journey eastward. "When it became dark, interesting enough, one of the ladies was aware that this was Friday night. She took out some candles she had prepared, lighted and blessed the candles, and said the prayers to welcome the Sabbath bride." The ceremony, normally conducted at home, marked Wollheim's memory of the journey to Auschwitz. "Here there was a group of one hundred people riding in that wagon, but still they were blessing God and welcoming the Sabbath."[49]

The Porajmos

Settela Steinbach was arrested in the Netherlands in a large roundup of 577 Roma in May 1944 (page 13). Of those, 279 were released because they did not fit the particular category of Roma to be deported. They were allowed to return to their caravans and were not bothered afterward.

Germans had an inconsistent policy concerning the fate of the Roma. In the summer of 1941, when the *Einsatzgruppen* began murdering Jews in the German-occupied Soviet Union, they also included in the massacres the Roma they encountered, killing at least thirty thousand. In Serbia the Germans made little distinction between Jews and Roma, murdering both indiscriminately. In the fall of 1941, five thousand Roma were sent to the Litzmannstadt ghetto, and when in December of that year the Kulmhof death camp went into operation, those Roma were its first victims. Chaim Rumkowski, the so-called Elder of the Jews in the Litzmannstadt ghetto, had been given the authority to decide which of the ghetto inmates would be deported to Kulmhof, and it was obvious to him that the Roma were to be at the top of

Roma memorial in Auschwitz-Birkenau, 2017.

the list—together with the German Jewish elderly. Yet, throughout 1942 the Roma of western and central Europe remained in limbo.

In December of that year Himmler made a decision concerning the Roma, the content of which is known from a circular issued by the Reich criminal police in January 1943: "Half-breed Gypsies, Roma Gypsies and non-German members of Gypsy families of Balkan background are to be selected according to certain guidelines and . . . committed to a concentration camp. From now on such people will be referred to as 'Gypsy-like Persons.' The committal will occur, without any consideration of the degree of miscegenation, family-wise to the Auschwitz concentration camp (Gypsy Camp)."[50] The somewhat confusing language of the circular of January 1943 suggests that not all Roma were to be deported. Indeed, those of the Sinti and Lalleri subgroups who were deemed to be racially pure were allowed to remain where they were. Dr. Robert Ritter, director of the Rassenhygienische und Kriminalbiologische Forschungsstelle (Research Office on Racial Hygiene and the Biology of Criminality), had decided that they were racially valuable. The 279 Roma arrested in May 1944 in the Netherlands but released after a few days belonged to that category. Settela, while she belonged to the Sinti subgroup, was obviously judged not to be of pure Sinti stock. Hence she ended up in Auschwitz-Birkenau.

Nine days before Settela arrived in Auschwitz a group of thirty-nine Roma children had arrived at the camp. In the early 1940s, Eva Justin (page 66), of the Research Office on Racial Hygiene, had assembled these children in a Catholic orphanage in Mulfingen, Germany, to serve as objects of her dissertation research. When she completed her PhD, the children had ceased to be useful to her. Film footage shows these children at Mulfingen in the

interval between Dr. Justin's graduation and their deportation to Auschwitz. They appear to be a lively and healthy group, full of potential. On May 12, 1944, all thirty-nine were admitted to Auschwitz. All but four died in the camp.

In total, thirty-two transports carrying 23,000 Roma arrived in Auschwitz . No selections took place upon arrival; families remained intact and were housed together in the so-called Gypsy Camp. It proved to be a deadly place: some 10,000 Roma died from illness, deprivation, and individual murders. Some 2,700 became sick with typhoid, and were "cured" in the gas chambers, while 2,897 were gassed when the Germans liquidated the Gypsy Camp on August 2, 1944. Of the remaining 7,000 Roma, some 4,000 were merged within the general camp population, while at least 2,500 were transferred to Buchenwald and Ravensbrück. Few survived.

In the history of the Porajmos, in which between 200,000 and 500,000 European Roma perished, Auschwitz played an important role. The camp accounted for around 21,000 of the victims. The circumstances of both their imprisonment in a dedicated camp in Auschwitz, the murder of many in the gas chambers, and the use of many Roma children as guinea pigs in medical experiments made the fate of the Roma the direct result of planned destruction. The first monument commemorating the Roma genocide was constructed in the ruins of the Auschwitz Gypsy Camp, and August 2, the day of the liquidation of the Gypsy Camp, is Roma Holocaust Memorial Day. And there is, perhaps, also some poetic justice in the fact that the most epigrammatic summary of the unprecedented experience of Auschwitz was articulated in the Romani language by a Roma survivor, Ceija Stojka: *Vi o merimo daral katar o Auschwitz* (Even death is terrified of Auschwitz).[51]

Disbelief and Indifference

Most people in German-occupied Europe tried to ignore the deportation trains of 1942 and 1943. When informed about the roundup and disappearance of Jews by messages from resistance organizations and couriers such as the Polish resistance member Jan Kozielewski (aka Jan Karski), the major Allied governments held that negotiations with the Germans would not happen. The Allies were committed to winning the war and accepting nothing less than the unconditional surrender of the German armed forces.

In April 1943 representatives of the United States and Britain met in Bermuda to discuss options to rescue European Jewry. A consortium of Jewish organizations proposed that neutral governments negotiate with Germany the release of a substantial number of Jews, the creation of sanctuaries for them in Allied and neutral countries, and the support of those who were to remain imprisoned, for the time being, within German-ruled Europe. The meeting ended inconclusively.

Jan Kozielewski (aka Jan Karski), 1943. United States Holocaust Memorial Museum, Washington, DC.

Studio portrait of Szmul Zygielbojm with his wife, Golda Sperling Zygielbojm, and their infant son, Yosef, ca. 1920. United States Holocaust Memorial Museum, Washington, DC.

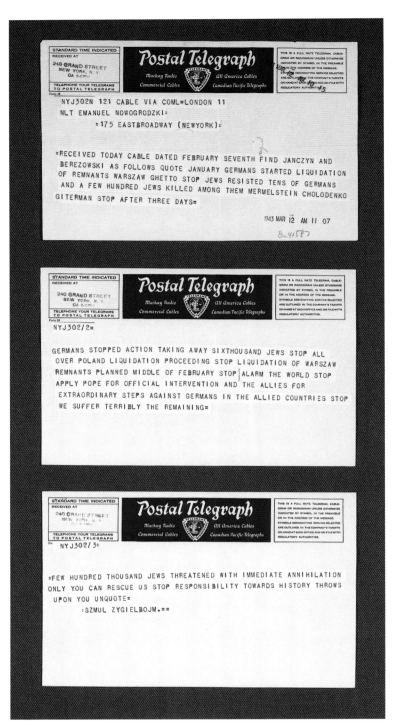

Telegram sent by Szmul Zygielbojm, March 1943. This telegram, covering three sheets, was among many of Zygielbojm's calls to save the Jews of Poland. One month later, in April, the remaining inhabitants of the Warsaw ghetto rose up, heroically and, from a military point of view, futilely, against the Germans. YIVO Institute for Jewish Research, New York.

In London, the Jewish Labor Bund representative on the Polish national council, Szmul Zygielbojm, tried to persuade officials of the destruction of Polish Jewry and the need for action. Despondent over news of the April 1943 failed Jewish uprising in the Warsaw ghetto and the subsequent murder of his wife and child, Zygielbojm committed suicide. In his suicide note he wrote: "By my death, I wish to give expression to my most profound protest against the inaction in which the world watches and permits the destruction of the Jewish people."[52]

In the United States, American Jewish leaders organized rallies in support of European Jews. The largest ones occurred at Madison Square Garden in New York City. Yet the leaders could not muster unity on how to persuade fellow Americans to act. In the fall of 1943 groups espousing active rescue, including the Va'ad Ha-Hatsala, organized a march of Orthodox and Haredi (ultra-Orthodox) rabbis on Washington DC. In the hope of a meeting with President Franklin D. Roosevelt, the rabbis walked to the White House—but the leader of the free world was not at home.

Arrival and Selection

Trains, traveling around the clock, brought 1.3 million Jews, Poles, Roma, and other enemies of the Third Reich, real or perceived, to Auschwitz: city dwellers and shtetl dwellers, young and old, rich and poor, poets and peddlers, teachers and students, doctors and rabbis, women, men, and children. Between March 1942 and April 1944 these trains stopped on the siding of the Auschwitz freight station. By May 1944, the trains were able to enter directly into Auschwitz-Birkenau on a newly built railway spur. After unlocking the doors of the trains, *Kapos* rushed out the passengers. Baggage containing household goods, clothes, and trinkets was left on the platform. Many of these suitcases and baskets that deportees took with them remain unidentified, but others can be traced back to particular people. One such suitcase carries the following painted information: *Dr. Stein. Kurt. Geb. 8.X.1912.*

Foreground: baggage and objects brought by those transported to the Auschwitz concentration camp; background: photograph of the disembarkation in Auschwitz from "The Auschwitz Album," 1944. Exhibition installation, Centro de Exposiciones Arte Canal, Madrid, 2017.

Suitcase of Dr. Kurt Stein, 1940s. Collection of Miroslav Ganobis, Poland. Exhibition installation, Centro de Exposiciones Arte Canal, Madrid, 2017.

Kurt Stein, ca. 1930. State Regional Archive, Plzeň, Czech Republic.

Who was this Dr. Kurt Stein? He was born in the Czech city of Plzeň (Pilsen) on October 8, 1912. He completed his medical degree in the late 1930s. In January 1942, the SS and police forced Kurt, along with his mother, Berta, his younger brother, Hanuš, and 2,000 other Plzeň Jews to leave their homes and deported them to the Theresienstadt (Czech, Terezín) ghetto in the German-ruled Czech lands. On October 26, 1942, Theresienstadt became an anteroom of Auschwitz, with the departure of a transport of 1,866 Jews to that ghetto. In the next two years, 46,000 Jews would leave Theresienstadt for Auschwitz. Hanuš's turn came in January 1943. Berta and Kurt survived until the SS initiated a final wave of deportations between September 28 and October 28, 1944, when eleven transports carrying 18,402 men, women, and children left the ghetto for Auschwitz. The SS forced Berta onto the transport of October 9 and Kurt onto the transport of October 19. Each, carrying one suitcase, was squeezed into a crowded freight wagon. Both mother and son were killed immediately after their arrival in the camp: Berta on October 10, and Kurt on October 20. Emptied of whatever was deemed to be of value, Kurt's suitcase was discarded, to find a place, seventy years later, in a private collection.

Hanuš, Berta, and Kurt were deported to Auschwitz separately. As adults they were consid-ered as single individuals, not as a family. Usually families with children were deported together. During the train journey, parents and children, brothers and sisters were still together, but on the camp's *Rampe* (ramp) the deepest ties were method-ically torn asunder. "Then came the order: leave all the luggage," Norbert Wollheim recalled. "But what was far more important and more gruesome was that the order came: men, one group, women with chil-dren to another group, and women without children, a third group. And I had to say a goodbye to my then wife and child. We waved to each other, and that's the last I have ever seen of her."[53]

Such farewells, if they occurred at all, happened amid a chaos of noise, dogs, and men—confident ones dressed in military uniforms and harried ones in striped clothing—shouting orders to line up in many languages to as many as five thousand dazed deportees.

Typically there were to be two columns: men and boys sixteen and older in one column, and the women, girls, and children in the other. "Five by five they walk down the street of arrivals," Charlotte Delbo (page 93) wrote. "It is actually the street of departures but no one knows it. This is a one-way street."[54] Prisoners often would whisper a very particular instruction to older boys. "I saw a skinny man in a striped uniform, dragging his feet. He was lumbering," Alex Gross told an interviewer fifty years after he had lined up for selection in Auschwitz. "Du bist achtzehn Jahre alt"—You're eighteen years old—the man said. Alex, who had arrived in Auschwitz with one of the first Hungarian transports, in May 1944, was fifteen at the time. Row by row, first the men and older boys and then the women, girls, and children were led to the camp doctors. In a few seconds, the doctor scanned the person standing before him and assessed his or her age, health, and strength, sometimes demanding a brief declaration as to age or occupation. "He said, in German, 'How old are you?' I said, 'Eighteen.'"[55] This answer saved Alex Gross's life—generally, children and the elderly were sent directly to the gas chambers. The criteria for selection changed from time to time, and the doctors conducting the selection had considerable latitude in deciding who was "fit for labor."

Of the 1.1 million Jews who were deported to Auschwitz, only 200,000 were admitted as registered prisoners into the camp; the other 900,000 were murdered shortly after their arrival. Of these,

The selection process, shown in a photograph from "The Auschwitz Album," 1944. Yad Vashem: The World Holocaust Remembrance Center, Jerusalem.

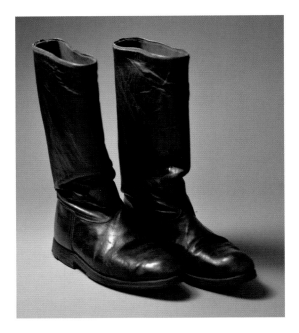

SS Jackboots, 1940s. Auschwitz-Birkenau
State Museum, Oświęcim, Poland.

On the Birkenau railway platform, after the selection of a
new transport of Jewish prisoners, SS officers make their way
out of the camp; photograph from "The Auschwitz Album,"
1944. Yad Vashem: The World Holocaust Remembrance
Center, Jerusalem.

Women and children on their way to the gas chambers, while
Crematorium 2 looms in the background; photograph from
"The Auschwitz Album," 1944. Yad Vashem: The World
Holocaust Remembrance Center, Jerusalem.

200,000 were children. With the exception of twins,
who were deemed useful for medical experiments,
and children on transports that were not subjected
to selection—a practice meant to hoodwink the Red
Cross—all Jewish children arriving in Auschwitz
were automatically condemned to death. In 2004
Oskar Gröning, a former SS man who served in
Auschwitz, explained to British documentary
filmmaker Laurence Rees how he and his colleagues
justified the murder of those children. He began by
justifying the murder of Jews in general:

"We were convinced by our world view that we
had been betrayed by the entire world, and that there
was a great conspiracy of the Jews against us—"

Rees interjected, "But surely, when it comes to
children you must realize that they cannot possibly
have done anything to you?"

"The children, they're not the enemy at the
moment," Gröning responded. "The enemy is the
blood inside them. The enemy is the growing up to be
a Jew that could become dangerous. And because of
that the children were included as well."[56]

During the selection the children were lined up
with the women. As the SS aimed to keep distur-
bance to a minimum, they decided not to separate
the children from their caregivers. Therefore they
also sent to the gas chambers the mothers, older
sisters, aunts, grandmothers, or friendly strangers
who carried or accompanied these children during
the selection process. Elderly people and those
judged to be infirm were sent immediately to the gas
chambers. These selection practices applied to Jews

only: all twenty-three thousand Roma who arrived in Auschwitz—men, women, and children—were initially admitted to the camp; the non-Jewish Poles who were sent to Auschwitz-Birkenau also were admitted and not subject to selection at arrival.

In May 1944 Bernhardt Walter and Ernst Hoffmann, who were in charge of the Auschwitz photography lab, recorded the arrival in Auschwitz-Birkenau of a transport of Jews from northern Hungary. They placed the photographs in an album, providing neatly written labels to identify the scenes. They labeled the photos showing the selection as *Aussortierung*. This German noun has two common meanings—"sorting" and "rejection"—the combination an appropriate designation, as some 80 percent of the arriving Jews depicted in those pictures were rejected during the selection process. In 1945 a nineteen-year-old survivor of that transport, Lilly (or Lili) Jacob, found the album in the abandoned SS barracks at the Dora-Mittelbau concentration camp in Germany. It became known as "The Auschwitz Album" and is probably the single most significant historical artifact concerning the history of the camp.

The arrival in Auschwitz of the trainloads of deportees, the separation of the families, the selection, and the quick dispatch of those who were to be murdered in the gas chambers—this process provides the core of the man-made catastrophe known as Auschwitz. It is here, above all, in its pivotal moment, the selection of the "useful" ones among the exhausted, thirsty, smelly, and disheveled arrivals by a German physician wearing an immaculate green uniform and polished black boots, that the order of humankind was violated in its most basic form. It is an order that assures a place to live and an opportunity for growth for every human born into a common world. In the story of Auschwitz, this is the point to which all earlier developments converge and from which all later ones diverge.

Array of objects brought to Auschwitz, 1942–44. Auschwitz-Birkenau State Museum, Oświęcim, Poland. Exhibition installation, Centro de Exposiciones Arte Canal, Madrid, 2017.

This Black Spot at the Core of Europe,

This Red Spot, This Spot of Fire . . .

MAP OF THE DEPORTATIONS OF JEWS TO AUSCHWITZ, 1942–1944

This map shows the major railway lines used to bring Jews from all over Europe to Auschwitz

Beginning in spring 1942, more than one million Jews and thousands of non-Jews from all the countries in German-ruled Europe—first from Slovakia (March), then France (March), Poland (May), Germany (May), the Netherlands (July), Belgium (August), Yugoslavia (August), Bohemia and Moravia (October), Norway (December), Greece (March 1943), Italy (October), Hungary (April 1944), and finally Rhodes (July)—were loaded onto trains for "resettlement." They ended up in what French

Aerial photograph of the Auschwitz area, 1944.
The US National Archives at College Park, Maryland.

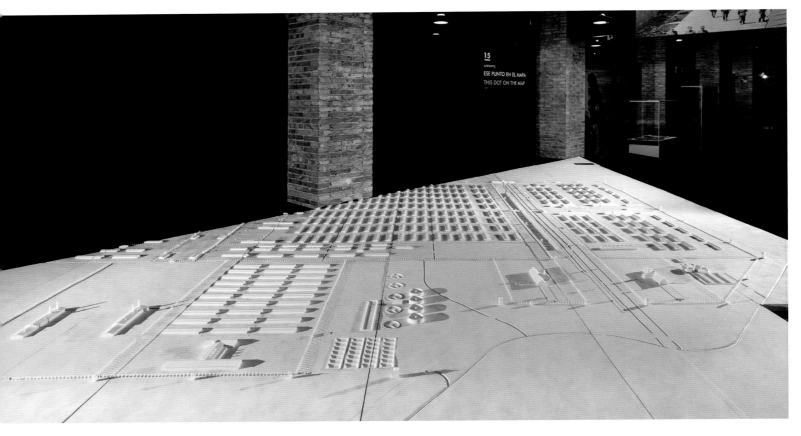

Model (scale 1:200) of the Auschwitz-Birkenau camp. The model shows the camp from the west. In the foreground are, at the far left, Crematoria 5 and 4, and at the right Crematoria 3 and 2. Adjacent to Crematorium 4 are the thirty barracks of Kanada, (pages 161–65). In the far back, right of the center of the picture, is the gate. Between the gate and Crematoria 2 and 3 is the railway platform. Musealia, San Sebastián, Spain. Exhibition installation, Centro de Exposiciones Arte Canal, Madrid, 2017.

deportee Charlotte Delbo (page 93), who arrived in Auschwitz in January 1943, defined in one of her poems as, "this black spot at the core of Europe / this red spot / this spot of fire this spot of soot / this spot of blood this spot of ashes / for millions / a nameless place." Almost no one had heard of the place where the doors of the freight wagons opened and everyone on board faced selection. "Today people know / have known for several years / that this dot on the map / is Auschwitz," Delbo wrote in 1965. She added: "This much they know / as for the rest / they think they know."[57]

Auschwitz is marked in the collective memory of the West by barbed-wire fences, by the *Arbeit Macht Frei* gate at the entrance of the *Stammlager*, by the Gate of Death through which the trains entered Auschwitz-Birkenau, by the shoddy horse-stable barracks that filled that camp, and above all by the four gas-chamber-equipped crematoria that, today, lie in ruins at the western edge of that camp. In 1946 David Olère, a surviving *Sonderkommando* of Crematorium 3, made an evocative drawing of this crematorium. It shows a line of deportees on their way into the basement of the building. None of them ever returned from that place.

The most striking part of Olère's drawing is the massive chimney with its crown of fire. This part of the drawing suggests the concept of Holocaust, an originally Greek word that means "burnt offering." It is remarkable that *burning* has became the central icon of the genocide of six million Jews in which the causes of death were starvation and disease (one million), bullets (two million), and gas (three million). To be sure, there are testimonies of living Jewish babies thrown on pyres in Auschwitz-Birkenau in the summer of 1944. There are also reports of some Jewish *Sonderkommandos* having been put in the ovens alive, but in the Holocaust the setting on fire of live human beings was exceptional. Nevertheless we refer to the genocide of the Jews as *Holocaust*, and, in the same vein, many people refer loosely to the "gas ovens" of Auschwitz, collapsing the gas chambers and the crematoria ovens into one spurious umbrella concept that equates killing and burning.

One of the first memoirs of Auschwitz, written by Sonia Landau and published in 1946 under the Polish Christian name she had adopted after her escape from

David Olère (1902–1985), drawing of Crematorium 3, 1945. Watercolor and ink on paper. Marc Oler, France, and the Ghetto Fighters' House Museum, Lohamei HaGeta'ot, Israel.

the Warsaw ghetto, Krystyna Zywulska, systematically conflated the killing and burning. Interestingly, her reasons for doing so are clearly revealed in the book. Sonia recalled that when she arrived in Auschwitz-Birkenau, her friend Zosha remarked, "We've entered hell," adding the question, "Do you think we'll roast?" For the Polish Catholic Zosha, who had been raised within the sacred topography of Christianity, the identification of Birkenau with hell was obvious. Sonia quickly internalized the Christian view. Later in her memoir she described the nighttime scene during the Hungarian Action (or Ungarn-Aktion, the mass deportation of Hungarian Jews—and the murder of most of them in the Auschwitz gas chambers—in 1944), when the crematoria ovens were overloaded and bodies were also burned on large pyres. "Every chimney was disgorging flames. Smoke burst from the holes and the ditches, swirling, swaying, and coiling above our heads. Sparks and cinders blinded us. Through the screened fence of the second crematory we could see figures with pitchforks moving against the background of flames. . . . I felt, as if at any moment, the earth would open and swallow us with this hell."[58]

The comparison between the camps and hell became routine. In 1971 critic and philosopher George Steiner noted that the death camps "are the deliberate enactment of a long, precise imagining. . . . In the camps, the millenary pornography of fear and vengeance, cultivated in the Western mind by Christian doctrines of damnation, was realized."[59] The comparison was, of course, not appropriate: hell has always been associated with the fires that burn the wicked. In the case of the camps, the fires burned the corpses of the innocent. A more appropriate reference would have been to recall the long association of fire and Jewish martyrdom. In Roman times, Jews such as Rabbi Akiva, Rabbi Shimon ben Gamliel, and Rabbi Hanina ben Teradion suffered martyrs' deaths on the pyre—the last, as the Mishnah records, wrapped in a Torah scroll, in the presence of his followers. "His students said to him: 'Our teacher, what do you see?' Rabbi Hanina ben Teradion said to them: 'I see the parchment burning, but its letters are flying to the heavens'" (Avodah Zarah 17a).

Finally the image of the crematorium makes it a specific symbol of the catastrophic interaction of the German and Jewish worlds in Auschwitz. At the beginning of the twentieth century, when Germany became the industrialized economy par excellence, Jewish religious authorities proclaimed an explicit injunction against cremation, which enjoyed increasing popularity. From rabbinical times onward, rabbis had tried to establish which acts of nonobservance of religious law led to a separation between an individual and the Jewish community. In the early twentieth century the act of cremation became an important boundary marker. Within the history of Jewish exile, burial had acquired central social significance in suggesting that the community as it gathered for a burial at a Jewish graveyard—often the only land Jews were allowed to own—represented the totality of a Jewish congregation at peace with itself. Cremation implied a willful severance from this community. Thus the Auschwitz crematoria are a symbol of the particularity of the *German* assault on the *Jews*.

The Lethal Core

Remains of the undressing room of Crematorium 3, 2018.

The crematoria—designed by SS architects and approved in Berlin, with their gas chambers and ovens manufactured by the engineering company Topf and Sons according to SS specifications—were at the core of the Auschwitz death factory. In the case of Crematoria 2 and 3, each of the buildings had an underground undressing room, equipped with benches, where the victims took off their shoes, clothes, and eyeglasses, and stored them—temporarily, they believed—by hanging them on numbered hooks. At the back of the undressing room was a door that led into a small vestibule, which gave access to the gas chamber. "At eye level of a man of average height, there was a round glass window in the door," former *Sonderkommando* Henryk Tauber testified in May 1945, when deposed by the Polish team charged with the forensic investigation of crimes committed in Auschwitz. He noted that on the gas-chamber side of the door, the window—or,

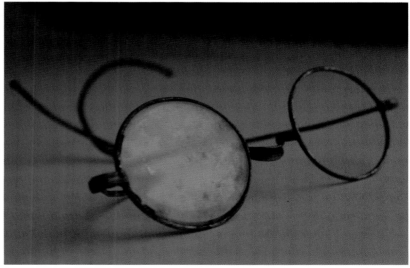

Eyeglasses brought into the Auschwitz camp by a deportee, 1940s. Auschwitz-Birkenau State Museum, Oświęcim, Poland.

Child's shoe, with sock, 1944. In the background is a photograph of Cremato-rium 4. Shoe from Auschwitz-Birkenau State Museum, Oświęcim, Poland. Exhibition installation, Centro de Exposiciones Arte Canal, Madrid, 2017.

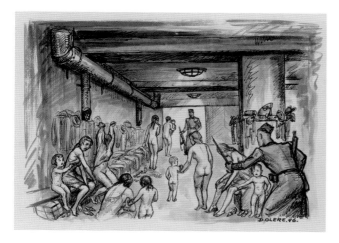

David Olère (1902–1985). Drawing of scene in undressing room of Crematorium 3, 1946. Watercolor and ink on paper. Marc Oler, France, and the Ghetto Fighters' House Museum, Lohamei HaGeta'ot, Israel.

better, peephole—was covered with a hemispherical grille. "The grille was installed because there had been cases of the people in the gas chamber breaking the glass before dying."[60]

The gas chamber itself was disguised as a shower room. It is a common misconception that the cyanide gas entered through the fake showerheads. This was not the case: the showerheads attached to the ceilings of the gas chambers were not connected to pipes. Instead SS medics, standing on the roof of the gas chamber, which projected beyond the footprint of the aboveground building, lowered a bucket with degassing Zyklon-B material into the chamber via wire-mesh columns (page 121). Death in the gas chambers was cruel and violent. "Once the [Zyklon-B] was poured in . . . it rose from the ground upwards," *Sonderkommando* and survivor Filip Müller recalled in the 1970s. "In the terrible struggle that followed . . . the strongest people tried to climb higher. . . . It was instinctive, a death struggle. Which is why children and weaker people, and the aged, always wound up at the bottom. The strongest were on top. Because in the death struggle, a father didn't realize his son lay beneath him."[61]

Tauber and Müller speculated what had happened during the gassing on the basis of what they saw after the cyanide had been sucked out of the room

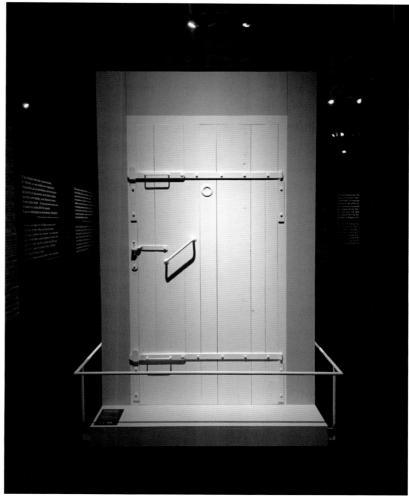

Model (scale 1:1) of the gas-chamber door used in Crematoria 2, 3, 4, and 5. Musealia, San Sebastián, Spain. Exhibition installation, Centro de Exposiciones Arte Canal, Madrid, 2017.

with powerful ventilators and after the gastight door was opened. When in early 1945 survivors of the Auschwitz death march arrived in the Buchenwald concentration camp, they told those whom they could trust, in whispers, what had happened back in Auschwitz. Buchenwald inmate Jorge Semprún immediately realized that the gas chambers had introduced something new in history. "There are no survivors of the gas chambers. No one can tell us that he was there, no one could ever, through the truthfulness of his story, make us say: It is as if I was there!" Throughout history, Semprún observed,

Zyklon-B tin and gas mask used in Auschwitz,
1942–45. Auschwitz-Birkenau State Museum,
Oświęcim, Poland. Exhibition installation,
Centro de Exposiciones Arte Canal, Madrid, 2017.

Fake showerhead once installed in an Auschwitz gas chamber, 1942–45. Auschwitz-Birkenau State Museum, Oświęcim, Poland.

Peephole into the crematorium ovens produced by Topf and Sons for Auschwitz Crematorium 2 and Crematorium 3, 1940s. Auschwitz-Birkenau State Museum, Oświęcim, Poland.

there were direct witnesses to massacres: survivors and perpetrators. But not of the death in the gas chambers. "We have the proofs, but not the testimonies. In Humanity's collective memory, legendary or historical, fable or document, there will always be this ontological vacuum: . . . no one could ever tell us that he has been there."[62]

If the gas chambers are an ontological vacuum, the history that unfolded in the incineration rooms has been described in detail by surviving *Sonderkommandos*. "Crematorium 2 had five ovens. Each oven had three receptacles for cremating corpses and was fired by two coke-generators," Tauber testified in 1945. "The corpses of 'muselmen,' which were emaciated and contained no fat, burned better in the side receptacles than in the central ones. When burning such corpses, we used coke suitable only for firing up the ovens. Fat corpses burned by themselves. . . . Each receptacle could in principle hold four to five corpses. Up to eight 'muselmen' could fit inside." Tauber also provided gruesome detail about the incineration of the bodies of children: they were placed on the bodies of adults. "We did it this way so that the children's corpses would not rest directly on the grates; the grates were widely spaced and a child's corpse could fall through into the ash box."[63]

David Olère (1902–1985), drawing of scene in incineration room of Crematorium 3, 1945. Olère's illustration shows the elevator for hoisting corpses, in the background, and six of the fifteen oven receptacles, to the left. Watercolor and ink on paper. Marc Oler, France, and the Ghetto Fighters' House Museum, Lohamei HaGeta'ot, Israel.

Bearing Witness: *Sonderkommandos*

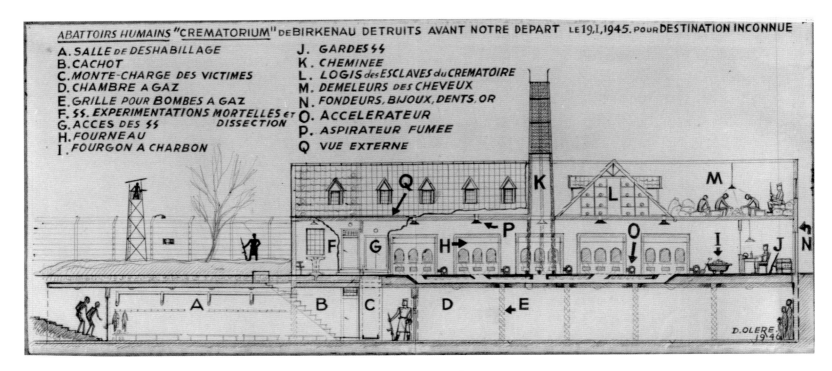

David Olère (1902–1985), cross section of Crematorium 3, 1946.
The caption reads: "Human slaughterhouses 'Crematorium' at
Birkenau destroyed before our departure on January 19, 1945, for
an unknown destination."

DRAWING LEGEND

A. Undressing room
B. Cell
C. Corpse hoist
D. Gas chamber
E. Gas column
F. Autopsy room for medical
    experiments and dissections
G. Entry for SS officers
H. Ovens
I. Coal trucks on tracks

J. SS overseers
K. Chimney
L. Living area for the Sonderkommandos
M. Hair combers
N. Casters: gold, jewelry, and teeth
O. Forced-air ventilators
P. Ventilation exhausts
Q. Outside view

Watercolor and ink on paper. Marc Oler, France, and the
Ghetto Fighters' House Museum, Lohamei HaGeta'ot, Israel.

The four crematoria at Auschwitz-Birkenau were operated under the control of the Political Office (the so-called Camp Gestapo). SS doctors supervised the gassings: they ordered SS medics to introduce the Zyklon-B into the gas chambers and, after the prisoners had been murdered, gave permission to open the gas-chamber doors. At any given time, a few dozen SS men were on-site to oversee the work of the camp's two hundred to eight hundred *Sonderkommandos*, who worked in twelve-hour shifts. At each crematorium, twenty *Sonderkommandos* gave instructions to the victims in the undressing room, ten cleaned out the gas chamber, six cut hair and harvested dental gold, six loaded the hoist for corpses that connected the ground floor to the basement, and eight maintained the oven fires and loaded the muffles. In the summer of 1944, when the Hungarian transports arrived at Auschwitz, the SS tripled the number of *Sonderkommandos* in order to cope with the workload.

The fate of the *Sonderkommandos* has been considered from different angles. In the first decades after the war, they were considered collaborators with the Germans who had purchased a slim chance at survival at the price of participation in the destruction of their own people. In her memoir published in 1946, Sonia Landau wrote that she and the other prisoners who saw them at work close to their barrack in the storehouse section of the camp assumed they were monsters. "Otherwise they would not work there. I felt contempt towards them."[64]

"The truth is that one wants to live at any cost, one wants to live because one lives, because the whole world lives," *Sonderkommando* Salmen Lewenthal wrote in a diary he kept secretly, which was found, buried in the soil, after the war. Many *Sonderkommandos* lost all sense of feeling. "They simply forgot what they were doing [illegible] and with time [illegible] they got so used to it that it was even strange [that one wanted] to weep and complain; that [illegible] such normal, average [illegible] simple and unassuming men [illegible] of necessity get used to

everything so that these happenings make no more any impression on them," Lewenthal wrote.[65] When Landau confronted a *Sonderkommando* about his work, he essentially told her the same, and added: "You think that the special squad are awful people. I assure you that they are like other people everywhere—only much more unhappy."[66]

In the mid-1980s Claude Lanzmann's ten-hour movie *Shoah* offered a second perspective: the surviving *Sonderkommando* as witness. This has become the dominant interpretation in our age, which, because of its commitment to right the wrongs against the marginalized, has been identified as "the era of the witness."[67] Filip Müller and Henryk Tauber provided oral testimony after the war; David Olère created visual testimony in drawings after his liberation. Salmen Lewenthal posthumously provided testimony by burying a record of what he had observed. Yet, even while the killings were happening, *Sonderkommandos* sought to inform the Polish resistance outside of the camp about the killings. "Somewhere about midway through 1944, we decided to take pictures secretly to record our work," *Sonderkommando* and survivor Alter Fajnzylberg (aka Stanislaw Jankowski) reported in 1945. "We all gathered at the western entrance leading from the outside to the gas-chamber of Crematorium V. . . . Alex, the Greek Jew, quickly took out his camera, pointed it towards a heap of burning bodies, and pressed the shutter. . . . Another picture was taken from the other side of the building, where women and men were undressing among the trees. They were from a transport that was to be murdered in the gas-chamber of Crematorium V."[68]

"Alex the Greek" was former Greek army officer Alberto Errera. A Sephardic Jew, Errera joined the resistance during the German occupation, assuming the name Aleksos (Alex) Michaelides. Captured, Errera was sent to Auschwitz in April 1944 and selected for the *Sonderkommando*. Risking his life, he took four photographs. The first shot was aimed too high and shows only the canopy of the trees

Auschwitz Sonderkommando *Alberto Errera, at great personal risk, shot these four photographs inside the camp, 1944.* TOP, LEFT TO RIGHT: *The first photograph missed its mark. The second photograph shows naked women being driven to the gas chamber.* BOTTOM: *These two photographs show the action around the top of a corpse-burning pit. Auschwitz-Birkenau State Museum, Oświęcim, Poland.*

Alberto Errera, 1930s. Jewish Museum of Greece, Athens.

near the crematorium. Photographing from the hip to conceal what he was doing, Errera had missed his subject. But the photograph provides in its failure to catch the intended scene the extreme pressure under which Errera operated. The second shows naked women on their way toward the gas chambers. Photographs three and four, taken from inside one of the gas chambers looking outside through the

open door, show the burning of bodies, which fill a deep pit. Corpse-burning pits were used when the number of corpses exceeded the cremation capacity of the ovens. In September 1944, the roll of film that contained the four photographs was smuggled to Kraków. By that time Errera had already been dead for a month; on August 9, he attempted an escape but was captured, tortured, and killed. The SS exposed his mutilated body at the camp gate as a final punishment for a man who had defied them.

A third perspective on the *Sonderkommandos* goes back to a more general observation on forced culpability and forced complicity made by Albert Camus. "He who kills or tortures will only experience the shadow of victory: he will be unable to feel that he is innocent," Camus observed in *The Rebel*. "Thus he must create guilt in his victim so that, in a world that has no direction, universal guilt will authorize no other course of action but the use of force and give its blessing to nothing but success. When the concept of innocence disappears from the mind of the innocent victim himself, the value of power establishes a definitive rule over a world in despair."[69] In the 1980s Primo Levi applied Camus's understanding to the *Sonderkommandos*. First he advised us to consider their fate "with pity and rigor, but that judgment of them be suspended." He assigned guilt to the perpetrators. In creating the *Sonderkommandos*, they had tried to deprive the victims of the solace of innocence. "Conceiving and organizing the squads was National Socialism's most demonic crime," Levi observed. "The existence of the squads had a meaning, contained a message: 'We, the master race, are your destroyers, but you are no better than we are; if we so wish, and we do so wish, we can destroy not only your bodies but also your souls, just as we have destroyed ours.'"[70]

Katharina Gruenstein (center, with kerchief tied under her chin) poses with friends before the war, 1939. Katharina Gruenstein survived thirteen selections. She was liberated in a subcamp of Ravensbrück and the only member of her family to survive. Yad Vashem: The World Holocaust Remembrance Center, Jerusalem.

Identification tag, 1942. Arriving in a transport of Slovak Jews in April 1942, Katharina Gruenstein was put to work in the Kanada sheds in August. Her tag indicates that she is prisoner 2851 of FKL (Frauenkonzentrationslager, or Women's Concentration Camp) Auschwitz. The red triangle indicates that she is a political prisoner from SL (Slovakia). Yad Vashem: The World Holocaust Remembrance Center, Jerusalem.

Höss was to ship currency, valuables, and precious metals to the SS headquarters in Berlin; rags and unusable clothes to the Reich Ministry of Economy for use as raw materials in industrial production; and all usable garments, shoes, blankets, bed linens, quilts, and household utensils to the Volksdeutsche Mittelstelle (Ethnic German Liaison Office, abbreviated as VOMI) for distribution among ethnic German settlers in the annexed territories.

Of course, those who arrived had been robbed of most of their property and possessions before they had boarded the trains. Businesses, workshops, professional licenses, academic diplomas, houses, savings, heirlooms, and anything else that did not fit into a suitcase or backpack had already been taken away. Nevertheless, the final depredation that happened in Auschwitz yielded much; in an interim report Pohl submitted to Himmler on February 6, 1943, he noted that 824 boxcars of goods had left Auschwitz: 569 were headed to the Reich Ministry of Economy, 211 to VOMI, and 44 to other concentration camps, various other Nazi organizations, and the IG Farben works at the other end of town.

The sorting of the belongings of the deportees and their temporary storage happened in a special section of the Birkenau camp known by the prisoners as "Kanada"—so named because Canada, the country, represented unlimited resources that were out of reach. At any time, Kanada overflowed with goods. "In the first row of the barracks were spread out dresses, blouses, coats," Sonia Landau remembered, a year after her liberation. "In another row were travelling bags, knapsacks; in the field under an awning were shoes, piles of shoes. Women's, children's shoes—all sizes and fashions. High heeled shoes, galoshes, wooden and leather shoes. Still further back stood baby carriages. . . . The girls in the barracks were ripping dress and coat linings in search for gold dollars and diamonds."[71]

Turnover was high. Valuable items stayed for only a short time in the Kanada storage sheds. Much of it was sent, according to the rules, to Berlin, but SS men at the camp also took things for themselves. "If a lot of stuff is piled up together, then you can easily stash away something for your personal gain," Oskar Gröning recalled, sixty years later. "Stealing things for yourself was absolutely common practice in Auschwitz."[72] Items

Four family pictures found in Auschwitz, 1930s and 1940s. The originals—special thanks to Ann Weiss, the daughter of survivors, who rediscovered them—are in the collection of the Auschwitz-Birkenau State Museum.

of perceived low value typically remained longer in Kanada; there was no urgency in finding a new home for them.

Most deportees carried one or more family photographs with them when they embarked on their journey. Typically these photographs were immediately destroyed, as they were without any value for the German Reich. Yet, thanks to the intervention

of David Szmulewicz, who was part of a resistance group within the camp, and some of the female sorters in Kanada, some twenty-four hundred photographs were hidden in the camp and survived the destruction of thirty Kanada barracks on January 23, 1945. These pictures were found after the liberation by former inmates and Soviet forensic investigators. They were forgotten until 1986, when Ann Weiss, a daughter of Polish Jewish Holocaust survivors, discovered the photographs in a locked storage room in the Auschwitz-Birkenau State Museum. Weiss began a search to identify the people in the pictures.

Possessions of deportees that were stored in Kanada, 1942–45. The exhibition of the Kanada artifacts in the Auschwitz-Birkenau State Museum was created in the 1950s. At that time the curators wanted to make a point about the masses of objects found, and they created large displays with mountains of suitcases, spectacles, bowls, and other artifacts. Such a scene both impresses and depresses. An alternative approach is to present these objects in such a way that the viewer might be able to discover, surely with some effort, why each artifact was treasured, once, by a particular human being, in the spirit of Margery Williams's 1922 children's classic The Velveteen Rabbit: *"Generally, by the time you are Real, most of your hair has been loved off, and your eyes drop out and you get loose in the joints and very shabby. But these things don't matter at all, because once you are Real you can't be ugly, except to people who don't understand." Exhibition installation, Centro de Exposiciones Arte Canal, Madrid, 2017.*

She discovered, among other things, that many of the pictures came from two adjacent Jewish communities in southern Poland: Będzin and Sosnowiec. In 1941 the Będzin and Sosnowiec ghettoes had been the destination of the Oświęcim Jews when they were deported from the Germanized town of Auschwitz. In August 1943 the Germans destroyed the Będzin and Sosnowiec ghettoes and sent the twenty thousand surviving Jews to Auschwitz in ten transports. Of these deportees sixteen thousand were murdered shortly after their arrival.[73]

On Innocence, Radical Loss, and Spiritual Stamina

From June 1940 to March 1942 more than thirty-eight thousand Polish men (mostly non-Jews) and fifteen thousand Soviet prisoners of war were incarcerated in Auschwitz. Almost all had arrived as individuals, without families. They were locked into a camp that, at least for the Polish inmates, was located in recognizable territory. Starting in March 1942, transports began to bring another 1.3 million people, mostly Jews, from all over Europe to Auschwitz, and, from among these, 230,000 men and 130,000 women were admitted as registered prisoners in the camp for the purpose of slave labor. Most of these deportees had arrived with their families and suffered the trauma of violent separation on the *Rampe* (ramp). These registered prisoners, designated "useful" during the selection process, were then admitted into a world that, paraphrasing the Dutch writer Etty Hillesum (who was killed at Auschwitz), was located on a hitherto unknown soil under a hitherto unknown sky. They came to a place marked by a confusing Babel of tongues and intranational rivalry that fomented an unparalleled sense of loss and confusion.

The disorientation of the Jewish deportees was reinforced by the circumstance that Jews could not help but understand their fate as haphazard and themselves as innocent of any crime that would have justified their arrest and deportation. When in 1933 the SA and the SS established the first concentration camps in Germany, those who found themselves inside as prisoners knew why they were there. These political prisoners knew that there was a relationship between their beliefs or actions and their imprisonment. The same applied to those convicted of crimes who, after their prison sentences, were sent to the camps, and to the Polish men who, in 1941 and 1942, were brought to Auschwitz as part of the German attempt to crush the Polish

spirit of resistance. Yet the Jews who were admitted to the camp from March 1942 onward did not have this privilege.

In the diary Philip Mechanicus kept in Westerbork he observed that those who pondered the *why* of their suffering could not accept that the simple fact that they were Jewish provided a satisfactory answer. "It contains no lesson for life, no incentive to take stock of his moral, spiritual or social attributes."[74] Some religious Jews found an answer for their dire situation in *Teshuvah* (repentance, as codified by Maimonides), as the communal consequences of the Jewish experience in the Diaspora, as stated in the beginning of the book of Deuteronomy. The more historically inclined tried to understand their own fate as part of Jewish history, with its ups and many downs.

Decades later Rabbi David Weiss Halivni, who was deported with his whole family to Auschwitz in 1944, pleaded that survivors not ask, "Why?" "There are events in history, such as Revelation to the believer, that exist without explanation; they just exist. They have no 'because.' The Holocaust should be treated as such an event—an event without explanation." Yes, investigate every aspect of the Holocaust; delve into its details. The facts should be recorded, including the key fact: during the Holocaust to be born a Jew meant to be born to be killed. "But when it comes to explanations, we should be careful, lest we justify what happened. Sometimes the line between explanation and justification is very thin."[75]

Indeed, the Jews in Auschwitz knew that, as long as the Third Reich was not defeated, they would never leave the camp except through the chimneys; they knew that it was very unlikely that they would ever see their loved ones again; they knew that, if they were to hang on until the arrival of Allied soldiers at the gates of the camp, they would return to a world in which there would be no homes to return to; they knew that if they were able to survive, and make a new beginning somewhere else, they would always be separated from their neighbors by an experience impossible to communicate, a reality few would want to believe to be true.

But yet. One way or another, in a situation in which there was no *why*, many Jews maintained their faith and tried to obey the commandments. "In the morning my father and I would rise before the general wake-up call and go to a nearby block where someone had traded a dozen rations of bread for a pair of phylacteries (tefillin)," Elie Wiesel recalled, half a century after his arrival in Auschwitz. "We would strap them onto our left arm and forehead, quickly recite the ritual blessings, then pass them on to the next person. A few dozen prisoners thereby sacrificed their sleep, and sometimes their rations of bread or coffee, to perform the mitzvah, the commandment to wear the tefillin."[76]

Each morning a pious Jewish man will say, before putting on the tallit, that he does so, "in fulfillment of the command of my Creator, as it is written in the Law, 'They shall make them a fringe upon the corners of their garments throughout their generations.' And even as I cover myself with the Tallith in this world, so may my soul deserve to be clothed with a beauteous spiritual robe in the world to come, in the garden of Eden. Amen."[77] There were no tallits in Auschwitz—except in the Kanada storehouses, of course. The Amud Aish Memorial Museum made available to us a tallit katan that was used by Mendel Landau in Auschwitz. Born in 1922 in Oświęcim to a family of Bobover Hasidim, Landau was sent in 1940 to the first of many forced-labor camps created for the construction of the Silesian tract of the Reichsautobahn (Reich Highway). When the construction of roads came to a halt, Landau was deported to Auschwitz. A devout man, he sought whatever means he could find to fulfill the religious commandments that framed his life. In 1944, he encountered a

Tallit katan used by Mendel Landau in Auschwitz, 1944. Amud Aish Memorial Museum, New York.

Hungarian Jew who had just arrived and had smuggled into the camp a tallit katan. Landau noticed the man's tzitzis (fringes) and asked if he could borrow the garment so he could make a blessing and thus observe a commandment. An SS guard spotted Landau wearing the tzitzis, beat him viciously, and threw down the now-bloody tallit, as a piece of trash, near the camp fence. When the guard had moved on, Landau risked his life for a second time—now in order to retrieve and return the tallit katan to its owner. However, the latter did not want it after having seen the price one paid for its possession. At great risk, Landau held on to it while in Auschwitz and brought it along with him during the death march in January 1945. He had it with him when he was liberated from Dachau on April 28, 1945.

The history of Jews in Auschwitz would not be complete if we did not note what Rabbi Norman Lamm defined as the "staggering psychological stamina and spiritual invincibility of those Jews who sought guidance in Halakhah (Jewish Law) from their few remaining rabbis."

> Questions (*she'elot*) on fine points of Jewish law were directed to a scholarly rabbi, and answers or response (*teshuvot*) were offered. Dedication to Torah was expressed not in the abstract, but in the minutiae of daily life *in extremis*. Thus, a semblance of normality was restored to the inmates of the vicious madhouses, as the norms of the Halakhah provided a minimal psychic structure of human dignity and morale. This was infinitely more than "foxhole faith" and empty consolation. . . . People stood ready to offer up not only their own lives but even the lives of their only surviving children if this was the decision of the Halakhah. The ancient *Akedah* motif—the sacrifice of Isaac by his father, Abraham—was played out in all its terrible magnificence.[78]

Lamm referred to a famous response given in Auschwitz by Rabbi Zevi Hirsch Meisels from Vác,

Hungary, concerning the question whether a father might try to save his son, who was included in a group of fourteen hundred boys of less than a certain height that was destined for the gas chambers, knowing well that his success in having his son released from that group would mean that another boy, hitherto "safe," would be selected to make up the predetermined number of fourteen hundred. When Meisels told the father that on the basis of Halakhah he could not say either yes or no, the man responded:

> Rabbi, I did what I could, what the Torah obligated me to do: I asked a question of a rabbi, and there is no other rabbi here. Since you cannot answer me that I am allowed to ransom my child, this is a sign that according to the law you may not permit it. . . . This is enough for me. It is clear that my only child will be burned according to the Torah and the law, and I accept this with love and rejoicing. I will do nothing to ransom him, for so the Torah has commanded.[79]

It is a modern reenactment of the Akedah, the most puzzling, the most distressing, and the most important of all the stories in the Torah. The parallel is only partial, of course. In the version of the story set in Auschwitz, the father was tested, and the son was murdered, while in the biblical one, the father was tested, and the son survived thanks to God's intervention. The Akedah includes mysteries: What did God intend when he commanded Abraham to sacrifice his son? What did Abraham think was going to happen? Elie Wiesel identified this as a game between God and Abraham, one in which Isaac was a mere object. Yet Isaac was aware of what was happening, and this gave him agency also—after God's intervention. Wiesel, the Auschwitz survivor, identified as the core mystery of the tale a simple fact commonly overlooked: "Isaac remained a believer."[80]

Stripped

Those Jews who passed selection were marched to a *Sauna* (delousing facility)—as were all non-Jewish arrivals (non-Jews were not subjected to the selection process). There the Jewish deportees who had been deemed "useful" at selection were stripped of whatever they had carried on their body into the camp. Their luggage had already been sent to Kanada. "SS men appeared and spread out blankets into which we had to throw all our possessions, all our watches and jewelry," Viktor Frankl recalled in 1946. Frankl realized that everything that might have any monetary value would have to be surrendered, but he hoped he might keep the manuscript of a book he was writing. He approached one of the prisoners working in the *Sauna*. "Approaching him furtively, I pointed to the roll of paper in the inner pocket of my coat and said, . . . 'I must keep this manuscript at all costs; it contains my life's work.' . . . A grin spread slowly over his face, first piteous, then more amused, mocking, insulting, until he bellowed one word at me in

Ring crafted out of tin, with inscription "Arno, 13-6 [June 13] 1942," 1942. Arnošt Levit made this engagement ring for Zdenka Fantlová, who kept it with her throughout her imprisonment at Auschwitz and after. Replica of the ring made for the exhibition by Musealia, San Sebastián, Spain.

answer to my question . . . : 'Shit!' At that moment I saw the plain truth . . . : I struck out my whole former life."[81]

The young Elli Friedmann hesitated to remove her bra; she felt ashamed to show her breasts. Years later, under the name Livia Bitton-Jackson, she recalled: "Just then a shot rings out. The charge is ear-shattering. Several women begin to scream. Others weep. I quickly take my bra off. . . . The shaving of hair has a startling effect. . . . A burden is lifted. The burden of individuality. The burden of associations. Of identity. The burden of the recent past."[82]

Very rare are stories about prisoners who proved able to smuggle a piece of their past into the camp. In 1942, in the Theresienstadt (Terezín) ghetto, twenty-six-year-old Arnošt "Arno" Levit made a ring for his twenty-one-year-old girlfriend, Zdenka Fantlová. When Arno heard that he would be included in a transport "to the East," he slipped the ring onto Zdenka's finger with the words: "That's for our engagement. And to keep you safe. If we're both alive when the war ends, I'll find you."[83] On October 16, 1944, Zdenka was deported to Auschwitz. Two days later she stood in a line awaiting registration—stripped naked, yet with the tin ring still on her finger. Ahead of her an SS man nabbed a girl concealing a ring in her mouth. She was dragged away and beaten. Zdenka decided not to drop her ring. Instead she slipped it under her tongue, taking the risk of a beating or even death. When the SS man began to search her, one of his superiors ordered him to move things along, and he turned to the next deportee. In the next six months in Auschwitz, on the death march, and in Bergen-Belsen, Zdenka clung to the ring, which indeed protected her. Arno, however, did not survive, nor did any of her family.

After having been stripped, the new arrivals were shaved. Beginning in the mid-1930s, all prisoners

Male deportees leave the shower room of the Zentralsauna (Central Sauna) in Auschwitz-Birkenau, 1943. This photograph was taken by Dietrich Kamann while he was documenting construction in the camp. It is therefore likely that he took it during a trial run of the Central Sauna and its equipment. Auschwitz-Birkenau State Museum, Oświęcim, Poland.

in the German concentration camps had their heads shaved, as a penal measure. When the camps became more crowded after the outbreak of war, and hygienic conditions became worse, prisoners also had their bodies shaved, as a preventive measure to avoid lice-borne typhus. This measure was psychologically painful for many women. And it was also painful in a literal way: the clippers used were not maintained and often made deep cuts.

The next step was the shower—an essential part of the delousing procedure. "While we were waiting for the shower, our nakedness was brought home to us," Viktor Frankl recalled, two years after going through the process. "We really had nothing now except our bare bodies—even minus hair; all we possessed,

Hungarian Jewish women after their registration into the camp, from "The Auschwitz Album," 1944. The woman in a black dress with a gray top who stands in the first row, fourth to the right from the pathway, is Lilly (or Lili) Jacob. In May 1945, in the abandoned SS quarters in the Dora-Mittelbau camp, Jacob found an album that contained this and other photos showing the arrival of her transport. Yad Vashem: The World Holocaust Remembrance Center, Jerusalem.

literally, was our naked existence."[84] From the shower room the prisoners were herded to a room where they were handed used striped uniforms and wooden clogs or shoes with wooden soles. None of the items fit, and prisoners had to try to assemble a somewhat suitable set of clothing through a quick exchange. When Primo Levi had dressed himself, he looked around and realized that he looked like everyone else, "a hundred miserable and sordid puppets." He knew he had reached the bottom. "If we speak, they will not listen to us, and if they listen, they will not understand. They will even take away our name: and if we want to keep it, we will have to find ourselves the strength to do so, to manage somehow so that behind the name something of us, of us as we were, still remains."[85]

And, yes, the next step was the transformation of men and women with names into numbered units. Primo Levi ceased to exist, at least to the world of the camp, and 174517 took his place. Number 174517 received a slip of cloth on which was stenciled his number and the double triangle forming a Star of David that indicated his crime of being a Jew, and then was put in a line that filed along to a prisoner who, with a special tool, tattooed the number 174517 in the left arm of unit *einhundert-vier-und-siebzig-tau-send-fünfhundert-siebzehn* (one hundred seventy-four thousand five hundred seventeen).

Auschwitz was the only Nazi concentration camp in which registered prisoners were tattooed with their prisoner numbers. Initially, prisoners carried their numbers on their uniforms only. When prisoners were admitted to the camp infirmary or were about to be executed, their numbers were also written in indelible ink on their chests or thighs, allowing for identification of their naked corpses. In the fall of 1941, Soviet prisoners of war received tattoos with their numbers upon registration, in anticipation of their certain deaths. This practice was extended to all new prisoners in March 1942—this was the time that transports with Jews began to arrive from Slovakia and France. Beginning in the spring of 1943,

Jan Komski (1915–2002), The Tattooing of Women, *1970–97. Pencil on paper. Auschwitz-Birkenau State Museum, Oświęcim, Poland.*

prisoners who had arrived earlier (including Polish prisoners) were also tattooed. Non-Jewish German prisoners, eleven thousand "reeducation" prisoners, four thousand police prisoners, and thirteen thousand Polish civilians caught in the Warsaw Uprising of 1944 were exempt—as were the seventy thousand Jews who survived the selection on arrival and were held only temporarily in Auschwitz-Birkenau before transport to other concentration camps.

"They lined us up for the tattooing," Sonia Landau recalled in 1946. "A few fainted, some screamed. My turn came. A political prisoner with a very low number and wearing a red *winkel* without the P (*volksdeutsch*), took my arm and began to tattoo number 55908. . . . In this minute, with every prick of the needle, one phase of my life vanished."[86] The tattoo meant not only that one's civilian identity had been obliterated but also that the new identity, embodied not in a name but in a number, carried a finality: it told the prisoner that, in the words of Charlotte Delbo (page 93), he or she was "destined to die naked."[87]

Upon his admission into Auschwitz on January 19, 1943, the Yugoslavia-born David Pollak was given a new name: 89896. After a few months in the camp he was sent to the Dora-Mittelbau camp. Like many

Alfred Kantor (1923–2003), Czech Family Camp, *1944. Pencil on paper. The Czech Family Camp was a section of Auschwitz-Birkenau where families sent from the Theresienstadt ghetto were housed. They were ordered, from time to time, to write postcards, the purpose of which was to provide an alibi to the outside world: deportation to Auschwitz did not mean death but life. But like all prisoners in Auschwitz, the inmates of the Czech Family Camp lived in the shadow of death, represented by the black smoke emanating from the crematorium chimneys. Almost all of them were murdered in the gas chambers. Museum of Jewish Heritage—A Living Memorial to the Holocaust, New York.*

prisoners, David sought to obtain an item that might allow him to anchor his identity. In exchange for a food ration he commissioned from a fellow prisoner a small medallion in which was engraved his name, birthplace, birthdate—and his Auschwitz name: 89896.

Only then were the numbers assigned billets in one of the hundreds of filthy and overcrowded barracks that made up a huge city of slaves. At the beginning of 1944, Auschwitz I (the *Stammlager*) and Auschwitz II (Auschwitz-Birkenau) together contained some forty-five thousand male and thirty thousand female prisoners, while five small satellite camps nearby housed two thousand prisoners work-ing the SS agricultural estate. In addition, the camp included many other prisoner compounds. The most important was Auschwitz III, located adjacent to IG Farben's Buna rubber factory. It held ten thousand inmates. Another seven camps held eleven thousand inmates all together. Thus the total camp population in early 1944 was close to one hundred thousand.

A mass of people, to be sure, making Auschwitz into the largest concentration camp in the Greater German Reich. But, of course, its size was much larger if we count not only the living but also those who had already died in that camp, and those who would die—some nine hundred thousand people who, at selection, were sent to the gas chambers.

Behind the Barrack Walls

In 1945, the Polish novelist Tadeusz Borowski, who had spent a year in Auschwitz, composed what remains one of the most remarkable literary echoes from life in the camp, "Auschwitz, Our Home." In it, he gave what became a classic description of living conditions in the camp.

> If the barrack walls were suddenly to fall away, many thousands of people, packed together, squeezed tightly in their bunks, would remain suspended in mid-air. Such a sight would be more gruesome than the medieval paintings of the Last Judgment. For one of the ugliest sights to a man is that of another man sleeping on his tiny portion of the bunk, of the space which he must occupy, because he has a body—a body that has been exploited to the utmost: with a number tattooed on it to save on dog tags, with just enough sleep at night to work during the day, and just enough time to eat. And just enough food so it will not die wastefully. As for actual living there is only one place for it—a piece of the bunk.[88]

The conditions in the barrack were, indeed horrible, and not only because of the overcrowding. Borowski did not mention the filth, which could not be tackled because of the lack of brooms, mops, pails, and water; he did not mention the stench; he

Barrack from the Auschwitz-Monowitz satellite camp, 1942–44. Musealia obtained this barrack in 2015 from the son of the man who received it in 1945 in compensation for the farm he lost due to the construction of the IG Farben plant. Musealia, San Sebastián, Spain. Exhibition installation, Centro de Exposiciones Arte Canal, Madrid, 2017.

Pocket knife, 1944. A fifteen-year-old Hungarian Jewish girl, Tova Glück, was deported to Auschwitz in June 1944. She survived the selection process. In the camp she "organized" this knife in exchange for a bread ration. Yad Vashem: The World Holocaust Remembrance Center, Jerusalem.

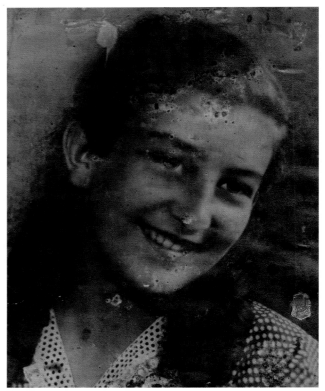

Kitchen pot from Auschwitz, 1940s. Each prisoner received two cups of boiled water mixed with chicory in the morning; four cups of unappetizing soup that contained (often rotten) potatoes, rutabaga, and small amounts of groats and rye flour in the afternoon; and ten ounces of black bread, served with either one ounce of sausage or margarine or a tablespoon of marma- lade or cheese, in the evening. This diet amounted to about thirteen hundred calories a day. The manual labor typically performed by Auschwitz inmates required a daily diet of more than three thousand calories. Auschwitz- Birkenau State Museum, Oświęcim, Poland. Exhibition installation, Centro de Exposiciones Arte Canal, Madrid, 2017.

Tova Glück, ca. 1943. Yad Vashem: The World Holocaust Remembrance Center, Jerusalem.

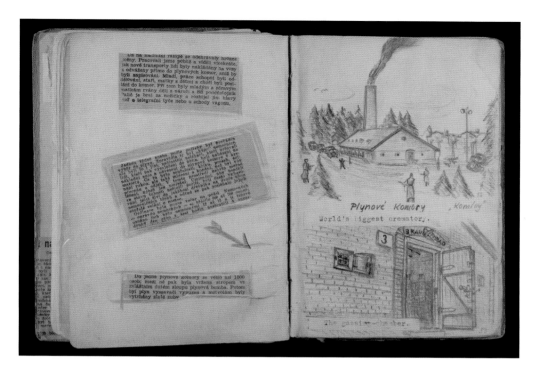

Alfred Kantor (1923–2003), two pages from sketchbook, 1944–45. Kantor kept the sketchbook in Auschwitz and later augmented it with relevant cuttings from newspapers and other publications. Museum of Jewish Heritage—A Living Memorial to the Holocaust, New York.

did not mention that many of the inhabitants were ill; he did not mention that the latrines were far away. Yet in an utterly dangerous world that can be best compared to a raging sea, the barrack was like a piece of flotsam that allowed the shipwrecked to hang on for a bit longer. No prisoner could be sure to survive the work outside, but between the evening and morning roll calls, the barrack walls provided a bit of protection against exposure, a bit of a clearing amid the beatings and the selections. It was the place where one could gather oneself, if one had the resources. The barrack walls protected the young Alfred Kantor when he sketched, in secret, what he saw in the camp, with the aim both to preserve the facts for a post-Auschwitz future and to hold on to himself. "My commitment to drawing came out of a deep instinct of self-preservation and undoubtedly helped me to deny the unimaginable horrors of life at that time," he would write.[89]

The interiority of the barrack provided the possibility for two inmates to share with each other whatever resources they had. "Stable pairing was the most common type of interpersonal relationship pattern," sociologist Elmer Luchterhand observed in his path-breaking study on inmate behavior in the concentration camps. "With all of the raging conflict in the camps, it was in the pairs that the prisoners kept alive the semblance of humanity. The pairs gave relief from the shame of acts of acquiescence and surrender. The pairs provided expertness in the survival skills known as 'organizing.'"[90] In the protective shell of the barrack, men cultivated a "comrade," and women adopted a "camp sister" or a surrogate "camp mother."

Sometimes the protection of the barrack provided space for a larger group of camp brothers and sisters to find a temporary niche of safety. "We were crouching on our tier, on the boards which were used by us as bed, table, floor," Charlotte Delbo (page 93) recalled years later. The space measured only eight feet by eight feet. "The roof was very low. You could only fit there sitting down, head lowered. There were eight of us, perched on a narrow platform, a group of friends death would separate."[91]

Annihilation Through Labor

Conditions in Auschwitz were brutal from the very beginning, and they remained so throughout the history of both the main camp, Auschwitz-Birkenau, and the satellite camps. Of the four hundred thousand people who were admitted to the Auschwitz camps as registered prisoners, half died as a result of starvation, disease, exposure, beatings, targeted collective punishments, and straightforward murder by means of phenol injections or cyanide gas. And then there was death through work. In April 1942 Oswald Pohl, the man who oversaw, among other things, all use of prisoner labor in the camps, issued a directive that instructed the commandant of each camp to maximize the labor output of each inmate. "This work must be exhausting in the true sense of the word in order to achieve maximum performance."[92] A few months later the true meaning of this instruction was articulated in a concept that occurs in an agreement made between Himmler and justice minister Otto Thierack. It concerns "the transfer of asocial elements from the prison service to the *Reichsführer SS* for annihilation through labor (*Vernichtung durch Arbeit*)."[93] In this particular agreement, the "asocial elements" referred to all Jews, Roma, Russians, and Ukrainians in German prisons.

This principle of annihilation through labor applied, from the end of 1942 onward, to all the camp prisoners. And it was applied in its most literal manner in Auschwitz. Regular selections within the camp determined which prisoners had ceased to be economically useful and were therefore targets for murder. These included all those labeled *Muselmänner*. "This word '*Muselmann*,' I do not know why, was used by the old ones of the camp to describe the weak, the inept, those doomed to selection," Primo Levi observed, in a discussion of the way many prisoners deteriorated to a point that they lost even the last spark of individuality. In normal society this hardly occurs, as few are left completely to themselves—there are always neighbors, always someone to help. "In the Lager things are different," Levi explained. "Here the struggle to survive is without respite, because everyone is desperately and ferociously alone."[94] Anything could trigger the transformation of a man into a *Muselmann*: forgoing a couple of food rations in exchange for a cigarette; suffering a cold, a blister on one's foot, or a small accident at work; or just the bad luck of crossing the path of a *Kapo* or SS man who happens to be in a very bad mood and seeks a convenient target for his anger and frustration. In a very short time, even the young and the strong could join what Levi identified as, "The backbone of the camp, an anonymous mass, continually renewed and

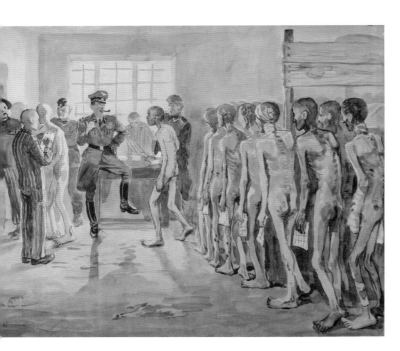

Jerzy Potrzebowski (1921–1974), Selection of Patients for the Gas, *1950. Watercolor on paper. Auschwitz-Birkenau State Museum, Oświęcim, Poland.*

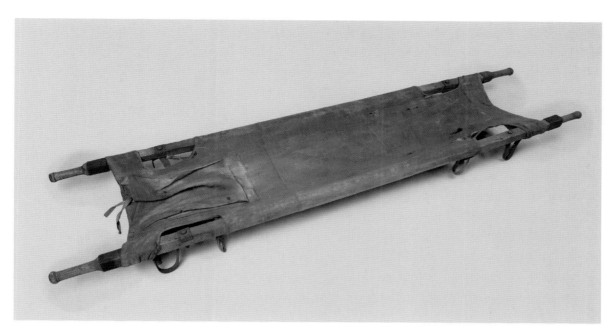

Stretcher, 1940s. Auschwitz-Birkenau State Museum, Oświęcim, Poland.

Alfred Kantor (1923–2003), Muselmann, *1944. Pencil on paper. Museum of Jewish Heritage—A Living Memorial to the Holocaust, New York.*

always identical, of non-men who march and labor in silence, the divine spark dead within them, already too empty to really suffer. One hesitates to call them living: one hesitates to call their death death, in the face of which they have no fear, as they are too tired to understand."[95]

Muselmänner were certain to die, but to the SS they did not die quickly enough. During regular selections held within the camp, SS doctors separated the *Muselmänner* from those who were still considered useful, and they were taken to a special barrack until there was room for them in the gas chambers—but many of them would have died by then.

Medical Experiments

Operating table, test tubes, and medical instruments, 1940s. Auschwitz-Birkenau State Museum, Oświęcim, Poland. Exhibition installation, Centro de Exposiciones Arte Canal, Madrid, 2017.

Every concentration camp had a medical department, which oversaw hygiene in the camp and ran the *Revier* (sick bay). In Auschwitz thirty SS physicians maintained the health of the SS garrison, oversaw prisoner doctors who attended to their fellow inmates, and conducted selections at the ramp and at regular intervals in the camp.

In addition to the tasks prescribed in official regulations, a number of SS doctors took advantage of their position, using inmates as "guinea pigs" in their own research. The gynecologist Dr. Carl Clauberg sterilized able-bodied Jews and Roma—men, women, and children. The most assiduous and notorious medical "researcher" was Dr. Josef Mengele. A medical doctor who also held a PhD in anthropology, Mengele had a special passion for the study of the genetic origins of various diseases and unusual conditions such as dwarfism—and for his "research" preferred using twins. Comparative autopsies of twins provided ideal study conditions, but twins rarely died simultaneously or at a location convenient for the researcher. Auschwitz offered Mengele an opportunity to do what was impossible anywhere else. Mengele set up a block for twins in the Gypsy Camp, where he conducted his experiments—which were wide ranging. Interested in eye color, he injected dye into the eyes of his human subjects; curious about the course of infectious disease and resistance to it, he inoculated inmates with infectious agents; he conducted sex-change operations. One twin served as the control while the other underwent medicalized torture. If one twin died during surgery, the other was killed by phenol injection, and comparative autopsies were performed.

Twins Eva and Miriam Mozes were ten years old when, in the spring of 1944, they arrived with a transport from Transylvania. They were immediately selected for inclusion in Mengele's experiments.

Children's barrack in the Auschwitz women's camp, 2017.

"Mengele came in every morning after roll call to count us. He wanted to know every morning how many guinea pigs he had," Eva recalled sixty years later. Regularly Mengele would draw blood from her and then administer a series of injections. "After one of those injections I became extremely ill and Dr. Mengele came in next morning with four other doctors. He looked at my fever chart and he said, laughing sarcastically, he said: 'Too bad, she is so young. She has only two weeks to live.'" Yet she was determined to survive. "Would I have died, my twin sister Miriam would have been rushed immediately to Mengele's lab, killed with an injection to the heart. Then Mengele would have done the comparative autopsies. That is the way most of the twins died."[96] Eva survived, and so did Miriam (page 194).

Mengele's zeal to identify twins on arriving transports prompted him to volunteer regularly to conduct selections. His became the face of the SS physician on the arrivals ramp who decided with a glance who would live and who would die.

Not all children that became the subjects of experiments were twins. "I was tattooed with the number 70072 and taken to the children's barrack in

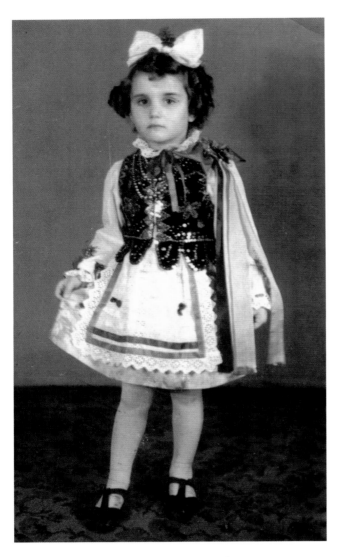

Lidia Maksymowicz, 1945. Galicia Jewish Museum, Kraków, Poland.

Birkenau," Lidia Maksymowicz recalled sixty years later. Born Ludmila Boczarowa and an ethnic Belarusian, Lidia had been transported to Auschwitz with her mother, who was captured in reprisal after her husband and her father (Lidia's father and grandfather) had joined the partisans.

I remember the murals on the walls of the barrack. They were to instill in us calm and order. The longing for my mother and the filth, cold, hunger were unbearable. But I learned from the other children through our camp jargon about something worse to come: Dr. Mengele. After one "visit" to the camp hospital so much blood had been drawn from me I was pale and weak. Soon my body was covered with sores and I couldn't see. I was three or four years old.[97]

Resistance

The Auschwitz SS aimed to destroy any possible solidarity among prisoners. Arbitrary divisions, impossible living conditions, the unrelenting threat of punishment, and routine killings in the gas chambers pitted every group against every other group, every person against every other person, and all against the prisoners at the bottom: the Jews.

Resistance in Auschwitz therefore consisted of acts in which prisoners, against all odds, showed solidarity with others. It included heroic actions made with a view to the larger world outside the camp, grand gestures of generosity, small acts of kindness and charity, and spiritual resistance. And it was expressed in the determination that—despite the best efforts of the SS—death in Auschwitz would not remain anonymous, and the victims would not remain without names.

On September 21, 1940, Witold Pilecki, who had been a second lieutenant in the Polish cavalry, purposely had himself arrested in Warsaw under the alias Tomasz Serafiński, anticipating that he would be sent to Auschwitz. Admitted as prisoner 4859, he began collecting intelligence about the camp for

Second Lieutenant Witold Pilecki of the Polish cavalry, 1930s. Auschwitz-Birkenau State Museum, Oświęcim, Poland.

Auschwitz mug shot of Witold Pilecki, imprisoned under the alias Tomasz Serafiński, 1940. Auschwitz-Birkenau State Museum, Oświęcim, Poland.

"The Heart of Auschwitz," 1944. Booklet (open) made by Auschwitz prisoner Zlatka Pitluk for fellow prisoner Fania Fainer's twentieth birthday. Montreal Holocaust Museum.

Esther Friedlander and her son, Ben, 1947. Collection of Shirley Kopolovic and Mark Levine, Canada.

Metal charms made from bullet casings by Auschwitz prisoner Esther Friedlander at the Weichsel-Union-Metallwerke munitions factory, 1944. Collection of Shirley Kopolovic and Mark Levine, Canada.

Comb made of metal fragments by Auschwitz prisoner Ruth Grunberger, 1940s. Museum of Jewish Heritage—A Living Memorial to the Holocaust, New York.

the Polish government-in-exile in London, while also organizing his fellow prisoners. Pilecki managed to smuggle out many messages about life and death in Auschwitz. In April 1943, Pilecki escaped and returned to Warsaw to convince the Polish resistance to attack Auschwitz in a coordinated effort with prisoners. In Warsaw, Pilecki learned that the commander of the resistance group who had sent him on his original mission had been arrested. The lead-

ership of the Armia Krajowa (Home Army), which had coordinated Polish resistance since 1942, judged an attack on the large and well-armed Auschwitz garrison to be suicidal—and also knew that it would not be able to shelter the tens of thousands of freed inmates. Subsequently, Pilecki wrote what would be the first full report on the conditions of Auschwitz and the mass murder of Jews in the gas chambers. The Allies received the report but ignored it. Pilecki

David Olère (1902–1985), Religious Service in Barrack, *1946. Watercolor and ink on paper. In Auschwitz, all religious practice was strictly forbidden. Nevertheless, many observant Jews and devout Christians tried to maintain religious practices as well as they could. David Olère's drawing shows both Christian prisoners (heads uncovered) and Jewish prisoners (heads covered) in prayer, while one inmate is on the lookout, ready to warn of an approaching SS guard or prisoner functionary. Marc Oler, France, and the Ghetto Fighters' House Museum, Lohamei HaGeta'ot, Israel.*

Madonna found in Auschwitz, 1940s. Auschwitz-Birkenau State Museum, Oświęcim, Poland.

continued to fight the Germans, participating in the 1944 Warsaw Uprising.

Fania Fainer and Zlatka Pitluk, two young Polish Jewish prisoners, were slave laborers at the Weichsel-Union-Metallwerke, a munitions factory operating adjacent to the camp that manufactured explosives. December 12, 1944, was Fainer's twentieth birthday, and Pitluk wanted to give her a present. She made a small booklet in the shape of a heart, and she and eighteen friends filled it with special wishes. The notes to Fainer are written in Polish, German, French, and Hebrew, and contain birthday wishes alongside messages of friendship and hope. Fainer's favorite inscription was "Freedom, Freedom, Freedom." Accompanying the heart was a small birthday cake made from the women's daily bread ration. Fainer kept the heart with her in Auschwitz, on the death march, and in the Ravensbrück and Malchow concentration camps.

In early 1944, Esther Friedlander, a trained seamstress, was engaged to be married. Months later, at age twenty-four, she entered Auschwitz. Born to an Orthodox Jewish family in the Czech town of Uzhhorod (now in Ukraine), Friedlander had lived under Hungarian rule since 1939. In April 1944, at the instigation of Adolf Eichmann, the Hungarian Action was launched, and Hungary began rounding up Jews. Between May 17 and May 31, five transport trains left for Auschwitz. Friedlander was selected to enter the camp; she ended up a slave worker in the Weichsel-Union-Metallwerke munitions factory. One day, she felt particularly unwell. A coworker told her to pretend to work. That day Friedlander crafted from a bullet casing two charms: a book and a four-leaf clover. Envisioning, in the midst of the horror, a happier future in which these charms would adorn someone's wrist, she drilled holes in them. She smuggled the charms out of the factory and kept them

Father Maksymilian Maria Kolbe, 1930s.
Auschwitz-Birkenau State Museum, Oświęcim, Poland.

with her until liberation. Friedlander held onto the charms until her death in 1985.

Shaved bald, dressed in rags, and tattooed with a number, prisoners tried to preserve a sense of identity and dignity. Like most women prisoners, sixteen-year-old Ruth Grunberger agonized over the loss of her hair. Secreting metal fragments from her work in the Weichsel-Union factory, she fashioned a small comb—a promise of a future day when, once again, she would have hair and freedom.

Maksymilian Maria Kolbe, born in 1894, was a Polish Franciscan. He was arrested in February 1941 and shortly thereafter deported to Auschwitz. Despite harsh prohibitions by the camp authorities, he secretly continued to hear confessions and encourage others to pray. Two months after his arrival, Kolbe volunteered to take the place on death row of another inmate, Franciszek Gajowniczek, who, after trying to escape, had been sentenced with nine others to death by starvation. Gajowniczek survived the war. Father Kolbe and the nine others were locked in cell 18 of Block 11. They were supplied with neither food nor water. Six died from dehydration. After three weeks of great suffering, Father Kolbe and the three other inmates still alive in cell 18 were killed by an injection of phenol into their hearts. Pope Paul VI beatified Father Kolbe in 1971, and Pope John Paul II canonized him as a martyr in 1982.

The World Must Know

In March 1944, Slovak Jewish inmates Walter Rosenberg (aka Rudolf Vrba) and Alfréd Wetzler observed the camp's preparations for the arrival of new transports and understood their import when they overheard SS men talking about the upcoming influx of Hungarian salami. With a lot of planning and even more luck, the two men managed to slip out of Auschwitz on April 7, 1944. They fled to Slovakia in the hope of warning the Jews of Hungary. They met up with the Slovak Working Group, an underground Jewish-rescue effort headed by Rabbi Michael Dov Weismandl and Zionist leader Gisi Fleischmann.

The testimony of Vrba and Wetzler, describing in detail the continuing massacres in the gas chambers, was added to information about the deportation of Hungarian Jews to Auschwitz supplied by Czesław Mordowicz and Arnost Rosin, who had escaped the camp on May 27, 1944. This testimony yielded the first substantial report on the use of Auschwitz as a death factory—but it did not reach the Hungarians in time. A summary of what came to be known as the "Auschwitz Protocols" reached the United States in July 1944.

This information led to diplomatic pressure on the Hungarian government to stop its program of mass deportation, which indeed happened, saving the lives of more than 150,000 Hungarian Jews. In addition, it triggered a debate among Allied political, military, and civic leaders about the question, what targets at Auschwitz should be bombed? On August 20, September 13, and December 18, 1944, Allied bombers attacked the IG Farben factory, which had been identified as a potential target many months earlier. But these planes did not bomb the Auschwitz camps.

The first proposal to bomb Auschwitz was made in May 1944 by Rabbi Weismandl. By that time the bombing of Auschwitz had become feasible, thanks to the Allied advance into Italy in the spring of 1944. On June 11, David Ben-Gurion and the rest of the Jewish leadership in Palestine met to discuss this issue. At that time they did not have the "Auschwitz Protocols," and decided that the lack of details and the likelihood that Jews would be killed argued against a bombing

LEFT: *Rudolf Vrba, 1946. Collection of Robin Vrba, United States.* RIGHT: *Alfréd Wetzler, 1960s. Collection of Wetzler family, Slovakia. In April 1944, Slovak Jewish prisoners Vrba and Wetzler escaped from Auschwitz and gave testimony about the Germans' program of mass murder. Their account was included in the widely disseminated report known as the "Auschwitz Protocols."*

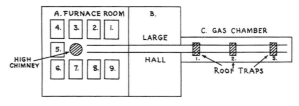

ROUGH GROUND PLAN OF CREMATORIA: TYPES I & II IN BIRKENAU

A composite plan of the crematoria from the first published edition of the "Auschwitz Protocols," The German Extermination Camps of Auschwitz and Birkenau (Washington, DC: War Refugee Board), 1944. Musealia, San Sebastián, Spain.

185

Departures and the Death March

Until the late spring of 1944, the road to Auschwitz had been largely a one-way street. In the first four years of the camp's existence, more than eight hundred thousand deportees had arrived in Auschwitz, while in that time only twenty-five thousand had been transported from Auschwitz to other camps. With the beginning of the Hungarian Action, Auschwitz also became the point of departure of many transports of Jews, deemed "fit for labor" during the selection, to other concentration and slave labor camps in the German Reich. The management of the labor-strapped armament industries eagerly employed as slave workers the inmates supplied by a now-burgeoning concentration camp system, which counted more than five hundred thousand inmates in August and seven hundred thousand four months later. The SS appreciated the massive cash flow that came its way.

By the fall of 1944 the number of prisoners on transports from Auschwitz to Sachsenhausen, Buchenwald, Mauthausen, Ravensbrück, and other camps far exceeded arrivals. Combined with the continuing high mortality, these departures caused the size of the Auschwitz camp network, which included by now forty-four subcamps, to shrink from over 105,000 registered prisoners (August 1944)

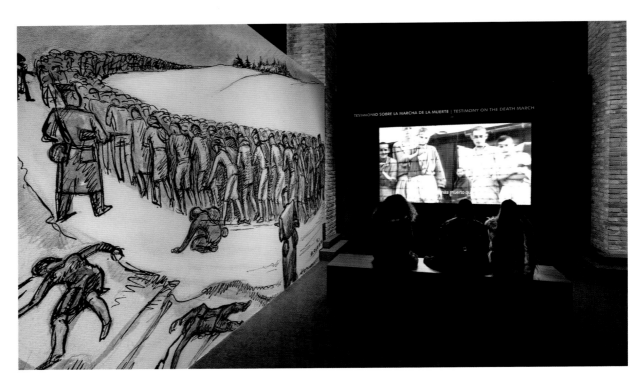

Film on the death march (background) and, to the left, a mural showing David Olère's drawing of the death march, 1945. Exhibition installation, Centro de Exposiciones Arte Canal, Madrid, 2017.

*Siegfried Fedrid's blanket, 1945. Holocaust Center
for Humanity, Seattle. Exhibition installation,
Centro de Exposiciones Arte Canal, Madrid, 2017.*

committed there, which was achieved through the dynamiting of the crematoria and burning of documents. All prisoners who could walk—some sixty thousand—were forced by the SS to march, without proper shoes, clothing, or food, to one of two collection points located at railway junctions some forty miles away. From there, open-wagon freight trains took them to concentration camps in the core of the Reich. Possibly as many as fifteen thousand of the prisoners who left Auschwitz on January 17, 1945, either died as a result of exposure and exhaustion or were murdered by the SS. Survival very much depended on receiving support from others, as Gizela Isserof received from two Hungarian Jewish girls. "And I always kept saying, 'I can't walk anymore.' And when I was ready to give in—'I'm not walking any further'—those two, Faiga Malka and Rivchu, would grab me by my sleeve. 'You have to go on. Your father's coming home, remember? You've got to walk a little longer. Let's walk.'"[103] Annie Glass walked while her sisters, one at each side, held her up. "And my feet were walking and I actually was sleeping and dreaming," she told an interviewer half a century later, adding: "You can do that, if you have to."[104]

One of the prisoners forced on the death march was the twenty-four-year-old deaf Austrian Jewish tailor Siegfried Fedrid. In 1942 Fedrid had been deported from his native Vienna to the Litzmannstadt (Łódź) ghetto, and in August 1944 he was sent, with the remaining sixty-five thousand ghetto residents, to Auschwitz. He survived selection and the next four months of camp life. When the SS ordered the evacuation of the camp, Fedrid grabbed a blanket. During the cold nights of the death march, he shared it with four other prisoners, saving his own and their lives.

Many of those who survived the death march from Auschwitz would find themselves on new death marches a few months later, when the SS tried to prevent their liberation by the Allied armies. Fedrid ended up in the Kaufering camp, a subcamp of the Dachau concentration camp, where he was liberated by the Americans in May 1945.

to 66,000 (January 1945). Among those who were sent away from Auschwitz were Margot and Anne Frank (page 128), who ended up in Bergen-Belsen. Like all the others who, until the middle of January 1945, were deported from Auschwitz, the Frank sisters traveled in a freight wagon, as did Alfred Kantor and Elie Wiesel.

After having slowly pushed back the German army throughout 1944, the Red Army decisively broke through the German lines in early January 1945. Around January 15, Heinrich Himmler ordered the full evacuation of Auschwitz and its subcamps and demanded the destruction of evidence of the crimes

Those who survived the death march did not necessarily experience liberation. Too many died in the last months of the war of disease or starvation. But the systematic annihilation of the Jews and the Roma had come effectively to an end. The German state, the SS, and the concentration camp system were in a state of collapse.

How did the survivors make it to this point, when everything had become random? Was it the result of some innate qualities or luck or both? Fifty years after his own liberation, Auschwitz survivor Rabbi David Weiss Halivni provided a simple answer: "Whereas those who perished perished more or less the same way and for the same reasons, those who survived survived in their own ways and for their own reasons." And he added: "The former is within the domain of scholarship. The latter defies scholarly capabilities."[105]

So be it.

After Auschwitz

Liberation

Auschwitz existed in a limbo during the ten days that separated the departure of the SS and the great majority of the prisoners and the arrival of the Red Army. In this period some of the remaining twelve hundred prisoners of the main camp broke into an SS warehouse and found two slaughtered pigs, bags of dried macaroni, and boxes containing tins of canned meat and condensed milk. They shared this supply with their comrades and with the fifty-eight hundred starving and sick prisoners in Auschwitz-Birkenau.

Finally, on January 27, 1945, the soldiers of the Red Army arrived at the gates of Auschwitz. "We ran up to them and they gave us hugs, cookies and chocolate," Eva Mozes remembered sixty years later. "Being so alone a hug meant more than anybody could imagine because that replaced the human worth that we were starving for. We were not only starved for food but we were starved for human kindness. And the Soviet Army did provide some of that."[106] With the arrival of the Red Army and the Polish Red Cross, significant medical resources, including three field hospitals, became available.

Red Army medics helping Auschwitz survivors, 1945. Auschwitz-Birkenau State Museum, Oświęcim, Poland.

Child survivors in Auschwitz, February 1945. The girl to the far right and the girl beside her (half-hidden), both wearing woolen hats, are Eva and Miriam Mozes. United States Holocaust Memorial Museum, Washington, DC.

Tin of condensed milk and an opener, 1945. Auschwitz-Birkenau State Museum, Oświęcim, Poland.

Amalgam of objects from Auschwitz, 1945. The SS set fire to the storage sheds known as Kanada. The heat of the fire that destroyed most (but not all) of Kanada soldered together the forks and spoons in the foreground. Objects from Auschwitz-Birkenau State Museum, Oświęcim, Poland. Exhibition installation, Centro de Exposiciones Arte Canal, Madrid, 2017.

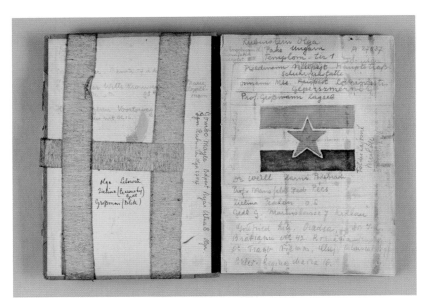

Manuscript, 1945. Immediately after his liberation, Dutch physician Eddy de Wind began writing a memoir of his time in the Auschwitz camp. Grateful to the Red Army, he decorated the manuscript with a Dutch flag carrying the red Soviet star. He joined the team of Red Army and Polish doctors taking care of the survivors. He published his book, entitled Eindstation Auschwitz *(Terminus Auschwitz), a year later. Collection of Sonja de Wind-Klijn, Netherlands.*

Eddy de Wind and others liberated from Auschwitz, 1945. De Wind, wearing glasses, is standing in the back, second from right. Collection of Sonja de Wind-Klijn, Netherlands.

Having suffered starvation, the patients had to be introduced gradually to normal meals. At the time, the liberation of Auschwitz was not a major news event; the Soviets were focused on their offensive operation in Berlin, while the Allied armies were advancing eastward. On April 30, Hitler committed suicide, and eight days later the Wehrmacht (German army) surrendered. The war in Europe was over.

Eva and Miriam Mozes and most of the other 180 children found in the camp—almost all twins—were brought to a convent in nearby Katowice, which was being used as an orphanage. Some of the liberated children were taken in by families in Oświęcim. Most of the other seven thousand Auschwitz inmates liberated by the Red Army struggled to recover in the field hospitals set up in the camp. The strongest began looking for ways to return home: by foot, by hitching rides, or by crowding onto trains.

Immediately after the arrival of the Red Army, the Soviet Extraordinary State Commission for Ascertaining and Investigating Crimes Perpetrated by the German-Fascist Invaders and Their Accomplices began a forensic investigation. The commission interviewed survivors, investigated the ruins of the crematoria, and studied the blueprints of buildings that they had found in the building of the Central Construction Office—the SS had forgotten to destroy those papers. And it created detailed inventories of the possessions of the murdered found in the remaining Kanada warehouses and in seven railway freight cars in the Auschwitz station: 1.7 million items of clothing and more than 43,000 pairs of shoes.

The commission secured 293 bales of women's hair. Its report noted, "The experts of the commission established that the hair was cut off the heads of 140,000 women."[107] The commission also calculated, erroneously, that more than 4 million people had been killed in Auschwitz. While in western Europe and North America calculations of the number of Auschwitz victims ranged between 1 million and 2.5 million, 4 million remained the official victim number in Soviet-dominated eastern Europe until 1989. The

Pajama bottoms taken from Kanada by an Auschwitz inmate after liberation, 1945. Museum of Jewish Heritage—A Living Memorial to the Holocaust, New York.

historians of the Auschwitz-Birkenau State Museum, led by Dr. Franciszek Piper, later revised the number, based on a variety of evidence. The number: 1.1 million people, of whom 90 percent were Jews.

The Soviet Extraordinary State Commission published its report in May 1945. By that time a Polish team of forensic investigators, acting on behalf of the Central Commission for Investigation of German Crimes in Poland, had started a separate investigation. Kraków judge Jan Sehn interviewed surviving *Sonderkommandos*. The detailed testimony of Henryk Tauber, who had worked for more than two years in Crematorium 2, proved crucial in establishing the killing and incineration procedures.

By the time the Soviet report appeared, tens of thousands of survivors from the Auschwitz death march had been liberated in Bergen-Belsen and other camps. The liberation of Auschwitz happened during a major military offensive and did not attract much attention at the time. Things were different in April and early May when the British entered Bergen-Belsen and the Americans entered Ohrdruf, Buchenwald, and Dachau. Large numbers of Western observers confronted the horrors of the camps for the first time. From the middle of April 1945 onward, photographs of starving inmates and mountains of emaciated corpses filled newspapers and magazines.

For the British and American public, the camps proved the war effort had been justified; soldiers had not died in vain. For many philosophers and theologians, the revelation of what had happened in Auschwitz triggered a lifelong search for the possible meaning of it—if any. "It was really as if an abyss had opened." Thus Hannah Arendt reflected, twenty years, later on her shock when, in 1945, she learned the details of the Auschwitz factory of death. Before then she had believed that humans could always make amends for the wrongs they committed. "But not for this. *This ought not to have happened.* And I don't mean just the number of victims. I mean the method, the manufacturing of corpses and so on—I don't need to go into that. This should not have happened. Something happened there to which we cannot reconcile ourselves."[108]

Those who were liberated in Auschwitz at the end of January, and those who were liberated in April and May, experienced the joy of freedom from captivity followed by the quiet in which all confronted the enormity of what had happened to them, the extent of their loss as they already knew it, and the terrible worry about what had happened to loved ones from whom they had been separated. Ana Tenenbaum found a pair of pajama bottoms in one of the few remaining storehouses of Kanada and took them with her as she left the camp to find her husband. She believed that by preparing a gift for him, she could ensure that they would somehow meet up again. And, indeed, that is what happened, amid the chaos of a destroyed and uprooted continent.

Survivors

Of all the German camps, Auschwitz had the largest number of murder victims: 1.1 million. It was also the camp with the greatest number of survivors: some two hundred thousand people brought to Auschwitz were sent to other camps before the war was over, and some seven thousand prisoners were liberated at the camp in January 1945.

Liberation may have ended the chaos of hatred, bigotry, and unreason these survivors had experienced, but another chaos of sorts took place. Tens of thousands walked hundreds of miles, tens of thousands piled onto the few available trains, all in an effort to return home, seeking to locate family, friends, past lives. A significant group of these Auschwitz survivors—especially non-Jewish survivors from Poland but also Jewish survivors from the Netherlands, Belgium, France, and Italy— were able to return to their original homes. Yet many non-Jewish survivors from Poland faced the political upheaval that came with the imposition of Communist rule in Soviet-occupied eastern Europe.

Mug shot of Witold Pilecki made by the Polish Ministry of Public Security after his arrest, 1947. Auschwitz-Birkenau State Museum, Oświęcim, Poland.

Tragic was the fate of Witold Pilecki, one of the true heroes in the history of Auschwitz (page 181). After the defeat of Germany, Pilecki remained loyal to the Polish government-in-exile in London, which did not recognize the Warsaw government. Arrested in Warsaw by Communist authorities in May 1947, Pilecki was tortured, sentenced in a show trial, and executed in 1948. He was posthumously rehabilitated after the fall of Communism.

Jewish survivors even from a western European country such as the Netherlands did not feel exactly welcome when they returned. Dutch society was traumatized by its own experience of the occupation. There was no recognition that the victimization of the Jews was of a different order of magnitude. Reintegration demanded a lie: Jews could be reintegrated only as long as they ignored the elephant in the room—the fact that the Dutch had not shown solidarity with them between 1940 and 1945 and did not do so after the war either. In addition, survivors found themselves in a situation of conflict with significant parts of Dutch society as they tried to regain what had been theirs. For years returnees fought with stock-exchange officials, insurance companies, bank presidents, and individual citizens who had taken possession of their property.

Very few Jewish survivors from Germany and Austria chose to go back to their countries of origin. Hanns Chaim Mayer, who had fled Austria in 1938, returned to the country that had offered him shelter, Belgium, and permanently changed his name to the one he had used when in hiding: Jean Améry. Speaking for all Jews who came from countries in which the population at large had either supported or at least condoned the persecution, Améry noted: "We . . . had not lost our country, but had to realize that it had never been ours. For us, whatever was linked with this land and its people was an existential misunderstanding. What we believed to have been our first love was, as they said there, racial disgrace." In regard to his Jewish identity, it had been imposed on him, as for many assimilated Jews, by outsiders, and the experience of Auschwitz had not brought him closer to God or the Jewish tradition. "On my left forearm I bear the Auschwitz number; it reads more briefly than the Pentateuch or the Talmud and yet provides more thorough information."[109]

Auschwitz survivor Jakob Grünbaum decided not to return to his hometown, Kraków. After twenty-two months in the Stalowa Wola slave labor camp, he had spent six months in the Płaszów concentration camp before he was transferred to Auschwitz in January 1945—just in time to be forced on a death march that brought him to Gleiwitz, and from there he was shuttled, by freight wagon, as far north in Germany as the Sachsenhausen camp and then down to the Flossenbürg and Regensburg camps in Bavaria. In April the SS forced Jakob on the road again as part of a contingent of five hundred, mostly former Auschwitz prisoners, toward Mauthausen. After a few days Jakob decided he could no longer go on. He hid in the Lehneckerhof farm near the Bavarian town of Neuötting, where the SS had interrupted the prisoners' march for a night's rest. The owner of the farm discovered Jakob after the departure of the SS and its prisoners and nursed him back to health. Two weeks later Germany capitulated, and Jakob made his way to the nearby town of Altötting, now under American army rule. With the help of the Americans, Jakob and a few hundred other camp survivors organized themselves—one of the many communities of displaced and stateless persons in the American occupation zone. First they needed to reestablish a civic identity; still wearing his now washed and pressed camp jacket over a new white shirt, Jakob had his first identity-card photograph taken since his imprisonment in February 1941. The occupation authorities recorded his date and place of birth, residency before the war, and the places where he had been imprisoned.

Robe made by Jakob Grünbaum (aka Jacob Greenbaum), ca. 1947. Collection of Miriam Greenbaum, Canada. Exhibition installation, Centro de Exposiciones Arte Canal, Madrid, 2017.

After discovering that not a single member of his immediate family had survived (page 119), Jakob decided to make a new life outside of Poland. Before the war Jakob had been a master tailor with his own atelier at 17 Saint Gertrude Street in Kraków. Without any formality the Germans had taken his business in 1940, and without much formality the ranking American officer in Altötting, Captain Raymond F. Goddard, restored Jakob's professional standing

Siegfried Fedrid (right foreground) taking English lessons in New York, 1948. United States Holocaust Memorial Museum, Washington, DC.

Lazar Kleinman, 1945. In 1944, fifteen-year-old Lazar Kleinman survived selection at Auschwitz by claiming that he was seventeen; put to work in Auschwitz III, he participated in two death marches, escaping in Bavaria on April 23, 1945. An American army sergeant found Lazar, wrapped him in his coat, and carried him to a field hospital. While Lazar was in the Kloster Indersdorf displaced children's camp, this photograph with his name was taken for the purpose of locating his family. In 1947 Lazar moved to Great Britain, where he was employed as a craftsman making handbags, buttons, bows, and belts. In the 1950s he opened his dress-manufacturing company, Roslyn Fashions. United States Holocaust Memorial Museum, Washington, DC.

by means of an improvised proof-of-employment document. Suggesting a new beginning, Captain Goddard Americanized Jakob's name: Jakob Grünbaum became Jacob Greenbaum.

Now Jacob opened an atelier in Altötting. He gained access to German military fabrics stored in a nearby Capuchin monastery. For his own use Jacob had made a pattern that hearkened back to the easier days before 1939. Visiting the storehouse, he chose a bolt of gray-green cloth used for Waffen-SS uniforms, and from this material he cut and fashioned a robe.

The twenty-year-old Berish Erlich, son of the famous Talmudic scholar Rabbi Nusyn Pinchas Erlich, had survived both the Warsaw Ghetto Uprising and Auschwitz to end up in the Landsberg displaced persons camp in Bavaria. There he wrote a memoir of his time in the ghetto and Auschwitz-Birkenau. Interestingly, his memoir looked not only backward but also to the present, in Germany, and to a new future, in North America. The memoir is in three languages, arranged triptych-like on each spread: first Erlich wrote in his native tongue, Yiddish; then in the language of the country

in which he found himself: German; and finally, in the middle panel, in the language of the country in which he expected to make a new beginning: English.

Siegfried Fedrid (page 191) was liberated by American soldiers in a subcamp of Dachau. He returned to his native Vienna to discover that his extended family and friends had been murdered and all his possessions were gone. Relatives in New York supported his immigration to the United States. He arrived in August 1947. Siegfried, now Fred, enrolled in English and citizenship classes sponsored by the New York Society for the Deaf. There he met

Doris Rosenstrauch, a deaf Holocaust survivor from Poland. Doris moved to Colorado, where she had family. Fred followed her; they married in 1948 and had three children. Fred died in 1963 at the age forty-two.

Many young survivors had become orphans, and the United Nations Relief and Rehabilitation Administration (UNRRA), which ran the many displaced persons (DP) camps that sheltered survivors, established a special DP camp for children in a Bavarian convent, Kloster Indersdorf. Before the war the nuns had operated an orphanage in the convent, so when UNRRA was looking for a place for one hundred child and adolescent survivors, they offered their space and help. Within a year one thousand youngsters—inclusive of Auschwitz survivors—lived at Kloster Indersdorf, in a remarkable self-organized community conceived by child psychologist Greta Fischer, a Czech Jew who had escaped to Britain in 1939 to become an assistant of Anna Freud. In the fall of 1945, for the purpose of locating the children's family members, UNRRA commissioned photographer Charles Haacker to take a picture of each orphan holding a nameplate. Unlike the Auschwitz mug shots, these were images of hope.

German homosexual men who had survived the camps returned to a country in which Paragraph 175 of the penal code remained on the books, and continued to be enforced, until the late 1960s. The fate of Richard Grune stands for many; immediately after his liberation from Flossenbürg, he began to record his memories of the camps in a remarkable series of lithographs (pages 51 and 202). In March 1946 he exhibited his work in a one-man show in the northern German city of Kiel. After four weeks, unknown men attacked the exhibition and destroyed all of Grune's art. Realizing that he was still unwelcome in Germany, Grune moved to Barcelona.

Interestingly, the history of male German homosexuals in the concentration camps has a remarkable legacy: in the 1970s those advocating for gay rights adopted an inverted pink triangle as a symbol of gay pride—making the pink triangle the only badge

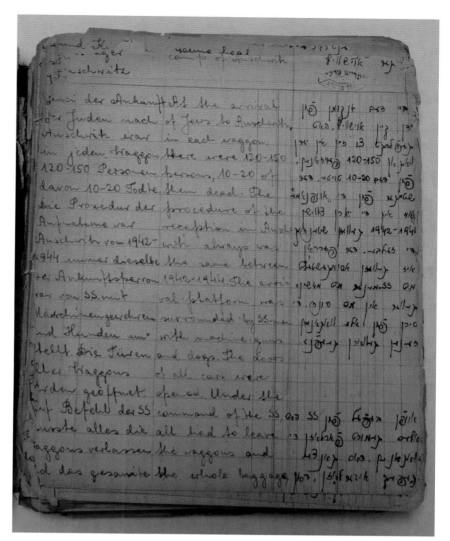

Memoir written by Berish Erlich in (left to right) German, English, and Yiddish, 1945. Amud Aish Memorial Museum, New York.

issued in concentration camps to be reclaimed by the victim group to which it had been issued.

Few of the handful of Soviet prisoners of war who had survived their imprisonment in Auschwitz ever testified about their experiences, which results in the fact that their history is *terra incognita*. The reason is simple: they were not welcomed back into Soviet society. "They invented that at Auschwitz, this Camp of Death, they were training spies," Pavel Stenkin recalled sixty years later. "So somebody got this idea in his head—what if they had turned me into

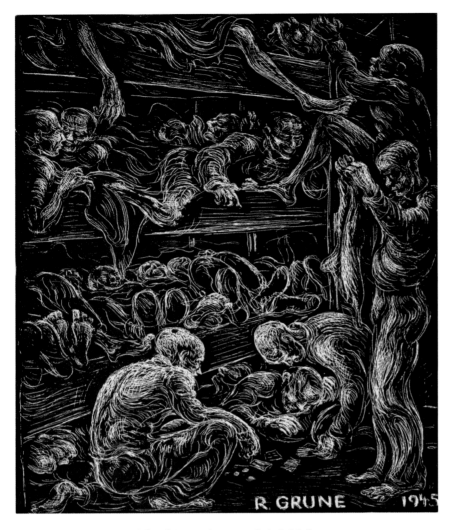

Richard Grune (1903–1983), Schlafraum
*(Dormitory), 1945. Lithograph. Collection of Robert
Jan van Pelt, Canada.*

a spy?" Initially Stenkin was sent as an exile to the Siberian city of Perm, but there he was subjected to lengthy interrogations. "They were tormenting and tormenting me. And then they decided to get rid of me. They sent me to prison."[110] Sent to the Gulag, he was released in 1953, after Stalin's death. Stenkin remained silent until, fifty years later, a British documentary filmmaker found him.

The few Roma survivors found themselves back in a life on the margins of a society that refused to acknowledge their suffering. Only the most determined, like Ceija Stojka (page 138), were willing to provide testimony. In 1943 Ceija, together with her mother and four of her five brothers, had been deported with other Roma to Auschwitz. By that time her father, Kurt, had already been killed in Hartheim Castle. Liberated in Bergen-Belsen, Ceija returned to her native Austria. Initially earning a living by peddling fabrics, she turned to writing and painting in her fifties. Together with the paintings made by her brother Karl, Ceija's drawn recollections of Auschwitz are among the most important legacies of the Nazi persecution of the Roma. Anna Kreutz (page 93), who had been transported from Auschwitz to Ravensbrück in the summer of 1944, was liberated by the American army while on a death march to Dachau. She married a Roma survivor of Buchenwald, Ignatz Mettbach, and after publishing a memoir, in 1999, became an advocate for Roma rights.

Forty-three-year-old David Olère, who for eighteen months had survived as a *Sonderkommando* in Crematorium 3, was liberated by the Americans at the Ebensee camp on May 6, 1945. Reunited with his wife, Juliette, in Paris, he tried to tell her what he had seen in Auschwitz. She believed he had gone insane. In order to reestablish communication, Olère began to draw what is now recognized as important visual testimony of life in the camp in general, and unique visual testimony of the operation of the gas chambers and crematoria (pages 119, 149, 153, 155, 156, and 183). From the early 1960s until his death in 1985, Olère produced many remarkable paintings on the same subjects as his postwar drawings, which are now part of the collection of the Auschwitz-Birkenau State Museum. At this time Olère's ambition was above all inspired by his pacifist stance. "I produced this testimony, all pure truth, so the next generations can be preserved from the horrors I have known in the war, and know peace."[111]

Nineteen-year-old Polish Catholic Marian Kolodziej had been captured in early 1940 by the Nazis while trying to join a Polish resistance group. He was sent to Auschwitz on June 14, 1940, in the first transport of prisoners. He spent more than four years in the camp.

Ceija Stojka (1933–2013), Was bleibt, nichts *(What remains, nothing), 2009. Collection of Miriam Greenbaum, Canada.*

Ceija Stojka, 1995. Collection of Christa Schnepf, Germany.

Marian Kolodziej (1921–2009), Labyrinth, 1995–2005.
Installation in the Franciscan church in Harmęże, Poland, 2012.

Liberated at Mauthausen, he returned to Poland, where he became known as a prominent set designer. For fifty years Kolodziej did not speak about his camp experiences. After suffering a stroke in the 1990s, he began to draw his memories of the camp. He continued to do so until his death in 2009. His drawings are assembled in the Franciscan church in Harmęże, one mile southwest of the ruins of the crematoria of Auschwitz-Birkenau. It is, without doubt, one of the most impressive memorials to the history of that camp.

Any memorial to Auschwitz can be but a cry into the enormous void created by the German murder of 1.1 million people at that place. In our exhibition we display the raw materials for the smallest of such memorials, never completed: two wedding rings and a small sapphire. Else van Dam and Leon Greenman, young and deeply in love, married in 1935. They

moved from London to Rotterdam, where Leon worked as a hairdresser and as a bookseller in his father-in-law's business and Else worked as a seamstress. In March 1940, Else gave birth to Barney. Leon registered the newborn at the British consulate in the Hague. A few months later, Germany invaded the Netherlands. During the hardships of the occupation, Else and Leon continued to take family photographs, taught Barney to play the piano, and made him toys.

On October 8, 1942, the police rounded up Jews living in Rotterdam. The Greenmans were taken to the Westerbork camp. Leon learned that his British papers, secreted with a friend, had been destroyed. He wrote to the Swiss legation, which represented British interests, for papers proving his British citizenship—the family's only hope for getting out of the camp. The papers never arrived. On January

Else, Barney, and Leon Greenman, 1942. Collection of Ruth-Anne Lenga, United Kingdom.

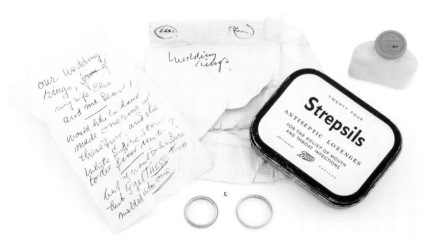

A tin, two wedding rings, a sapphire, and a note, left by Leon Greenman. Collection of Ruth-Anne Lenga, United Kingdom

18, 1943, Leon, Else, and Barney were deported to Auschwitz. During the train journey to Auschwitz they agreed that if one of them were to die, the other ought marry again if they found a partner who would be a good stepparent to their child. They did not consider the possibility that Barney might die. On arrival three days later, Leon was separated from his wife and child: "I could see Else clearly for she was wearing a thick red cape over her head and shoulders to keep her warm. She gestured a kiss to me with her hand, partly holding up Barney so that I could see him also."[112] Else and three-year-old Barney were loaded onto a truck, and the truck departed. Leon entered the camp as 98288—*acht-und-neunzig-tausend-zwei-hundert-acht-und-achtzig.*

Returning in 1945 to the Netherlands, Leon realized he alone had survived. He collected some objects he and his family had left behind and moved to London. Perturbed by the rise of neo-Nazism, Leon became active in Holocaust education and the fight against racial and ethnic prejudice, accompanying students to Auschwitz. His message, as articulated in one of the audiovisual displays in this exhibition, was simple: "Stay away from hate. It's not necessary. Whether you're white, whether you're black, whether you're yellow. You are a human being, you weren't asked to come into this world, you were made. And while you're here, do the right thing. Create love and understanding. And that will create happiness."[113] Leon never remarried. At his death, a friend found a throat-lozenge tin in his bedside table. It contained his and Else's wedding rings and a small white sapphire. Leon's handwritten note enjoined the finder to perform a last act on his behalf: "Our wedding rings, of my wife Else and me. Please I would like to have made one ring of these two, and the white sapphire stone to be fixed unto. But I want to be sure that I get THESE two melted into one."

The Site

By the early summer of 1945 almost all survivors had left the Auschwitz camp. A small group remained behind to ensure the preservation of what remained of the complex. In 1947 the Polish government created the Państwowe Muzeum w Oświęcimiu (State Museum in Oświęcim). It included most of the main camp and most of Auschwitz-Birkenau—470 acres in total. The *Stammlager* was, more or less, in the state in which the SS had left it in January 1945; but Auschwitz-Birkenau was in bad shape: the SS had blown up the four crematoria, and most of the prefabricated wooden barracks had been dismantled and reconstructed elsewhere to shelter people made homeless by the war. The compound constructed near the IG Farben Buna factory, and all the other satellite camps, were not included in the state museum.

The museum had modest beginnings, and during the height of the Cold War its staff had to negotiate a difficult path between the desire to present the history of the camp as it could be established on the basis of the evidence and the ideological perspective imposed by the Communist regime. In 1991 the Auschwitz-Birkenau State Museum in Oświęcim made the most important step toward becoming a globally significant institution, when its chief historian, Franciszek Piper, published in *Yad Vashem Studies* a revised assessment of the total number of victims: not 4 million dead, as the Soviet forensic investigators had established in 1945 and which had been the official figure ever since, but 1.1 million. An international fund-raising campaign, initiated by American businessman Ronald S. Lauder, generated sufficient capital to create a modern preservation laboratory for the large collections of artifacts and documents, and the conservation of the remaining fences, buildings, and ruins was brought up to international standards. Today the museum is a state-of-the-art institution that maintains the physical legacy

Entrance of the Auschwitz-Birkenau State Museum in Oświęcim, Poland, 1950s. Auschwitz-Birkenau State Museum, Oświęcim, Poland.

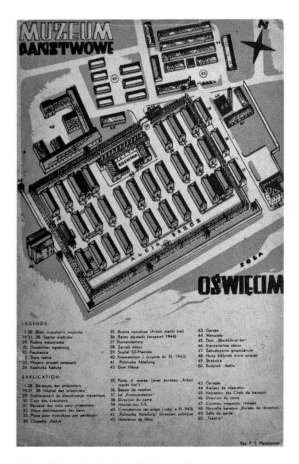

Map of the Auschwitz-Birkenau State Museum in Oświęcim, Poland, 1950s. Florence and Laurence Spungen Family Foundation, Santa Barbara, California.

Auschwitz-Birkenau, 2017.

Graffiti on the north wall of the delousing barrack in the women's camp, Auschwitz-Birkenau, 2012. Marta Goldstein was twenty-two years old when she left, on July 25, 1944, a trace of her life on this brick.

Preserving a Zyklon-B tin in the Auschwitz-Birkenau State Museum preservation lab, 2017.

of Auschwitz, conducts research into its history, and manages an annual flow of over 2 million visitors, of whom 10 percent come from the United States.

Nevertheless friction remains. This is rooted in the paradox that almost everyone who arrives at the gates of the Auschwitz-Birkenau State Museum for a visit has "seen" Auschwitz before: through books, movies, TV documentaries, and the Internet. This,

unavoidably, creates a situation in which, during the visit, there will be a ticking-off of the mental to-see list prepared in advance: fence: √; guard tower: √; gate: √ barrack: √; suitcase exhibit: √; hair exhibit: √; crematorium: √. This, of course, is the effect of living in a world saturated with images and information. The result is a tension between the ethical demand that emerges when we think *Auschwitz*, and the experience of a visit to the physical relics of Auschwitz, which are managed by a museum and shared with, at times, crowds of other people. Initially this tension may confound the expectations of the visitor.

Yet, as I have seen over thirty years of visiting the site, this tension will not define the experience. Most visitors give the site their attention and, especially among the remains of Auschwitz-Birkenau, allow themselves to become attuned to the landscape and its relics, encountering unexpected and touching reminders of lives lived and lost, and discovering within themselves a new mindfulness about the terrible history that the site embodies, and a new responsiveness to the world at large—a broken world that remains in urgent need of repair.

Architect(ure)'s Weakest Moment

Or, When *Not* to Learn from Architects

DJAMEL ZENITI, CURATOR

A concentration camp is built, like a stadium or a big hotel. You need contractors, estimates, competitive bids. And no doubt a bribe or two. Any style will do. . . . The architects calmly plan the gates through which no one will enter more than once.
— *Nuit et brouillard* (*Night and Fog*), Alain Resnais, director, 1956

"Nothing can replace a visit to the authentic site of the biggest crime of the twentieth century," states Dr. Piotr Cywiński, director of the Auschwitz-Birkenau State Museum.

April 2018, first visit to Battery Park, New York. A simple, austere, and dignified building houses the permanent exhibition of the Museum of Jewish Heritage—A Living Memorial to the Holocaust, which tells the story of the Jews before, during, and after the Holocaust and commemorates the victims.

Built by Pritzker Architecture Prize laureate Kevin Roche in the 1990s, the original building of the MJH conjures up associations with a beehive, a Sumerian ziggurat, a Chinese pagoda, or an Italian baptistery, but in fact it looks like *nothing* ever built before, by either beast or man. Compared to the nearby skyscrapers it appears small, but its presence daunts. Architects can learn from it!

Directly after the attacks on the World Trade Center on September, 11, 2001, the museum building functioned as a shelter, a safe place, and a command post for the rescue operations starting at Ground Zero. In relation to the fallen skyscrapers, the dwarfish building transcended itself and was *transformed*—it embodied encouragement.

January 2016, first visit to the Centro de Exposiciones Arte Canal, Madrid. Since late 2014, I have been part of a small team that aims to create a traveling exhibition on Auschwitz. The subjects of touring exhibitions vary wildly, from children's books to science-fiction blockbusters, from historic periods or moments to the works of individual artists, from treasures through the centuries to the collections of museums. They are conceived and designed from the outset to be packed, transported, unpacked, reassembled, and dismantled many times, so that they can be seen and enjoyed by visitors in many different places. They need to be flexible, to accommodate different venues, many of which are not yet known when the design process begins.

From the beginning of the design endeavor, I realized that we faced a difficult task: to create a physical layout that was evocative and allowed for a historically correct visitor experience while avoiding the pitfalls of overzealous design. How could we allow the setting of the exhibition to remain a modest background for the often apparently modest artifacts shown, the heartbreaking testimonies heard? One thing was clear: the design process was not going to be a routine job, like the planning of a stadium, a big hotel, or, apparently, a concentration camp.

By early 2016 we had a site: a twenty-seven-thousand-square-foot decommissioned water tank located mostly underground near the Plaza de Castilla in Madrid. Built in the late nineteenth century, it had been converted a decade earlier into an underground exhibition hall. It was a distinctive space filled with brick columns about fourteen feet apart in every direction. Now the work of design could begin, and as I tried to fit the narrative and the artifacts into this labyrinth of columns, I could not help but think about my German colleagues who, three-quarters of a

PAGES 210–211: Buttons. Auschwitz-Birkenau State Museum, Oświęcim, Poland.

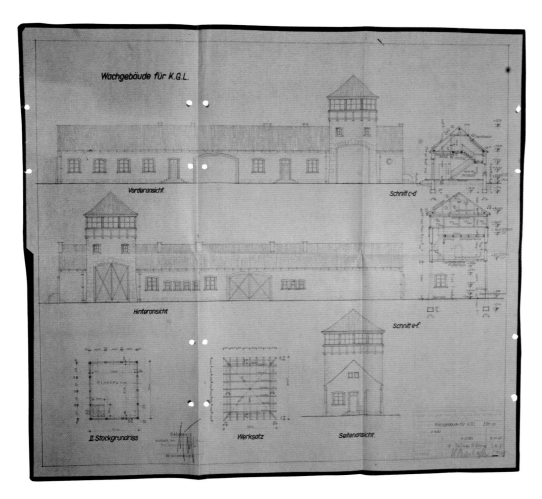

Wachgebäude für KGL *(Guardhouse for the prisoner of war camp),*
1941. This design shows elevations and section of the gate building
(the so-called Gate of Death) leading into Auschwitz-Birkenau. Yad
Vashem: The World Holocaust Remembrance Center, Jerusalem.

century ago, "calmly" produced their own drawings,
for "gates through which no one will enter more than
once." As I put final details on paper to make the dead-
line, I often thought about one of the key architectural
drawings in our exhibition: labeled *Wachgebäude für*
KGL (Guardhouse for the prisoner of war camp), it
shows the first design for what became widely known
as the Gate of Death. Through this gate locomotives
pulled trains of freight wagons to the place of selection; the crematoria were visible down the line. It was
a major passage in the historical axis of extermination,
constructed by the architects, my late colleagues who
worked for the SS.

5.11.1941. That date, November 5, 1941, appears
three times on the drawing of the Gate of Death.
That day, prisoner 538 completed the drawing, and
that same day SS architects Walther Dejaco and Karl
Bischoff checked and approved the drawing. It must
have been an important job. Was it?

April 2000, Vienna Technical University. An
architecture theory course titled "The Architecture
of Genocide" is held by Robert Jan van Pelt. Students
are given an assignment: to design a perfect killing
machine. Will they take the task? Professor van Pelt
puts a mirror in front of the architects-to-be. Is every
design job acceptable?

June 1971, State Court House, Vienna. Not one of the Auschwitz architects was born a mass murderer. But step-by-step, with drawing after drawing, at the behest of their superior Karl Bischoff, Austrian-born architects Walther Dejaco and Fritz Ertl arrived at the point where they planned and executed the horror. "From the outset, their construction activity was aimed at short-term vegetation of the prisoners, and represented a mockery of the most elementary principles of building technology," the 1971 indictment of Dejaco and Ertl stated. "Given their effort to improve the barracks intended for the guard dogs and cows by providing appropriate ventilation, to guarantee the health of the animals, it is clear that the accused were very well aware that the barracks built by them, which had neither windows nor sufficient ventilation and which were constructed closely adjacent to each other, did not offer sufficient living space [for humans]."[1]

May 2019, Museum of Jewish Heritage—A Living Memorial to the Holocaust, New York. From an at-first-sight inconspicuous venue in Madrid, our exhibition will move to one of the most prestigious and showy locations on the planet: the tip of Manhattan. From a square tank with too many brick columns to a hexagonal sanctuary with too many blunt angles and a circular polished-stainless-steel escalator linking three floors that creates in the interior a sensation of being in a snail shell. Another labyrinth.

The Madrid exhibition was a success in terms of the number of visitors (450,000 in nine months) and the amount of time the visitors spent in the exhibition

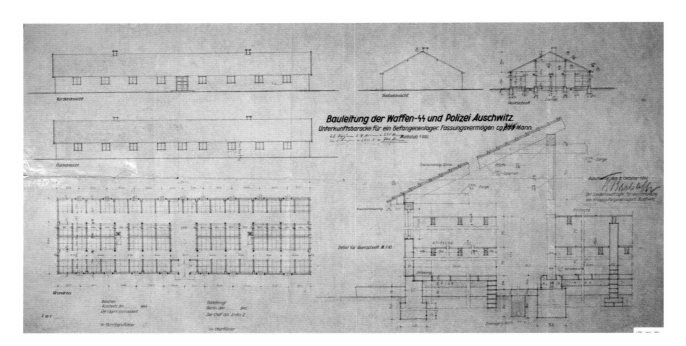

Unterkunftsbarracke für ein Gefangenenlager ca. 550-Mann *(Accommodation barrack for a prison camp for about 550 people), a plan for a barrack at Auschwitz-Birkenau, 1941. In penciled notes beneath the title, SS architect Karl Bischoff changed the plan's nine prisoners per bunk to twelve, thus increasing the barrack's capacity by a third without any redesign. Auschwitz-Birkenau State Museum, Oświęcim, Poland.*

Interior of a barrack in Auschwitz-Birkenau, 2017.

The architects of the Auschwitz Central Construction Office, 1943. Karl Bischoff stands fourth from the right, and Walther Dejaco third from the right. Fritz Ertl stands in the second row, fourth from the left. Auschwitz-Birkenau State Museum, Oświęcim, Poland.

(three hours on average). Yet its very success caused traffic jams in places, and as an emergency measure we had to lower the number of people admitted every hour. And feedback told us that it was not only the topic that slowed people down; the design proved to be a culprit also: it was too overwhelming, too tough, too tight.

It became clear that at the MJH the flow and pace of visitors needed to be rethought, and the result is an exhibition that does not, as it did in Madrid, provide a single path but has a more layered texture, with multiple paths for, as the saying goes, skimmers, swimmers, and divers. We'll be offering a freer flow than we did in our first venue in Madrid, yet at the same time we'll present an augmented assemblage of artifacts, as we'll include important objects in the collection of the MJH relating to the story we tell within our exhibition. And we have less space than in Madrid—a hexagonal Rubik's Cube, to be sure.

October 1941, Auschwitz. As I worked on the MJH design and calculated the occupancy numbers for each floor, I could not help but think about *one*

dreadful decision concerning occupancy that left me in awe when I first heard about it, in 1997, in Yad Vashem, in Jerusalem, at a lecture given by Dr. van Pelt. On October 8, 1941, SS architect Karl Bischoff reviewed a plan drawn by Fritz Ertl of the brick barracks at Auschwitz-Birkenau entitled *Unterkunftsbarracke für ein Gefangenenlager ca. 550-Mann* (Accommodation barrack for a prison camp for about 550 people). Bischoff made a small calculation, visible on the blueprint exhibited, assuming that each of the sixty-two triple-level berths, measuring six by six feet, would hold twelve instead of nine prisoners. Thus he increased, with the stroke of a pencil, the barrack capacity from 550 to 744.

Indeed: Himmler's order, given at the beginning of October 1941, to expand the capacity of Auschwitz-Birkenau, still in the planning phase, by a third provided a problem to the SS, but the architect provided a quick and convenient solution. A ghost from construction past. And a *ghastly* important job done, solved . . . indeed. Have a close look at the picture of the architects who opened Pandora's design box and found a solution. But did they?

Searching for Meaning in Traces of the Past

PAUL SALMONS, CURATOR

Unlike most exhibitions, *Auschwitz. Not long ago. Not far away.* does not display the story we usually like to tell about ourselves, with beautiful artworks and sacred relics touting the great accomplishments of humankind, the wonders of our past. Rather, the objects displayed are the traces of genocide, the remnants of a murdered people, and the material evidence of crimes against humanity. They are what remain despite the perpetrators' attempts to conceal their crimes. Many of the objects have never before been on public display.

Some are seemingly ordinary things. A simple woolen blanket appears unremarkable, yet its familiarity is misleading. To most of us, a blanket is associated with a warm, comfortable bed—a safe place in which to curl up at the end of a busy day, to rest, to sleep, or to retreat in times of illness. A bed is where, as a child, you are read bedtime stories; where, as an adult, you hold your lover. But this thing that is so familiar takes on a radically different

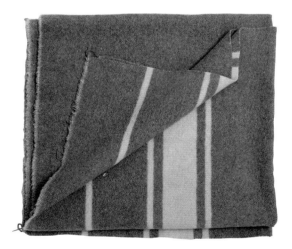

The blanket that Siegfried Fedrid carried with him on the death march from Auschwitz, 1945. Holocaust Center for Humanity, Seattle.

meaning in the story of Auschwitz. There, a bed was a hard, three- or four-tiered wooden bunk, a place where human beings lay their broken bodies after days of backbreaking and brutal work. It was a space shared with the dying and the dead. And in these beds in winter, thin blankets were all the exhausted prisoners had to guard against a cold so severe they could not get warm.

Tens of thousands of such blankets were distributed in Auschwitz, and each anonymous, mass-produced one speaks to the suffering of countless prisoners.

But this blanket, while indistinguishable from the others, also has its own unique story: we know the person who sheltered beneath it. It is a tangible artifact that connects us to twenty-four-year-old Jewish tailor Siegfried Fedrid (pages 191 and 200). It was this blanket that Fedrid grabbed in January 1945, as he and sixty thousand other prisoners were evacuated from Auschwitz and forced to march for days, for nearly forty miles, in wooden clogs and thin striped uniforms, without food—with guards shooting those who were too exhausted to keep up—before arriving at a railway junction and the train that would take them deeper into the German Reich. It was this blanket that Fedrid wrapped around himself on the bitterly cold nights of the death march, as thousands perished from exhaustion and exposure, freezing to death.

Despite enduring a concentration camp system designed not only to kill through work but also to degrade and dehumanize, Fedrid chose to share this blanket with four others, who huddled together with him against the cold. Instead of thinking only of self-preservation, in this act Fedrid showed a generosity that saved not only the lives of these men but also, perhaps, something of our own faith in human nature. This simple blanket, then, is certainly no

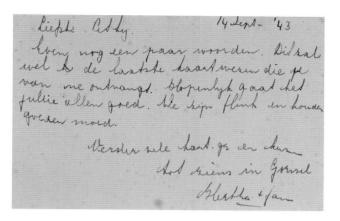

A note written by Hertha Aussen and thrown from a deportation train bound for Auschwitz-Birkenau, 1943. Herinneringscentrum Kamp Westerbork, Hooghalen, Netherlands.

Hertha Aussen, 1940s. Herinneringscentrum Kamp Westerbork, Hooghalen, Netherlands.

high point in the history of human creative arts, but what object speaks more to the human capacity for selflessness, the ability to care for one another, even in the most desperate of circumstances?

Each object, then, can tell many stories and can reveal many different issues, questions, and meanings. The cattle car has become a symbol of the Holocaust. It conveys the horror of deportation to the death camps: men, women, and children crowded into a rough wooden wagon for days and nights at a time, with no room to sit down, no food, and just one bucket for water and another to use as a toilet. But a letter cast from one of these freight wagons reminds us that those crammed inside were not a faceless mass but individuals, with lives and loves, hopes and dreams.

"Dearest Kitty," wrote seventeen-year-old Hertha Aussen, on a scrap of paper addressed to Netty Rènes and thrown from a train leaving the Westerbork camp in the Netherlands, heading for Auschwitz. "Briefly a few words. Most likely this will be the last card you'll receive from me. I hope you will all be fine. We're brave and keep our spirits up. For the rest: many warm greetings and kisses. See you again in Gorssel. Hertha and family."

This note is the last trace of Hertha Aussen. The last mark she made on this world was that of her pen on this paper—a reaching out to wish her friend well, to say goodbye, not to completely disappear. Aussen reached Auschwitz three days later and was murdered on arrival.

The freight wagon holds a further story, however. The personal items that deportees carried with them were plundered, and the trains returned from the camps laden with the belongings of murdered people, to be sold and reused. People across Europe became complicit in the looting of their neighbors' lives. Clothing, spectacles, wristwatches, jewelry, hairbrushes, cutlery, pots and pans—everything that people brought with them to Auschwitz was deemed to be of some value. Except, of course, their lives.

And so, in the world of Auschwitz, a little shoe was

A child's shoe and sock, 1940s. This small shoe was discovered in January 1945 among the thousands of pairs that remained at Auschwitz-Birkenau when it was abandoned by the Nazis as the Red Army approached. Auschwitz-Birkenau State Museum, Oświęcim, Poland.

deemed to be of more worth than the small child who wore it. The shoe was kept, while the child—perhaps a boy of three or four years old—was murdered, his body turned to ash in the crematorium ovens. He tucked his little sock into his shoe as he undressed for what he was told was a shower, then entered the gas chamber.

We do not know this child's name or where he came from. But perhaps we can sense something of what we lost in Auschwitz. What life would this child have led, had he lived? Who would he have loved, what lives would he have touched, what things would he have done? And in contemplating the world that created Auschwitz—our world, not long ago and not far away—how should we think about ourselves?

Conserving Testaments to Human Survival

DR. ANA GALÁN PÉREZ, COLLECTIONS MANAGER, MUSEALIA

When this music plays, we know that our comrades, out in the fog, are marching like automatons; their souls are dead and the music drives them, like the wind drives dead leaves, and takes the place of their wills.

—Primo Levi

In 1925, the Regina-Verlag, a publishing house in Berlin, printed the score of Mozart's Symphony No. 35 in D Major, also known as the *Haffner Symphony*.[1] One of the copies of the score ended up in Auschwitz, where a clerk stamped it with the words *HAFTL. KAPELLE K.L. AUSCHWITZ N°__* (Auschwitz concentration camp prisoner band no.__). Composed to be performed in freedom, Mozart's score, through this copy, became a small part of the system of oppression and destruction. When in January 1945 the SS destroyed all incriminating papers before they abandoned the camp, this score escaped the pyre. Obviously the SS believed that a Mozart symphony represented no threat in a future forensic investigation into the crimes committed in Auschwitz. Nor, in the SS's view, did the tempered steel tuning fork that one of the Auschwitz camp orchestras used for tuning instruments before playing such scores. Inscribed with the number *870* and the letters *SCHW* (*Schwingungen*, or vibrations per second), it produced an A. It also survived the destruction of evidence.

In 1934, Louis Bannet, a gifted student at the Rotterdam Conservatory, formed his own jazz band, Rhythm Five, and earned the nickname "the Dutch Louis Armstrong" (page 104). In January 1943, Bannet was arrested and deported to Auschwitz-Birkenau, carrying his trumpet with him in the deportation train from the Westerbork camp. When he arrived at Auschwitz, Polish prisoner Heinz Frank told him, "Louis, play for your life." Bannet recalled this comment after the war, noting, "I'll never forget that." Succeeding in his audition, Bannet became a member of one the camp's orchestras. Aided by his skill as a musician, his optimism, and a good dose of luck, he survived Auschwitz,

*Score of Mozart's Symphony No. 35 in D Major (*Haffner Symphony), *stamped HAFTL. KAPELLE K.L. AUSCHWITZ N°__, 1920s. Auschwitz-Birkenau State Museum, Oświęcim, Poland.*

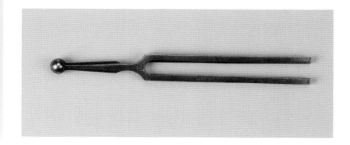

Tuning fork used in Auschwitz, 1930s. Auschwitz-Birkenau State Museum, Oświęcim, Poland.

Trumpet played by Louis Bannet in Auschwitz, 1930s. Museum of Jewish Heritage—A Living Memorial to the Holocaust, New York.

with his trumpet still in his possession. Decades later, Bannet's family gave it to the Museum of Jewish Heritage—A Living Memorial to the Holocaust, New York.

In Auschwitz, the sound of music marked the rhythm of the inmates as they returned from work. It could also be heard inside a prefabricated wooden barrack, where Mozart was played for SS members who enjoyed classical music—or jazz was played, if Bannet's group was performing. These barracks were not designed and produced to function as concert halls or officers' casinos. Instead, they had been designed to accommodate the men of the Reich Labor Service while they lived in the countryside, working the German soil. But they proved to be useful as prisoner shelters also. In the same manner, the scores, tuning forks, and instruments used to produce music had a previous origin and function; they had not been printed, forged, and put together to produce music in a death camp. They, like the barrack, were ordinary items. But when put to use in Auschwitz, which denied in its every aspect the idea of safety as embodied in shelter or the aspiration of delight as embodied in music, these artifacts were charged with the weight of history.

Today such artifacts are part of the historic and cultural heritage of the twentieth century, and they are preserved by the institutions that currently

hold them. The Auschwitz-Birkenau Memorial and Museum, also known as the Auschwitz-Birkenau State Museum in Oświęcim (in Polish, it was known until the 1990s as the Państwowe Muzeum w Oświęcimiu, or PMO), owns and manages the musical score as artifact PMO-II-4-367/1-8 and the tuning fork as artifact PMO-R6-3. The museum is a UNESCO World Heritage site, and thus these two objects are officially classified as part of a shared human heritage. Bannet's trumpet is registered at the Museum of Jewish Heritage in New York as artifact MJH-2235.89. The barrack from Auschwitz III, which provides the physical context for the display of the score, the tuning fork, and the trumpet at the Museum of Jewish Heritage, is not part of a public collection. Identified, acquired, and restored by Musealia in 2016, it is—at least for now—part of a corporate collection.

These four artifacts presented in the exhibition *Auschwitz: Not long ago. Not far away.* are sourced from different places and owned by different institutions and organizations, each with its own standards and requirements as to the way its artifacts should be treated, conserved, and displayed. Yet, for a seven-year period, they are part of a collection of collections, in which the particular rules governing the maintenance of each artifact, agreed on in contracts, must be harmonized in a general approach that allows these very different objects, both in ownership and material conditions, to be presented together. Thus an apparently simple display of a sheet of music, a tuning fork, and a trumpet within the context of a reconstructed barrack that stands within a gallery in a museum necessitates close cooperation between different institutions in different countries—in this case Poland, Spain, and the United States. Conservators have to swap information concerning the technical requirements for conserving and displaying the score, the tuning fork, the trumpet, and the barrack. What is the allowable range in the temperature, air quality, illumination, and humidity in the exhibition galleries as a whole and in the individual display case

Barrack from Auschwitz III, 1940s. Musealia, San Sebastián. Exhibition installation, Centro de Exposiciones Arte Canal, Madrid, 2017.

in which the artifact in particular is to be held? Various international standards regulating the transport and display of cultural artifacts come into play—the most important of which are articulated by the International Memorial Museums Charter and by the European Confederation of Conservator-Restorers' Organisations. In the special case of the Auschwitz artifacts, the guidelines established by the International Committee of Memorial Museums in Remembrance of the Victims of Public Crimes also apply.

All of this requires considerable planning long before the exhibition is opened. During the installation phase, artifacts must travel under special, agreed-upon conditions, and various protocols govern the arrival, registration, documentation, and temporary housing in a secure climate-controlled storage room at the exhibition venue. Other protocols define who may handle artifacts during installation, and a careful coordination of staff is essential to install the artifacts in a synchronized manner, ensuring they spend as little time as possible between the secure storage room and the secure display case, that each ends up in the correct position, and that the cabinets are properly closed. All of this needs to be documented in detail for conservation purposes. And

once the artifacts are in place, the daily monitoring of the physical environment begins: temperature, air quality, illumination, and humidity—and, of course, the human environment.

During the exhibition, each of the lenders—institutions and private persons—receives a regular update on the condition of their artifacts, including updated photographs and reports on any change in the display. In the case of the *Haffner Symphony* musical score, it was initially displayed closed, showing the cover, and later displayed opened, presenting the pages that bear the inscription *HAFTL. KAPELLE K.L. AUSCHWITZ N°__*.

This exhibition brings these four objects together for the first time, allowing them to take on a new meaning and transmit the message of oppression by and survival through music. Their management is conducted with custom software developed for Musealia that provides full control of every detail of the conservation and handling of this special collection. It helps Musealia adhere to preventive conservation and documentary management standards agreed to with the official institutions, museums, and private collections that joined together to make the unique collection of collections that is *Auschwitz: Not long ago. Not far away*.

Testimony in the Exhibition

DR. MICHAEL BERENBAUM, CURATOR, WITH KEN WINIKUR

Elie Wiesel, the bard of Auschwitz, was fond of saying, "Only those who were there will ever know, and those who were there can never tell." We honor Wiesel's memory, but we respectfully disagree. *Those who were there can tell.*

This exhibition marks the interplay between a place and a process, the killers and their victims. Recorded testimony gives the victims—survivors all but surely victims as well—the chance to tell their story; we, in turn, have the responsibility to listen.

Those murdered during the Holocaust cannot be heard, at least not directly. We do not have video or audio of their testimony. In ghettos and in hiding, in concentration camps and even in the vicinity of the crematoria, however, some wrote diaries and letters, determined to have their say. Sometimes they buried these documents, hoping against hope that at least their memories would survive. Historian Emanuel Ringelblum led a group of writers, scholars, rabbis, scientists, poets, and philosophers in an effort to create archives for the Warsaw ghetto, so that its fate would not be written by the perpetrators alone. He buried the writings in milk cans, two of which were discovered after the war. *Sonderkommando* Salmen Gradowski (page 188) buried his memoir near one of the Auschwitz crematoria. While we might not be able to witness their testimony, their words live on.

Survivors are another matter. Fortunately, for us and for history, the technology for video recording became inexpensive in the late 1970s. This enabled the gathering of survivor testimony at a time when survivors had achieved a certain distance from their experience. They could look back. They were willing to speak. Equally important, we were willing to listen. The Holocaust Survivors Film Project, based in New Haven, Connecticut, pioneered the recording of survivor testimony. In 1994 Steven Spielberg established the Survivors of the Shoah Visual History Foundation, now the University of Southern California (USC) Shoah Foundation. In the 1990s, the foundation recorded fifty-two thousand testimonies in thirty-two languages of people from fifty-seven countries, compiling the most massive video testimony of any event in history.

Quantity also begot quality. Because so many said so much, we have pearls of wisdom, gems of insight, and access to dimensions of the Holocaust that documents, diaries, and memoirs alone could not allow us to understand or even to describe.

Historians can be skeptical of oral histories, most especially of those recorded well after the event. As we see with eyewitness testimonies in the courtroom, memory can condense and blur the facts. Survivors may incorporate into their recollections what they have learned later or heard from elsewhere. This makes the task of assessment so very important. Audiences are less skeptical and more trusting of survivors' words than historians are. For our exhibition, we selected testimony with both an eye to historical accuracy and an eye to the testimony's capacity to offer entry into the events of the Holocaust. From our selections, we created six films that take us through the world of Auschwitz.

Deportation. The forced evacuation from home and community was the beginning of the journey, one families most often took together. The experience has at least three dimensions: 1) the known that was left behind—home, however crowded; ghetto, however squalid; possessions, however meager; 2) the unknown destination to which one is being sent; 3) the arduous, tension-filled journey to the unknown. Survivors take us into the cattle cars where, herded together, often with no provisions for food and only a bucket for water and sanitation, they faced the unknown. They describe the heat of summer and the cold of winter. They offer us an

Video presentation, showing the testimony of Auschwitz survivor Magda Bader (pictured) and others. Exhibition installation, Centro de Exposiciones Arte Canal, Madrid, 2017.

understanding of their anxiety and their uncertainty as to where they were going, but also a glimpse of the last moment when a family was intact, when parents had children and children had parents.

Arrival. In this film, survivors tell of getting off the train, leaving behind its stench. Prisoners now, they were separated—men to one side, women and children to the other—only to face a Nazi physician who, with a signal of his hand, determined who would live and who would die. We hear of the final words said between husband and wife, parents and child, that last moment when they were together, when they had one another.

Life in the Camp. This film presents daily life in Auschwitz-Birkenau: waking up, roll call, work, starvation, life in the barracks. We learn of the prisoners' solidarity and of their isolation and of the small tricks they learned to increase their chances of survival. We also learn of the *Muselmänner*, the walking dead, those who can no longer take what life has become and have given up all hope.

The Sonderkommandos. This movie presents the testimonies of those prisoners who were intimate with the killing process, working in the undressing room, the gas chambers, and the crematoria, feeding the flames, collecting the discarded clothes, witnessing murder day after day. Listen to the words of Dario Gabbai, a Greek survivor still alive in his nineties in 2018. He was a young man when he was given his assignment, and he decided to shut off his emotions. "'I am a robot.' I did just this to my mind and I said, 'From now on close your eyes and do whatever needs to be done without asking too much.' I didn't know what I was doing." Dario mentions that he and the other *Sonderkommandos* lived in relative comfort, but that didn't matter much. "It's the inside of your soul." Sam Itzkowitz, a Polish survivor, describes a Hungarian rabbi put to work in the incineration room, burning the corpses. "I think he was very delirious. He took it upon himself to throw every child into the fire. And his job, he was going back and forth picking out children, saying the prayer of death for every child, kissed every child, and threw it into the fire." Morris Venezia, a Greek Jew who was deported to Auschwitz in 1944, provides testimony from the killing in the gas chambers. "After they closed the door, I could hear the people's voices . . . crying and screaming. You could hear 'Sh'ma yisrael, adonai eloheinu.' They were calling God. And these voices are still in my ears."

Death Marches. As Soviet troops pushed westward toward Auschwitz in January 1945, tens of thousands of camp inmates were forcibly evacuated on what became known as death marches. In the frigid winter they walked mile after mile, with no provisions, no shelter, no place for sleep, no way to relieve themselves. If prisoners paused they were shot; if they weakened they were killed. Few documents or photographs give us access to this experience. Survivor testimony, however, allows us to understand the struggle between life and death, the necessity to push oneself beyond all human endurance. So we present the voices of some who were there. "We took the first step, and I guess we all knew that this was going to be the first step to the end of the road— either to liberation or to, to doom." Thus Gerda Weissmann Klein remembered her departure on a death march in testimony recorded by the United States Holocaust Memorial Museum and featured in the 1995 documentary film *One Survivor Remembers: The Gerda Weissmann Klein Story.* Alice Lok Cahana,

a Hungarian teenager, spoke of her hunger in the Shoah Foundation's 1998 film *The Last Days.* "Once we arrived to a place, it was not covered with snow. It was a field, and I remember they let us for a minute sit down. And the grass [was] eaten up in a matter of seconds. We were that hungry."

Rabbi Menachem Rubin, the Muzhar'er Rebbe, a Hasidic master in Hungary before being deported to Auschwitz, who rebuilt his life and his community in Brooklyn, New York, could not talk of his experience. It was too painful, so he alluded to it with the words of Psalms. "The Lord has afflicted me greatly but he has not given me to die," he said. "The worse affliction is that we did not die."

All the voices of the survivors guide us into this chamber of hell. They fulfill their most important mission: to speak for the dead. And in what we witness—as we become witnesses to the witnesses— we also learn of those who never lived to tell the story, but whose story is told only by those who not only entered the gates of Auschwitz-Birkenau but also exited.

Let us give Filip Müller, a Czech survivor featured in Claude Lanzmann's classic documentary *Shoah* (1985), the last word:

> We asked ourselves many times: What's more important in this moment, these thousands of people whom we can't help or the lives of a hundred witnesses, who are still alive today? And one day could inform the world of what happened there. And we ask ourselves this question many times.

He could not answer the question, nor can we. But like Müller, we can—and we must—ponder that question.

From Generation to Generation

JOSÉ ANTONIO MÚGICA AND MARÍA TERESA AGUIRRE, EXECUTIVE PRODUCERS

In the late summer of 2009, Musealia director Luis Ferreiro gathered us to explain his vision for creating an exhibition on the history of Auschwitz. We had, back then, only a limited knowledge of this topic.

Being one generation older than Luis, we grew up in post–Civil War Spanish society. Our parents had told us about the pain and suffering that the war had brought, how siblings had killed one another in bitter conflict, and we experienced ourselves the public silence that framed the first three decades of our lives.

The Spanish catastrophe became a connection point to Auschwitz. This, and Luis's conviction of the need to tell this story, brought us to the Auschwitz-Birkenau State Museum in Oświęcim. Like many visitors, we were struck by the family pictures on display in the Central Sauna building in Auschwitz-Birkenau. The photographs had been found among the belongings of the hundreds of thousands of victims. They are images of life before the war—moments, attitudes, and feelings in which we easily recognized ourselves. We stared at them, as if we could still hear their subjects' voices, enjoy their laughs, admire the music played, the jokes told—as if they were still alive.

For us, the picture illustrating this essay is one that strikes us *nos llegó al alma*—as if a sword pierces our soul. It shows a father and his young son. The boy looks directly at us, the observers, holding a picture of what, likely, are his grandparents: a picture within a picture that brings together three generations and tells a single story.

In our exhibition, we encounter parents and grandparents with their children and grandchildren, trying to make sense of the story of Auschwitz together, in a conversation *l'dor v'dor*, from generation to generation.

Display of family photographs found in Auschwitz, in the Zentralsauna (Central Sauna) of Auschwitz-Birkenau, 2012.

Three generations, 1930s. Auschwitz-Birkenau State Museum, Oświęcim, Poland.

You Who Are Passing By

Among the smallest artifacts on loan from the Auschwitz-Birkenau State Museum are buttons. They arrived at Musealia accompanied by a series of photographs documenting each and every one and the following description:

PMO-II-1-2470/0.5 kg — A set of 334 buttons, weighing 0.5 kg. The objects are of different colors and sizes, mostly metal and synthetic material.

Some of them are attached to pieces of paper, some have trademark names embossed on them, as well as other inscriptions. Some objects are convex with a loop, others are lined with fabric or thread. With most of them, traces of usage can be seen—small fabric damages, stains, stabilized corrosion. Material: metal, synthetic material, fabric, paper, thread. Measurements: various, ø largest button: 3.5 cm, ø smallest: 1.1 cm. State of preservation: good.

Buttons, 1930s and 1940s, Auschwitz-Birkenau State Museum, Oświęcim, Poland.

Woman's red shoe, 1940s. Auschwitz-Birkenau State Museum, Oświęcim, Poland. Exhibition installation, Centro de Exposiciones Arte Canal, Madrid, 2017.

YOU WHO ARE PASSING BY

I BEG YOU

DO SOMETHING

LEARN A DANCE STEP

SOMETHING TO JUSTIFY YOUR EXISTENCE

SOMETHING THAT GIVES YOU THE RIGHT

TO BE DRESSED IN YOUR SKIN IN YOUR BODY HAIR

LEARN TO WALK AND TO LAUGH

BECAUSE IT WOULD BE TOO SENSELESS

AFTER ALL

FOR SO MANY TO HAVE DIED

WHILE YOU LIVE

DOING NOTHING WITH YOUR LIFE.

—Charlotte Delbo, Auschwitz survivor (1971)

Notes

The Heart of the Matter

1. Aleksandr Solzhenitsyn, *The Gulag Archipelago, 1918–1956: An Experiment in Literary Investigation* (London: Collins and Harvill Press, 1974), 168.

Auschwitz Stories and the Story of Auschwitz

1. Tadeusz Borowski, *This Way for the Gas, Ladies and Gentlemen*, trans. Barbara Vedder (New York: Viking, 1967), 112–13.
2. Heinrich Heine, "Almansor: Eine Tragödie," in *Sämtliche Werke*, 10 vols. (Leipzig: Insel, 1911), 1:314.
3. Hannah Arendt, *Eichmann in Jerusalem: A Report on the Banality of Evil* (New York: Viking, 1963), 43, 44.

AUSCHWITZ: Not Long Ago. Not Far Away.

The Encounter

1. Primo Levi, *The Truce: A Survivor's Journey Home from Auschwitz*, trans. Stuart Woolf (London: Bodley Head, 1965), 12.
2. Primo Levi, *The Drowned and the Saved*, trans. Raymond Rosenthal (New York: Simon and Schuster, 1986), 199.

Before Auschwitz

3. Jean Améry, *At the Mind's Limits: Contemplations by a Survivor on Auschwitz and Its Realities*, trans. Sidney Rosenfeld and Stella P. Rosenfeld (Bloomington: Indiana University Press, 1980), 86.
4. David Weiss Halivni, *Peshat and Derash* (Oxford: Oxford University Press, 1991), 97.
5. Heinrich von Treitschke, "Unsere Aussichten," *Preussische Jahrbücher* 44 (1879), 573.
6. John Keegan, *The First World War* (New York: Knopf, 1999), 9, 3–4.
7. Adolf Hitler, *Mein Kampf*, trans. Ralph Manheim (Boston: Houghton Mifflin, 1943), 118.
8. Sebastian Haffner, *Defying Hitler: A Memoir*, trans. Oliver Pretzel (New York: Farrar, Straus, and Giroux, 2002), 285, 291.
9. Manfred Overesch et al., eds., "Dokument 101: Schrift des SS-Hauptamtes beim Reichsführer SS über 'Untermenschentum' (1935)," in *Das Dritte Reich: Daten-Bilder-Dokumente* (Berlin: Directmedia Publishing, 2001), CD-ROM.
10. Ernst Hiemer, *Der Giftpilz* (Nuremberg, Stürmerverlag, 1938), 8.
11. Elvira Bauer, *Trau keinem Fuchs auf grüner Heid und keinem Jud auf seinem Eid* (Nuremberg: Stürmerverlag, 1936), [40].
12. Améry, *At the Mind's Limits*, 86.
13. Hannah Arendt, *The Origins of Totalitarianism*, new ed. (New York: Harcourt, Brace, and World, 1966), 477.

14. Hannah Arendt, "The Aftermath of Nazi Rule: Report from Germany," *Commentary* 10, no. 10 (1950), 344.
15. Haffner, *Defying Hitler*, 195.
16. Kim Wünschmann, *Before Auschwitz: Jewish Prisoners in the Prewar Concentration Camps* (Cambridge, MA: Harvard University Press, 2015), 230–34.
17. George Orwell, "Review of *Gypsies* by Martin Block," in *Essays*, ed. John Carey (New York: Knopf, 2002), 103.
18. Martin Broszat, "The Concentration Camps," in Helmut Krausnick et al., *Anatomy of the SS State*, trans. Richard Barry, Marian Jackson, and Dorothy Long (New York: Walker and Company, 1968), 455.
19. Orwell, "Review of *Gypsies* by Martin Block," 104.
20. Haffner, *Defying Hitler*, 142.
21. Hannah Arendt, "'What Remains? The Language Remains': A Conversation with Günter Gaus," in *Essays in Understanding, 1930–1954*, ed. Jerome Kohn (New York: Harcourt, Brace, and Company, 1994), 10–11.
22. These examples come from photographs of antisemitic signs taken in 1935, on instigation of Dr. Alfred Wiener, by Werner Fritz Fürstenberg while driving his motorcycle through Germany; *The Motorcycle Album*, Wiener Library, London.
23. United States Chief Counsel for the Prosecution of Axis Criminality, *Nazi Conspiracy and Aggression*, 8 vols. (Washington, DC: United States Government Printing Office, 1946), 4:7, 9.
24. Ian Kershaw, *Hitler*, 2 vols. (London: Allen Lane / Penguin, 1998–2000), 1:529–31.
25. Henry Bauer, "My name is Henry (Heinz) Bauer," ms. AR 6347, Leo Baeck Institute Archives, New York, [3].
26. Ibid.
27. Max Domarus, *Hitler: Speeches and Commentary*, 4 vols. (Wauconda, IL: Bolchazy-Carducci, 1990–2004), 3:1449.
28. SS-Hauptamt-Schulungsamt, *Der Kampf um die deutsche Ostgrenze: Ein Langsschnitt von der friihgermanischen Zeit bis zur Jetztzeit* (Berlin: SS-Hauptamt, 1941), 43, 41.

Auschwitz

29. Rudolf Höss, *Death Dealer: The Memoirs of the SS Kommandant at Auschwitz*, ed. Steven Paskuly, trans. Andrew Pollinger (Buffalo NY: Prometheus, 1992), 168.
30. Oskar Gröning, testimony in Laurence Rees, dir., *Auschwitz: The Nazis and the "Final Solution"* (TV miniseries), episode 4, "Corruption," BBC, February 1, 2005.
31. Emmanuel Levinas, *Totality and Infinity: An Essay on Exteriority*, trans. Alphonso Lingis (The Hague: Martinus

Nijhoff, 1979), 194, 199.

32. As quoted in Alan Taylor, "World War II: The Holocaust," *Atlantic*, October 16, 2011, https://www.theatlantic.com/photo/2011/10/world-war-ii-the-holocaust/100170/, accessed October 6, 2016.

33. Levi, *The Drowned and the Saved*, 36–38.

34. Wolfgang Sofsky, *The Order of Terror: The Concentration Camp*, trans. William Templer (Princeton, NJ: Princeton University Press, 1997), 17, 88.

35. Primo Levi, *If This Is a Man*, trans. Stuart Woolf (New York: Orion Press, 1959), 31.

36. Charlotte Delbo, *Auschwitz and After*, trans. Rosette C. Lamont (New Haven, CT, and London: Yale University Press, 1995), 106.

37. Pavel Stenkin, testimony in Rees, *Auschwitz: The Nazis and the "Final Solution,"* episode 2, "Orders and Initiatives," BBC, January 18, 2005.

38. Quoted in Ernst Klee, Willi Dressen, and Volker Riess, *"The Good Old Days": The Holocaust as Seen by Its Perpetrators and Bystanders* (Old Saybrook, CT: Konecky and Konecky, 1991), 118.

39. Joseph Goebbels, *Die Tagebücher von Joseph Goebbels: Teil II*, ed. Elke Fröhlich, 15 vols. (Munich: Saur, 1996), 2:498–99.

40. Raul Hilberg, as quoted in Claude Lanzmann, *Shoah: An Oral History of the Holocaust; The Complete Text of the Film* (New York: Pantheon Books, 1985), 55.

41. Höss, *Death Dealer*, 290.

42. Fritz Sander's testimony given during his interrogation of March 7, 1946, in Gerald Fleming, *Hitler and the Final Solution*, 2d ed. (Berkeley and Los Angeles: University of California Press, 1994), 205.

43. Höss, *Death Dealer*, 256.

44. Zygmunt Bauman, *Modernity and the Holocaust* (Ithaca, NY: Cornell University Press, 1989), 122, 134.

45. Anne Frank, *The Diary of Anne Frank*, ed. David Barnouw and Gerrold van der Stroom, trans. Arnold J. Pomerans, B. M. Mooyaart-Doubleday, and Susan Massotty (New York: Doubleday, 2003), 321.

46. Philip Mechanicus, *Year of Fear: A Jewish Prisoner Waits for Auschwitz*, trans. Irene R. Gibbons (New York: Hawthorne, 1968), 26–27.

47. Etty Hillesum, *Etty: The Letters and Diaries of Etty Hillesum, 1941–1943*, ed. Klaas A. D. Smelik, trans. Arnold J. Pomerans (Grand Rapids, MN, and Cambridge: Eerdmans, 2002), 654.

48. Norbert Wollheim, Oral History RG-50.030.0257, 1991, United States Holocaust Memorial Museum Collection, Washington, DC.

49. Ibid.

50. Michael Zimmermann, *Rassenutopie und Genozid: Die national-sozialistische "Lösung der Zigeunerfrage"* (Hamburg: Christians, 1996), 301ff.

51. Lith Bahlmann and Matthias Reichelt, eds., *Ceija Stojka (1933–2013): Sogar der Tod hat Angst vor Auschwitz* (Nuremberg: Verlag für modern Kunst Nürnberg, 2014), 11–12.

52. The text of Zygielbojm's suicide note can be read on the Yad Vashem website; "The Last Letter from Szmul Zygielbojm, The Bund Representative with the Polish National Council in Exile," http://www.yadvashem.org/docs/zygielbojm-letter-to-polish-national-council-in-exile.html, accessed October 6, 2018.

53. Wollheim, Oral History RG-50.030.0257, USHMM.

54. Delbo, *Auschwitz and After*, 7.

55. Alex Gross, interview 11272, 1996, Visual History Archive, USC Shoah Foundation, Los Angeles.

56. Oskar Gröning, testimony in Rees, *Auschwitz: The Nazis and the "Final Solution,"* episode 3, "Factories of Death," BBC, January 25, 2005.

57. Delbo, *Auschwitz and After*, 137–38.

58. Krystyna Zywulska, *I Came Back*, trans. Krystyna Cenkalska (New York: Roy Publishers, 1951), 16, 179–80.

59. George Steiner, *In Bluebeard's Castle: Some Notes Towards the Redefinition of Culture* (London: Faber and Faber, 1971), 47–48.

60. "Deposition of Sonderkommando Member Henryk Tauber," in Wacław Dlugoborski and Franciszek Piper, *Auschwitz 1940–1945: Central Issues in the History of the Camp*, trans. William Brand, 5 vols. (Oświęcim: Auschwitz-Birkenau State Museum, 2000), 3:251–52.

61. Filip Müller, as quoted in Lanzmann, *Shoah*, 125–26.

62. Jorge Semprún, "Une petite lampe s'est allumée dans la baraque des contagieux . . . ," as quoted in Caroline Fournet, *The Crime of Destruction and the Law of Genocide: Their Impact on Collective Memory* (Aldershot: Ashgate, 2007), 32.

63. "Deposition of Sonderkommando Member Henryk Tauber," 254–55, 261.

64. Zywulska, *I Came Back*, 175.

65. Salmen Lewenthal, "Diary," in *Amidst a Nightmare of Crime: Manuscripts of Members of Sonderkommando*, ed. Jadwiga Bezwińska (Oświęcim: The State Musem at Oświęcim, 1973), 139.

66. Zywulska, *I Came Back*, 176.

67. Annette Wieviorka, *The Era of the Witness*, trans. Jared Stark (Ithaca, NY, and London: Cornell University Press, 2006).

68. As quoted in Teresa Swiebocka, Jonathan Webber, and Connie Wilsack, *Auschwitz: A History in Photographs* (Oświęcim: State Museum in Oświęcim, 1993), 42–43.

69. Albert Camus, *The Rebel: An Essay on Man in Revolt*, trans. Anthony Bower (New York: Knopf, 1954), 155.

70. Levi, *The Drowned and the Saved*, 60, 53–54.

71. Zywulska, *I Came Back*, 160.

72. Oskar Gröning, in Rees, *Auschwitz: The Nazis and the "Final Solution,"* episode 4, "Corruption," BBC, February 1, 2005.

73. The quotation in the caption accompanying the photographs of the deportees' possessions is from Margery Williams,

The Velveteen Rabbit; Or, How Toys Become Real (London: Heinemann, 1922), 4.

74. Mechanicus, *Year of Fear*, 18

75. David Weiss Halivni, *The Book and the Sword* (Boulder, CO: Westview Press, 1996), 155–56.

76. Elie Wiesel, *All Rivers Run to the Sea* (New York: Knopf, 1995), 82.

77. *The Standard Prayer Book: Authorized English Translation*, trans. Simeon Singer (New York: Bloch, 1958), 17.

78. Norman Lamm, editor's foreword, in Irving J. Rosenbaum, *The Holocaust and Halakhah* (New York: Ktav, 1976), xiii–ix.

79. As quoted in Robert Kirschner, ed., *Rabbinic Responsa of the Holocaust Era* (New York: Schocken, 1985), 118.

80. Elie Wiesel, "The First Survivor," in *Against Silence: The Voice and Vision of Elie Wiesel*, ed. Irving Abrahamson, 3 vols. (New York: Holocaust Library, 1985), 1:385.

81. Viktor Frankl, *Man's Search for Meaning: An Introduction to Logotherapy*, trans. Ilse Lasch, rev. ed. (London: Hodder and Stoughton, 1964), 12.

82. Livia Bitton-Jackson, *I Have Lived a Thousand Years: Growing Up in the Holocaust* (New York: Simon and Schuster, 1997), 77–78.

83. Zdenka Fantlová, *The Tin Ring: How I Cheated Death*, trans. Deryck Viney (Newcastle upon Tyne: Northumbria Press, 2010), 84.

84. Frankl, *Man's Search for Meaning*, 13.

85. Levi, *If This Is a Man*, 21.

86. Zywulska, *I Came Back*, 18.

87. Delbo, *Auschwitz and After*, 13.

88. Borowski, *This Way for the Gas*, 130–31.

89. Alfred Kantor, *The Book of Alfred Kantor* (New York: McGraw Hill, 1971), [22].

90. Elmer Luchterhand, "Prisoner Behaviour and Social System in the Nazi Camp," *International Journal of Social Psychiatry* 13 (1967), 259–60.

91. Delbo, *Auschwitz and After*, 17.

92. International Military Tribunal, *Trial of the Major War Criminals before the International Military Tribunal: Nuremberg, 14 November 1945–1 October 1946*, vol. 38, document 129-R, 366.

93. As quoted in Nikolaus Wachsmann, "'Annihilation Through Labor': The Killing of State Prisoners in the Third Reich," *Journal of Modern History* 71, no. 3 (September 1999), 631.

94. Levi, *If This Is a Man*, 101.

95. Ibid., 103.

96. Eva Mozes Kor, in Rees, *Auschwitz: The Nazis and the "Final Solution,"* episode 4, "Corruption," BBC, February 1, 2005.

97. Lidia Maksymowicz, in a presentation given in July 2013 at the Galicia Jewish Museum, Kraków, as recorded by Miriam Greenbaum.

98. As quoted in David Wyman, *The Abandonment of the Jews: America and the Holocaust* (New York: Pantheon Books, 1984), 296.

99. Libuša Breder, in Rees, *Auschwitz: The Nazis and the "Final Solution,"* episode 5, "Frenzied Killing," BBC, February 8, 2005.

100. David A. Wyman, "Why Auschwitz Was Never Bombed," *Commentary* 65 (May 1978), 37–46; Dino A. Brugioni and Robert G. Poirier, *The Holocaust Revisited: A Retrospective Analysis of the Auschwitz-Birkenau Extermination Complex* (Washington, DC: Central Intelligence Agency, 1979).

101. Lewenthal, "Diary," in *Amidst a Nightmare of Crime*, ed. Bezwińska, 154–55.

102. Salmen Gradowski, "Letter," in *Amidst a Nightmare of Crime*, ed. Bezwińska, 77.

103. Gizella Isserof, interview 36780, 1997, Visual History Archive, USC Shoah Foundation, Los Angeles.

104. Annie Glass, interview 15188, 1996, Visual History Archive, USC Shoah Foundation, Los Angeles.

105. Halivni, *The Book and the Sword*, 169.

After Auschwitz

106. Eva Mozes Kors, in Rees, *Auschwitz: The Nazis and the "Final Solution,"* episode 6, "Liberation and Revenge," BBC, February 15, 2005.

107. Union of Soviet Socialist Republics, "Statement of the Extraordinary State Committee for the Ascertaining and Investigation of Crimes Committed by the German-Fascist Invaders and Their Associates on Crimes Committed by the German-Fascist Invaders in the Oswiecim Death Camp," *Information Bulletin, Embassy of the Union of Soviet Socialist Republics* (Washington DC), vol. 5, no. 54 (May 29, 1945), 8.

108. Arendt, "'What Remains? The Language Remains,'" in *Essays in Understanding*, 14.

109. Améry, *At the Mind's Limits*, 50, 94.

110. Pavel Stenkin, in Rees, *Auschwitz: The Nazis and the "Final Solution,"* episode 6, "Liberation and Revenge," BBC, February 15, 2005.

111. David Olère, as quoted in Agnieszka Sieradzka, *David Olère: Ten, który ocalał z Krematorium III / The One Who Survived Crematorium III* (Oświęcim: Auschwitz-Birkenau State Museum, 2018), 3.

112. "Leon Greenman," Jewish Museum, London, https://jewishmuseum.org.uk/about-us/history/leon-greenman/, accessed November 2, 2018.

113. Leon Greenman, interview 6966, 1995, Visual History Archive, USC Shoah Foundation, Los Angeles.

Architect(ure)'s Weakest Moment. Or, When *Not* to Learn from Architects.

1. Hans Schafranek, "Eine unbekannte NS-Tätergruppe: Biografische Skizzen zu Österreichern in der 8. SS-Totenkopf-Standarte (1939–1941)," in *Österreichische Akteure im Nationalsozialismus*, ed. Christine Schindler (Vienna: Dokumentationsarchiv des österreichischen Widerstandes, 2014), 99–100.

Conserving Testaments to Human Survival

1. The epigraph on this page is from Levi, *If This Is a Man*, 52.

Further Reading

This list includes only books in English that are readily available in public and college libraries or can be purchased either through brick-and-mortar bookstores or through online marketplaces for new or used books.

Collection of Documents

Noakes, Jeremy, and Geoffrey Pridham. *Nazism, 1919–1945: A Documentary Reader*. 3d rev. ed., 4 vols. Liverpool: Liverpool University Press, 2001.

On the History of Oświęcim

Dwork, Debórah, and Robert Jan van Pelt. *Auschwitz: 1270 to the Present*. New York and London: W. W. Norton and Company, 1996.
Wolnerman, Chaim, Aviezer Burstin, Meir Shimon Geshuri, eds. *Sefer Oshpitsin: Oswiecim; Auschwitz Memorial Book*. Jerusalem: Oshpitsin Society, 1977. Available online at JewishGen, https://www.jewishgen. org/yizkor/oswiecim1/ oswiecim.html.

On Jews and Judaism

Baskin, Judith R. and Kenneth Seeskin, eds. *The Cambridge Guide to Jewish History, Religion, and Culture*. Cambridge: Cambridge University Press, 2010.
Brenner, Michael. *A Short History of the Jews*. Trans. Jeremiah Riemer. Princeton, NJ: Princeton University Press, 2012.

Kriwaczek, Paul. *Yiddish Civilisation: The Rise and Fall of a Forgotten Nation*. London: Weidenfeld and Nicolson, 2005.

On Jewish-Gentile Relations, Anti-Judaism, and Antisemitism

Cohn, Norman. *Warrant for Genocide*. New York and Evanston, IL: Harper and Row, 1967.
Klier, John D., and Shlomo Lambroza, eds. *Pogroms*. Cambridge: Cambridge University Press, 1992.
Laqueur, Walter. *The Changing Face of Anti-Semitism: From Ancient Times to the Present Day*. Oxford: Oxford University Press, 2008.
Mosse, George L. *Toward the Final Solution*. New York: H. Fertig, 1978.
Nirenberg, David. *Anti-Judaism: The Western Tradition*. New York: Norton, 2014.

On World War I

Grady, Tim. *A Deadly Legacy: German Jews and the Great War*. New Haven, CT, and London: Yale University Press, 2017.
Herwig, Holger H. *The First World War: Germany and Austria-Hungary*. London: Bloomsbury, 2009.
Keegan, John. *The First World War*. New York: Knopf, 1999.
Sloterdijk, Peter. *Terror from the Air*. Trans. Amy Patton and Steve Corcoran. Los Angeles: Semiotext(e), 2009.

On the Weimar Republic

Haffner, Sebastian. *Failure of a Revolution: Germany 1918–1919*. Trans. Georg Rapp. London: Deutsch, 1973.
Hett, Benjamin Carter. *The Death of Democracy: Hitler's Rise to Power and the Downfall of the Weimar Republic*. New York: Henry Holt, 2018.
Weitz, Eric D. *Weimar Germany: Promise and Tragedy*. Princeton, NJ: Princeton University Press, 2007.
Widdig, Bernd. *Culture and Inflation in Weimar Germany*. Berkeley, Los Angeles, and London: University of California Press, 2001.

On the Third Reich

Arendt, Hannah. *The Origins of Totalitarianism*. New ed. New York: Harcourt, Brace, and World, 1966.
Burleigh, Michael. *The Third Reich: A New History*. New York: Hill and Wang, 2001.
Evans, Richard. *The Third Reich in Power, 1933–1939*. New York: Penguin, 2005.
Haffner, Sebastian. *Defying Hitler: A Memoir*. Trans. Oliver Pretzel. New York: Farrar, Straus, and Giroux, 2002.
Johnson, Eric A. *Nazi Terror: The Gestapo, Jews, and Ordinary Germans*. New York: Basic Books, 1999.
Kühne, Thomas. *Belonging and Genocide: Hitler's Community, 1918–1945*. New Haven, CT, and London: Yale University Press, 2010.

Biographies of Key Nazis

Cesarani, David. *Eichmann: His Life and Crimes*. New York: Vintage, 2005.
Gerwarth, Robert. *Hitler's Hangman: The Life of Heydrich*. New Haven, CT, and London: Yale University Press, 2011.
Kershaw, Ian. *Hitler*. 2 vols. London: Allen Lane/ Penguin, 1998–2000.
Longerich, Peter. *Heinrich Himmler: A Life*. Trans. Jeremy Noakes and Lesley Sharpe. New York: Oxford University Press, 2012.

On German Concentration Camps

Krausnick, Helmut, et al. *Anatomy of the SS State*. Trans. Richard Barry, Marian Jackson, and Dorothy Long. New York: Walker and Company, 1968.
Sofsky, Wolfgang. *The Order of Terror: The Concentration Camp*. Trans. William Templer. Princeton, NJ: Princeton University Press, 1997.
Wachsman, Nikolaus. *KL: A History of the German Concentration Camps*. New York: Farrar, Straus, and Giroux, 2015.
Wünschmann, Kim. *Before Auschwitz: Jewish Prisoners in the Prewar Concentration Camps*. Cambridge, MA: Harvard University Press, 2015.

On the Expulsion of the Jews

Dwork, Debórah, and Robert Jan van Pelt. *Flight from the Reich: Refugee Jews, 1933–1946*. New York: W. W. Norton, 2008.

On World War II

Beevor, Antony. *The Second World War*. London: Weidenfeld and Nicolson, 2012.

Evans, Richard. *The Third Reich at War: How the Nazis Led Germany from Conquest to Disaster*. London: Allen Lane, 2008.

Snyder, Timothy. *Bloodlands: Europe Between Hitler and Stalin*. New York: Basic Books, 2010.

On the German Occupation of Poland

Gross, Jan T. *Polish Society under German Occupation: The Generalgouvernement, 1939–1944*. Princeton, NJ: Princeton University Press, 1979.

Rutherford, Philip T. *Prelude to the Final Solution: The Nazi Program for Deporting Ethnic Poles, 1939–1941*. Lawrence: University Press of Kansas, 2007.

On the History of the Holocaust (general)

Bauman, Zygmunt. *Modernity and the Holocaust*. Ithaca, NY: Cornell University Press, 1989.

Browning, Christopher R. *The Origins of the Final Solution: The Evolution of Nazi Jewish Policy, September 1939–March 1942*. Lincoln: University of Nebraska Press, 2004.

Cesarani, David. *Final Solution: The Fate of the Jews 1933–1949*. New York: St. Martin's Press, 2016.

Confino, Alon. *A World Without Jews: The Nazi Imagination from Persecution to Genocide*. New Haven, CT, and London: Yale University Press, 2014.

Dwork, Debórah, and Robert Jan van Pelt. *Holocaust: A History*. New York: W. W. Norton, 2002.

Hilberg, Raul. *The Destruction of the European Jews*. 3rd ed., 3 vols. New Haven, CT, and London: Yale University Press, 2003.

On the History of the Holocaust (topics)

Aly, Götz, and Susanne Heim. *Architects of Annihilation: Auschwitz and the Logic of Destruction*. Trans. Allan Blunden. London: Weidenfeld and Nicolson, 2002.

Blatman, Daniel. *The Death Marches*. Trans. Chaya Galai. Cambridge, MA: Harvard University Press, 2011.

Browning, Christopher R. *Ordinary Men*. New York: HarperCollins, 1992.

Fleming, Gerald. *Hitler and the Final Solution*. 2nd ed. Berkeley and Los Angeles: University of California Press, 1994.

Hallie, Philip. *Lest Innocent Blood Be Shed: The Story of the Village of Le Chambon and How Goodness Happened There*. New York: Harper and Row, 1979.

Kirschner, Robert, ed. *Rabbinic Responsa of the Holocaust Era*. New York: Schocken, 1985.

Lifton, Robert Jay. *The Nazi Doctors: Medical Killing and the Psychology of Genocide*. New York: Basic Books, 1986.

Wyman, David. *The Abandonment of the Jews: America and the Holocaust*. New York: Pantheon Books, 1984.

On the Porajmos

Lewy, Guenter. *Forgotten Victims: The Nazi Persecution of the Gypsies*. New York and Oxford: Oxford University Press, 2000.

Margalit, Gilad. *Germany and Its Gypsies: A Post-Auschwitz Ordeal*. Madison: University of Wisconsin Press, 2002.

Weiss-Wendt, Anton. *The Nazi Genocide of the Roma: Reassessment and Commemoration*. New York: Berghahn, 2015.

On the History of Kulmhof and the Operation Reinhard Camps

Arad, Yitzhak. *Belzec, Sobibor, Treblinka: The Operation Reinhard Death Camps*. Bloomington: Indiana University Press, 1987.

Lanzmann, Claude. *Shoah: An Oral History of the Holocaust; The Complete Text of the Film*. New York: Pantheon Books, 1985.

Montague, Patrick. *Chelmno and the Holocaust: The History of Hitler's First Death Camp*. Chapel Hill: University of North Carolina Press, 2012.

On the History of Auschwitz (general)

Cywiński, Piotr M. A., Jacek Lacendro, and Piotr Setkiewicz. *Auschwitz from A to Z: An Illustrated History of the Camp*. Trans. William Brand. Oświęcim: Auschwitz-Birkenau State Museum, 2013.

Czech, Danuta. *Auschwitz Chronicle 1939–1945: From the Archives of the Auschwitz Memorial and the German Federal Archives*. Trans. Barbara Harshav, Martha Humphreys, and Stephan Shearier. New York: Henry Holt, 1990.

Dlugoborski, Wacław, and Franciszek Piper. *Auschwitz 1940–1945: Central Issues in the History of the Camp*. Trans. William Brand. 5 vols. Oświęcim: Auschwitz-Birkenau State Museum, 2000.

Dwork, Debórah, and Robert Jan van Pelt. *Auschwitz: 1270 to the Present*. New York and London: Norton, 1996.

Gutman, Yisrael, and Michael Berenbaum, eds. *Anatomy of the Auschwitz Death Camp*. Bloomington and Indianapolis: Indiana University Press, 1994.

Langbein, Hermann. *People in Auschwitz*. Trans. Harry Zohn. Chapel Hill and London: University of North Carolina Press, 2004.

Rees, Laurence, dir. *Auschwitz: The Nazis and the "Final Solution."* TV miniseries. BBC, January 11–February 15, 2005.

———. *Auschwitz: A New History*. New York: Public Affairs, 2005.

Steinbacher, Sybille. *Auschwitz: A History*. Trans. Shaun Whiteside. London: Penguin, 2005.

On the History of Auschwitz (topics)

Bartosik, Igor, Łukasz Martyniak, and Piotr Setkiewicz. *The Beginnings of the Extermination of Jews in KL Auschwitz in the Light of the Source Materials*. Trans. William Brand. Oświęcim: Auschwitz-Birkenau State Museum, 2014.

Bezwińska, Jadwiga, ed. *Amidst a Nightmare of Crime: Manuscripts of Members of Sonderkommando*. Oświęcim: The State Musem at Oświęcim, 1973.

Brasse, Wilhelm. *Wilhelm Brasse, Photographer, 3444, Auschwitz 1940–1945*. Brighton: Sussex Academic Press, 2012.

Des Pres, Terrence. *The Survivor: An Anatomy of Life in the Death Camps*. Oxford: Oxford University Press, 1976.

Greif, Gideon. *We Wept Without Tears: Testimonies of the Jewish Sonderkommando from Auschwitz*. New Haven, CT, and London: Yale University Press, 2005.

Greif, Gideon, and Peter Siebers. *Todesfabrik Auschwitz: Das Konzentrations- und Vernichtungslager Auschwitz 1940–1945*. Cologne: Emons Verlag, 2016.

Gutman, Israel, and Bella Gutterman. *The Auschwitz Album: The Story of a Transport*. Jerusalem and Oświęcim: Yad Vashem and the Auschwitz-Birkenau State Museum, 2002.

Lagnado, Lucette Matalon, with Sheila Cohn Dekel. *Children of the Flames: Dr. Josef Mengele and the Untold Story of the Twins of Auschwitz*. New York: Penguin, 1992.

Neufeld, Michael J., and Michael Berenbaum, eds. *The Bombing of Auschwitz: Should the Allies Have Attempted It?* New York: St. Martin's Press, 2000.

Piper, Franciszek. *Auschwitz Prisoner Labor*. Trans. William Brand. Oświęcim: Auschwitz-Birkenau State Museum, 2002.

Pressac, Jean Claude. *Auschwitz: Technique and Operation of the Gas Chambers*. New York: Beate Klarsfeld Foundation, 1989.

Setkiewicz, Piotr. *The Histories of Auschwitz IG Farben Werk Camps, 1941–1945*. Trans. Witold Zbirohowski-Kościa. Oświęcim: Auschwitz-Birkenau State Museum, 2008.

Sieradzka, Agnieszka. *David Olère: Ten, który ocalał z Krematorium III/The One Who Survived Crematorium III*. Oświęcim: Auschwitz-Birkenau State Museum, 2018.

Świebocki, Henryk. *London Has Been Informed: Reports by Auschwitz Escapees*. Trans. Michael Jacobs and Laurence Weinbaum. Oświęcim: Auschwitz-Birkenau State Museum, 1997.

Testimony and Memoirs (Auschwitz)

Améry, Jean. *At the Mind's Limits: Contemplations by a Survivor on Auschwitz and Its Realities*. Trans. Sidney Rosenfeld and Stella P. Rosenfeld. Bloomington: Indiana University Press, 1980.

Borowski, Tadeusz. *This Way for the Gas, Ladies and Gentlemen*. Trans. Barbara Vedder. New York: Viking, 1967.

Delbo, Charlotte. *Auschwitz and After*, trans. Rosette C. Lamont. New Haven, CT, and London: Yale University Press, 1995.

Frank, Anne. *The Diary of Anne Frank*. Ed. David Barnouw and Gerrold van der Stroom. Trans. Arnold J. Pomerans, B. M. Mooyaart-Doubleday, and Susan Massotty. New York: Doubleday, 2003.

Frankl, Viktor. *Man's Search for Meaning: An Introduction to Logotherapy*. Trans. Ilse Lasch. Rev. ed. London: Hodder and Stoughton, 1964.

Höss, Rudolf. *Death Dealer: The Memoirs of the SS Kommandant at Auschwitz*. Ed. Steven Paskuly. Trans. Andrew Pollinger. Buffalo, NY: Prometheus, 1992.

Kantor, Alfred. *The Book of Alfred Kantor*. New York: McGraw Hill, 1971.

Levi, Primo. *The Drowned and the Saved*. Trans. Raymond Rosenthal. New York: Simon and Schuster, 1986.

———. *If This Is a Man*. Trans. Stuart Woolf. New York: Orion Press, 1959.

———. *The Truce: A Survivor's Journey Home from Auschwitz*. Trans. Stuart Woolf. London: Bodley Head, 1965.

Mechanicus, Philip. *Year of Fear: A Jewish Prisoner Waits for Auschwitz*. Trans. Irene R. Gibbons. New York: Hawthorne, 1968.

Müller, Filip, with Helmut Freitag. *Eyewitness Auschwitz: Three Years in the Gas Chambers*. Trans. Susanne Flatauer. Chicago: Ivan R. Dee, 1979.

Nyiszli, Miklos. *Auschwitz: A Doctor's Eyewitness Account*. Trans. Tibère Kremer and Richard Seaver. New York: Frederick Fell, 1960.

Pilecki, Witold. *The Auschwitz Volunteer: Beyond Bravery*. Trans. Jarek Garliński. Los Angeles: Aquila Polonica, 2012.

Venezia, Shlomo. *Inside the Gas Chambers: Eight Months in the Sonderkommando of Auschwitz*. Trans. Andrew Brown. Cambridge: Polity Press, 2009.

Vrba, Rudi, and Alan Bestic. *I Cannot Forgive*. London: Sidgwick and Jackson and Gibbs and Phillips, 1963.

Wiesel, Elie. *Night*. New York: Hill and Wang, 1960.

Zywulska, Krystyna. *I Came Back*. Trans. Krystyna Cenkalska. New York: Roy Publishers, 1951.

Aftermath

Citroen, Hans, and Barbara Starzyńska. *Auschwitz-Oświęcim*. Rotterdam: Post Editions, 2011.

Cywiński, Piotr. *Epitaph*. Trans. Witold Zbirohowski-Kościa. Oświęcim: Auschwitz-Birkenau State Museum, 2015.

Emilewicz-Pióro, Magdalena, and Piotr M. A. Cywiński. *Auschwitz Legacies*. Oświęcim: Auschwitz-Birkenau State Museum, 2015.

Huener, Jonathan. *Auschwitz, Poland, and the Politics of Commemoration, 1945–1979*. Athens: Ohio University Press, 2003.

Langer, Lawrence L. *The Holocaust and the Literary Imagination*. New Haven, CT, and London: Yale University Press, 1975.

Pendas, Devin O. *The Frankfurt Auschwitz Trial, 1963–1965*. Cambridge: Cambridge University Press, 2006.

Stone, Dan. *The Liberation of the Camps: The End of the Holocaust and Its Aftermath*. New Haven, CT, and London: Yale University Press, 2015.

Thaler, Henri Lustiger, and Habbo Knoch, eds. *Witnessing Unbound: Holocaust Representation and the Origins of Memory*. Detroit: Wayne State University Press, 2017.

van Pelt, Robert Jan. *The Case for Auschwitz: Evidence from the Irving Trial*. Bloomington and Indianapolis: Indiana University Press, 2002.

Wieviorka, Annette. *The Era of the Witness*. Trans. Jared Stark. Ithaca, NY, and London: Cornell University Press, 2006.

Wyman, David S., ed. *The World Reacts to the Holocaust*. Baltimore and London: Johns Hopkins University Press, 1996.

Index

Credits and Acknowledgments

Catalogue

Musealia: Robert Jan van Pelt, with Luis Ferreiro and Miriam Greenbaum (editors). Beverley Slopen Literary Agency: Beverley Slopen (agent). Abbeville Press: Amy K. Hughes (project editor); Misha Beletsky (designer); Louise Kurtz (production manager); Patricia Fogarty (proofreader).

PHOTOGRAPHY CREDITS
Akg-images/Abraham Pisarek: 70. José Barea: 15, 18, 20, 26, 28, 35 (top right), 43, 52, 56, 62, 79, 82 (right), 96, 97, 99 (bottom), 121, 136, 141, 142 (top left), 145, 148, 152, 153, 154, 155 (top left), 165 (top), 173, 174, 178, 182 (bottom left), 190, 191, 195, 196 (top left), 199, 203 (top), 205 (right), 210–11, 221, 223, 227. Izaskun Cámara: 25, 58, 59, 63, 101, 169, 182 (top left), 206 (bottom), 216. Luis Ferreiro: 11. Peter Goldberg: 7. Miriam Greenbaum: 164 (bottom). John Halpern: 71, 115, 140. Fred Hunsberger: 120 (top). Galerie KaiDikhas: 203 (bottom). Carlos Reijnen: 204. Aaron Rezny: 167. Jennifer Rodewald: 38, 42 (bottom), 47 (left), 66 (top), 69, 73 (left), 78 (left), 80 (top), 84, 117, 126, 133, 172, 175, 177 (bottom), 182 (bottom right), 186, 197, 220. Paweł Sawicki: 9, 53 (right), 88, 89, 101, 102 (right), 107 (bottom), 123, 137, 144, 151, 155 (top right), 177 (top), 179, 183 (right), 194 (bottom left), 207 (top left), 207 (bottom), 215 (left), 218, 219 (both), 226. Robert Jan van Pelt: 41 (bottom), 106 (top), 108, 113 (top), 207 (top right), 225 (left). Jesús Varillas: 27, 46, 86, 98, 99 (top), 100, 113, 164 (top), 165 (bottom).

GRAPHICS
Anna Biedermann and Victor Figuerola: 23, 24, 25, 44, 118, 146, 147. Peter Siebers: endpapers.

Exhibition as Presented in New York City

Musealia, San Sebastián, in collaboration with the Auschwitz-Birkenau State Museum, Oświęcim, and the Museum of Jewish Heritage—A Living Memorial to the Holocaust, New York.

MUSEALIA
Curatorial team: Robert Jan van Pelt, Canada (chair); Michael Berenbaum, United States; Miriam Greenbaum, Canada; Paul Salmons, United Kingdom; Djamel Zeniti, Luxembourg. Executive team: Luis Ferreiro (project director), José Antonio Múgica and María Teresa Aguirre (executive producers). Managers: Ana Galán Pérez (collections); Icíar Palacios (communications and public relations); Amaia Múgica (accounts); Marisa Ruiz (human resources); Javier Galán (production). Office: Andrea Calleja (communications assistant). Museography: Anna Biedermann, Víctor Figuerola (assistant).

AUSCHWITZ-BIRKENAU STATE MUSEUM
Executive team: Piotr M. A. Cywiński (director), Rafał Pióro (deputy director). Senior managers involved with the exhibition: Piotr Setkiewicz (head research), Wojciech Płosa (head archives), Elżbieta Cajzer (head collections), Jolanta Banaś-Maciaszczyk (head preservation), Aleksandra Papis (head conservation laboratories). Press office: Bartosz Bartyzel (spokesman). Special Musealia liaison: Paweł Sawicki. Preparation and administration of artifacts for the Musealia exhibition: Agnieszka Sieradzka, Andrzej Jastrzębiowski, Marta Paszko.

MUSEUM OF JEWISH HERITAGE—A LIVING MEMORIAL TO THE HOLOCAUST
Board: Bruce C. Ratner (chair); Peter S. Kalikow (first vice chair), Abraham H. Foxman, Stephen E. Kaufman, George Klein, Manfred Ohrenstein, Ann Oster, Ingeborg Rennert, Howard J. Rubenstein (vice chairs); Simon Bergson, Howard J. Butnick, Robert Dombroff, Marian Klein Feldt, Nancy Fisher, Matthew Goldstein, Judah Gribetz, H. Dale Hemmerdinger, Patti Askwith Kenner, Jack Kliger, Rita G. Lerner, Robert P. Morgenthau, Sheila Nevins, Irving Paler, Gladys Pickman, Lily Safra, Larry A. Silverstein, Regina Skyer, Ronald B. Sobel, Steven Spielberg, Eliot Spitzer, Jeffrey E. Tabak, Michele Cohn Tocci, Ruth Westheimer, Gary Zwerling. Select staff: Michael S. Glickman (president and CEO), Elaine Valby and Rita Iosefson (office of the president), Elizabeth Edelstein (education), Miriam Haier, Lisa Safier, Margot Lurie and Mara Sonnenschein (external affairs), Michael Stafford (operations), Susan Woodland, Treva Walsh and Michael Morris (collections), Maggie Radd and Bryn Jayes (exhibitions).

LENDERS OF ARTIFACTS, IMAGES, AND COPYRIGHT HOLDERS
Akg-images, Berlin; Amud Aish Memorial Museum, Brooklyn; Anne Frank House, Amsterdam; Auschwitz-Birkenau State Museum, Oświęcim; Auschwitz Jewish Center, Oświęcim; BiG Productions, New York; Katharina Brand, Germany; Bundesarchiv, Berlin; Burgerbibliothek Bern, Bern; Canadian War Museum, Ottawa; Centropa, Vienna; Christian Schad Museum, Aschaffenburg; Creative Differences, Pasadena; Czartoryski Museum and Library, Kraków; Deutsches Historisches Museum, Berlin; Dokumentationsarchiv des österreichischen Widerstandes, Vienna; Facing History and Ourselves, Brookline, Massachusetts; Zdenka Fantlová-Erlich, United Kingdom; Eleanor Fedrid-Corner, United States; Feng Shan Ho family, United States; Florence and Laurence Spungen Family Foundation, Santa Barbara, California; Förderkreis Elfriede Lohse-Wächtler, Hamburg; Friends of the March of the Living, Miami; Klaus Fritsch, Vienna; Galicia Jewish Museum, Kraków; Miroslav Ganobis, Poland; Gedenkstätte Buchenwald, Weimar; Gedenkstätte Haus der Wannseekonferenz, Berlin; Gedenkstätte und Museum Sachsenhausen, Oranienburg; the George and Adele Klein Foundation, New York; Ghetto Fighters' House Museum, Kibbutz Lohamei Hagetaot, Israel; Greenbaum family, United States and Canada; Irene Guttmann Hizme and Rene Guttmann Slotkin, United States; Hamburger Institut für Sozialforschung, Hamburg; Hamburger Kunsthalle, Hamburg; Stella Hasson DeLeon family, United States; Herinneringscentrum Kamp Westerbork, Hooghalen; Historisches Museum, Frankfurt am Main; Rainer Höss, Germany; Holocaust Center for Humanity, Seattle; Imperial War Museum, London; Institut für Zeitgeschichte, Munich; Institute of National Remembrance, Warsaw; Joods Cultureel Kwartier—Joods Historisch Museum, Amsterdam; Jewish Museum, London; Jewish Museum of Greece, Athens; William Kaczynski, United Kingdom; Klarsfeld Foundation, Paris; Shirley Kopolovic and Mark Levine, Canada; KZ-Gedenkstätte Mauthausen, Mauthausen; Ruth-Anne Lenga, United Kingdom; Lern- und Gedenkort Schloss Hartheim, Alkoven; Les Éditions de Minuit, Paris; Ministerio de Asuntos Exteriores, Unión Europea y Cooperación, Madrid; Montreal Holocaust Museum, Montreal; Musealia, San Sebastián; Museum of Jewish Heritage—A Living Memorial to the Holocaust, New York; Museumsquartier Osnabrück—Felix Nussbaum Haus, Osnabrück; National Archives, College Park, Maryland; Nationaal Onderduikmuseum, Aalten; National Center for Jewish Film, Waltham, Massachusetts; Nederlands Fotomuseum, Rotterdam; NIOD Instituut voor Oorlogs-, Holocaust- en Genocidestudies, Amsterdam; Marc Oler, France; Rijksarchief Brussel, Brussels; Rodgers Center for Holocaust Education, Chapman University, Orange, California; Sanz-Briz family, Spain; Alexander Savin, Russia; Paweł Sawicki, Poland; Christa Schnepf, Germany; Schweizerisches Bundesarchiv,

Bern; Schwules Museum, Berlin; Shoah Foundation, University of Southern California, Los Angeles; Peter Siebers, Germany; Slovak National Archive, Bratislava; Staatsbibliothek, Berlin; State Regional Archives, Pilsen; Stiftung Neue Synagoge Berlin—Centrum Judaicum, Berlin; St. Maximilian Kolbe Centre, Harmęże; Ceija Stojka Estate—Hojda Stojka, Germany; Terezin Initiative Institute, Prague; Transit Film GmbH, Munich; United States Holocaust Memorial Museum, Washington, DC; United States Naval History and Heritage Command, Washington, DC; University of South Carolina, Columbia; Robert Jan van Pelt, Canada; Robin Vrba, United States; Daniel Weihs, Israel; Ann Weiss, United States; Alfréd Wetzler family, Slovakia; Wiener Library for the Study of the Holocaust and Genocide, London; Sonja de Wind-Klijn, Netherlands; Yad Vashem: The World Holocaust Remembrance Center, Jerusalem; Yale University Library, New Haven, Connecticut; YIVO Institute for Jewish Research, New York; Zoyda Art Production, Ząbki; Zweite Deutsche Fernsehen (ZDF)—Zur Person, Mainz.

PRODUCTION
Architectural models: University of Waterloo School of Architecture, Cambridge, Canada—Anna Longrigg, Bob Intini, Madeleine Reinhardt, Michael Nugent, Piper Bernbaum, Tom Nugent, Tristan van Leur; Escuela Superior Técnica de Arquitectura de la Universidad del País Vasco en San Sebastián. Audio tour: David McFetridge, with Sandy Goldberg and Paul Salmons, United Kingdom, and Jesús Sánchez, Spain; Ludovico Einaudi, Italy (music); Rec Estudio, San Sebastián (production). Frames and lightboxes: Printit BCN, Barcelona. Insurance: Mapfre. Interior display: Feltrero, Madrid. Legal matters: Izaskun Porres, San Sebastián; Uría Menéndez, Madrid; Clarick,

Gueron & Reisbaum, New York. Lighting: Intervento, Madrid. Photography: José Barea, Madrid; Jesús Varillas, Madrid; Izaskun Cámara Pozuelo, San Sebastián; Paweł Sawicki, Oświęcim. Picture framing: Marcos Cano, Madrid. Replicas: Laura Elvira Martínez, United Kingdom; El Taller de Piñeiro, Alcoy. Restoration and preservation: Die Schmiede, Duisburg; Julian Zawada Usługi Budowlane, Oświęcim. Showcases: Frank Europe, GmbH, Bad Kreuznach. Software: WEGETIT, San Sebastián. Text editors, exhibition, English: Claire Crighton, United States; Kiel Majewski, United States; Spanish: Icíar Palacios, Spain. Translations: Diego León, Spain; Políglota, SL, Madrid. Transportation: ArtTransit, Wodzierady; TTI Transportes, Madrid. Videos for the exhibition: Winikur Productions, Boston; Zoyda Art Production, Ząbki. Video (promotion and exhibition): MorganCrea, San Sebastián. Web design and graphics: Studio Itxaso Mezzacasa, San Sebastián.

COLLABORATING INSTITUTIONS
Association of Holocaust Organizations, Hollis, New York; Battery Park City Authority, New York; Centro Sefarad-Israel, Madrid; Canal de Isabel II, SA, Madrid; Centro de Exposiciones Arte Canal, Madrid; International Holocaust Remembrance Alliance, Berlin.

ACKNOWLEDGMENTS
Robert E. Abrams, Juan Aguilar, Pilar Aguilar, Maria Aguirre, Morgan Ahern, Julio Martín Alarcón, Fernando Arlandis, Irati Arrieta, Juan José Arrizabalaga, Izaskun Aseguinolaza, José Luis Auger, Frank Bajohr, Ben Barkow, Gerhard Baumgartner, Eva Benatar, Joanna Berendt, Alicja Bialecka, Thomas Blatt, Erica Blumenfeld, Anne Bordeleau, Verena Borgmann, Anat Bratman-Elhalel, Tom Brink, Martina Caspers, Judith Cohen, Imogen Dalziel, Teresein da Silva, Caroline Davis, Delores Delgado, Melcher de Wind, Tamira de Wind, Peter Eigelsberger, David Fabricant, Raquel Fernández, Raúl Fernández, Unai Fernández de Betoño, Anna

Fischer, Andrzej Folwarczny, Robert Frey, Sholom Friedmann, Sandra González, Elly Gotz, Esme Gotz, Shoshana Greenwald, Diny Griffioen-Drenthel, Marilyn J. Harran, Michael Haupt, Marie-Claude Hawry, Anabel Hernandez, Alice Herscovitch, Cinita Herzberger, Roberta Hyman, Zuzanna Janusik, Mary Johnson, Roman Kent, Sarah Kindermann, Elisabeth Klamper, Guido Knopp, Agnieszka Kocur-Smoleń, Anton Kras, Maren Krüger, Tomasz Kuncewicz, Luis Lafuente Batanero, Klaus Lankheit, Yariv Lapid, Noga Lebovitz, Irene Leitner, Ronald Leopold, Astrid Ley, Henry Lustiger Thaler, Bartek Majda, Lidia Maksymowicz, Piotr Malarek, Władysław Malarek, Eugenie Martens, Álvaro Martínez Bueno, Alice Marxova, Paula Matellanes, Ewa Matlak, Donald McKay, Christina Meri, Rosa Mettbach, Theodor Michael, Stella Nina Michaelis, Joanna Millick, Anna Miszewska, Günther Morsch, Dirk Mulder, Fernando Navarro, Sarah Nichols, Jacek Nowakowski, Jakub Nowakowski, Michael Nugent, Mirosław Obstarczyk, Anna Odi, Maria José Olaizola, Julia Ortmeyer, Moritz Pankok, Jadwiga Pinderska-Lech, Oliver Plöger, Karen Polak, Rafael Prieto Martín, Dovid Reidel, Emily Reisbaum, Milan Richter, Thomas Richter, Andrea Rodríguez, Menachem Rosensaft, Nuria San Román, José Sánchez Tortosa, Christine Schmidt, Beata Schulman, Florian Schwanniner, Anne Sibylle Schwetter, Natalia Semanova, Edward Serotta, William Shulman, Dee Simon, Anna Skrzypińska, Wojtek Smoleń, Vanda Mikolowska Solomon, Toby Sonneman, Stanlee Stahl, Tereza Štěpková, Paula Stern, Sora Stöckl, Karl Stojka, Helena Svojsikova, Artur Szyndler, Nechama Tec, Javier Tortuero Ortiz, Caecilia Thoen, Julia Thompson, Marian Turski, Vivian Uria, Alexandra von Würzen, Małgorzata Walczak, Barbara Warnock, Thomas Weber, Vital Zajka, Ariana Zwiers.

Auschwitz: Not Long Ago. Not Far Away. is published in conjunction with the exhibition of the same name at the Museum of Jewish Heritage—A Living Memorial to the Holocaust, New York (mjhnyc.org).

The exhibition is organized by Musealia, San Sebastián (musealia.net), in collaboration with the Auschwitz-Birkenau State Museum, Oświęcim (auschwitz.org/en/), and the Museum of Jewish Heritage—A Living Memorial to the Holocaust, New York.

Visit the exhibition online at auschwitz.net/en/.

First edition
10 9 8 7 6 5 4 3 2 1

ISBN 978-0-7892-1331-0

Library of Congress Cataloging-in-Publication Data available upon request

For bulk and premium sales and for text adoption procedures, write to Customer Service Manager, Abbeville Press, 655 Third Avenue, New York, NY 10017, or call 1-800-ARTBOOK.

Visit Abbeville Press online at www.abbeville.com.

01 Bunker 2
02 Corpse-burning pits
03 Narrow-gauge tracks
04 Warehouse
05 Undressing barrack
06 Bunker 1
07 Barn used as warehouse
08 Temporary sewage plant
09 Drainage channel
10 Sewage plant
11 Pump house
12 Crematorium 2
13 Ash pits
14 Grinding site
15 Entry to the yard of Crematorium 3
16 Crematorium 3
17 Prisoner clothing warehouse
18 "Kanada," storage area
19 Sewage sedimentation basin
20 Central Sauna
21 Medics
22 Women's accommodation in Kanada
23 Men's accommodation in Kanada
24 Crematorium 4
25 Crematorium 5
26 Fire water reservoir
27 Camp B1b: Men's camp (March 1942–July 1943)
28 Camp B1b: Women's camp (July 1943–November 1944)
29 Fire water reservoir
30 Barrack of punishment company
31 Potato-peeling barrack
32 Bread warehouse
33 Kitchen
34 Kitchen barrack
35 Delousing facility
36 Location of women's orchestra
37 Block leader office
38 Camp B1a: Women's camp (August 1942–November 1944)
39 Delousing facility
40 Barrack 25: waiting room for the gas chambers
41 Location of women's orchestra
42 Potato storage
43 Quarantine barrack for prisoners to be released
44 Rampe (May 1944–January 1945)
45 Gate building
46 Camp BIIf: Men's camp hospital
47 Soccer field
48 Volleyball court
49 Camp BIIe: Gypsy Camp
50 Delousing facility
51 Children's playground
52 Camp BIId: Men's camp (July 1943–January 1945)
53 Location of men's orchestra
54 Water tank and place of execution
55 Barrack of punishment company
56 Barrack of Sonderkommandos
57 Camp BIIc: Transit camp for Jewish women (from June 1944 onward)
58 Camp BIIb: Czech Family Camp (September 1943–July 1944)
59 Camp BIIa: Quarantine camp (August 1943–November 1944)
60 Air-raid dugout
61 Off-limit "neutral zone" or death strip
62 Camp BIII: "Mexico" transit camp for Jewish prisoners (June 1944–October 1944)
63 Dog kennels
64 Old Rampe (Spring 1942–May 1944)
65 Auschwitz freight station
66 Cabbage storage
67 Potato storage
68 Camp for civilian workers
69 New building yard
70 Union munitions factory
71 Fenced walkway
72 Commandant's office and SS barracks
73 SS hospital
74 Block 30: sterilization
75 Road connecting the Rampe to the north road
76 Meadow
77 Woodlot
78 Undressing barrack (March 1943)
79 Death block (men)
80 Water treatment plant